At the Edge

The Sustainability and the Environment series provides a comprehensive, independent, and critical evaluation of environmental and sustainability issues affecting Canada and the world today.

SUSTAINABILITY
AND THE
ENVIRONMENT

Ann Dale
in collaboration with S.B. Hill

At the Edge:
Sustainable Development
in the 21st Century

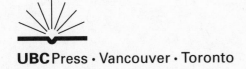
UBCPress · Vancouver · Toronto

Printed in Canada on acid-free paper ∞

ISBN 0-7748-0836-5 (hardcover)
ISBN 0-7748-0837-3 (paperback)
ISSN 1196-8575 (Sustainability and the Environment)

National Library of Canada Cataloguing in Publication Data

Dale, Ann, 1948-
    At the edge

    (Sustainability and the environment, ISSN 1196-8575)
    Includes bibliographical references and index.
    ISBN 0-7748-0836-5 (bound)
    ISBN 0-7748-0837-3 (pbk.)

    1. Sustainable development. I. Title. II. Series.
HC79.E5D34 2001   333.7   C00-911349-5

This book has been published with the help of a grant from the Humanities and Social Sciences Federation of Canada, using funds provided by the Social Sciences and Humanities Research Council of Canada.

UBC Press acknowledges the financial support of the Government of Canada through the Book Publishing Industry Development Program (BPIDP) for our publishing activities.
Canada

We also gratefully acknowledge the support of the Canada Council for the Arts for our publishing program, as well as the support of the British Columbia Arts Council.

UBC Press
The University of British Columbia
2029 West Mall, Vancouver, BC V6T 1Z2
(604) 822-5959
Fax: (604) 822-6083
E-mail: info@ubcpress.ca
www.ubcpress.ca

For Daniel James

In nature, the normal way in which trees flourish is by their association in a forest. Each tree may lose something of its individual perfection of growth, but they mutually assist each other in preserving the conditions for survival ... A forest is the triumph of the organization of mutually dependent species.

– Alfred North Whitehead, *Science and the Modern World*

Contents

Preface

We appear to be living in the best of times and the worst of times, a time of paradoxes. Much of what appears to be progress may actually be decline. The collapse of the Berlin Wall and the Soviet Union offer unparalleled opportunities for democracy worldwide, while, at the same time, the level of ethnic and regional conflicts has never been greater (Head 1992). Although we increasingly recognize the importance of plurality and the

---

While I was finalizing my research proposal in the summer of 1996, one of my best friends died very suddenly and at a young age. Once in a while, a special person or animal walks into your life. Odessa Mamut was such a being; he was the gentlest creature I have ever had the privilege of knowing. Since his death, the words "compassion for all living beings" and "doing no harm" keep reverberating.

---

diversity of human societies worldwide, homogenization through globalization appears to be accelerating. Postmodernist thought is paralleled by a worldwide trend in fundamentalism. We live in an information age, and yet many people remain fundamentally ignorant of most key ecological processes. Overall wealth is increasing at the same time as income disparities are widening. We have the technology to travel to the moon, yet we do not know anything about, nor have we even named, most of the species on our planet – many of which are threatened with extinction. We can explore Mars, and yet the internal combustion machine continues to pollute our planet. We produce arms and sell them to countries who then turn around and use them against us. Many of the world's scientists are engaged in arms and war-related research. It is, indeed, a paradoxical time, as biophysical evidence continues to mount that human growth and consumption patterns are slowly destroying the habitat on which survival depends, earth.

Paradoxes, however, can be viewed as both crises and opportunities. The solutions we seek for moving towards more sustainable societies may well lie in learning to reconcile the tensions within the paradoxes rather than in denying their existence simply because we feel powerless to change our current planning, decision-making, and activity systems. Whether a paradox is perceived as a crisis or an opportunity depends very much on where one is located in what Foucault (1980) refers to as "power/knowledge" systems (Lather 1991). As the following chapters outline, feelings of powerlessness allow us to continue living in massive denial of our present ecological reality, as we degrade our current and, some analysts would argue, our future ecological capital at an unprecedented rate and scale (Capra 1996; Daily 1997; Earle 1995; Ehrlich and Ehrlich 1997; Gordon and Suzuki 1990; Hill 1975; Meadows et al. 1992; Odum 1973; and Wackernagel and Rees 1996).

The central assumption of my story is that the implementation of sustainable development is the human imperative of the twenty-first century, requiring strong leadership by local, regional, and national governments, and that governments must move beyond simply being governments to governance, actively engaging all sectors of society in its implementation. How? Through reconciliation and dialogue. Sustainable development can be regarded as a process involving the reconciliation of three imperatives: (1) the ecological imperative to live within global biophysical carrying capacity and to maintain biodiversity; (2) the social imperative to ensure the development of democratic systems of governance that can effectively propagate and sustain the values by which people wish to live, and (3) the economic imperative to ensure that basic needs are met worldwide. And equitable access to resources – ecological, social, and economic – is fundamental to its implementation.

Human activity, as implied in the notion of sustainable development, affects three broad external systems: the ecological, the social, and the economic, all of which are ultimately dependent on the development of one internal system: the individual. It is counter-productive to debate which is more fundamental. Addressing all four is both necessary and sufficient. The three external imperatives are causally interdependent: it is not possible to change the direction or nature of one without also affecting the other two. Given this interconnectedness, failure to properly consider any one will make it impossible to address the other two. And failure to integrate the personal and the professional may well prove, in the long run, to impede any real progress in reconciling these three imperatives.

There are two inter-related levels of human activity – the personal and the political – and these are often mistakenly separated. This book focuses on the latter and its organizational implications, as I believe that sustainable development will not be realized without effective government leadership – leadership that will enable us, over the next decade, to diffuse sustainable development concepts and practices before we reach irreversible thresholds. I have also assumed that the socio-economic system is a closed rather than an open system and that human activity systems are a part of natural systems, with biospheric limits.

Government leadership will not ensue, however, unless a framework based on the reconciliation of ecological, social, and economic imperatives is implemented across governments at all levels. Such a framework is critical for consistent and effective government leadership in all sectors of Canadian society, ultimately leading to new forms of governance if sustainable development is to be effectively implemented at all levels of human activity. So far, in the absence of an organizing concept, efforts to coordinate natural resource policies either have been largely ineffective or have been used to favour one use over others (Caldwell 1970).

This story begins, in Chapters 1 through 3, with a discussion of the overall context of sustainable development, including the specific research context that led to my writing this narrative. Although sustainable development is still a fairly amorphous paradigm (Pierce 1999), I argue that, because of its integrative potential, it offers the best possibilities for reconciling human activity systems and natural systems over both the short and the long term. In Chapters 4 through 6, I offer a global discussion of the three sustainable development imperatives – the ecological, the social, and the economic. There are numerous debates as to whether the glass is half empty or half full. I have chosen, however, to focus on the half-empty glass, because although numerous positive examples of sustainable development are now emerging in all sectors of society and in a number of communities, the condition of our world and its continuing deterioration is so great that it requires special attention. Particularly notable failures are the Kyoto Convention on Climate Change and the 1992 Biodiversity Convention. In the case of the former, in spite of enormous government efforts and measures, it is now clear that we will not even meet the new greenhouse gas reductions of 6 percent below 1990 levels by 2012. With respect to the Biodiversity Convention, as is discussed in Chapter 4, it has neither slowed the destruction of habitat nor slowed the rate of human-induced species extinction rates. Therefore, I argue that, given the global ecological, social, and economic evidence, it is clear that human societies everywhere must embrace a new paradigm, adopt new metaphors, and create new space for policy alternatives that re-direct human activity systems to face our critical ecological realities.

I then turn from the global to the Canadian context. In Chapter 7, I detail the systemic restraining forces working against the implementation of sustainable development at the federal level – namely, the solitudes, silos, and stovepipes that characterize Canada. By solitudes I am referring to the deep cleavages that separate us by language, geography, and gender. Stovepipes are the great divides between sectors – between the research community and governments, between the research community and the private sector, and between each of these and non-governmental organizations (NGOs). Silos are the separations within and between government departments, and in universities between academic disciplines. I believe that a failure to address such restraining forces would make any proposed framework for reconciliation merely theoretical. In Chapter 8, I discuss the centrality of social actors and their institutions, since sustainable development must be socially constructed, that is, social and economic arrangements must be made purposively and responsibly (Cernea 1994). Chapter 9 looks at purposeful decision making for sustainable development. The last chapter, entitled Reflections, shares some of my thoughts on my own context while writing this book.

Some understanding of my own location and context may enhance your appreciation of the arguments put forth in this book. Most of my career has been spent in a large bureaucracy, working with very senior decision makers. For over twenty-three years I was exposed, on a daily basis, to a dominant male system that placed a high value on rational, objective behaviour that was, in turn, based on an expert model of modern science. In large bureaucracies, often in order to meet brutal political deadlines, aggression is seen as positive. Detachment and emotional neutrality are the preferred professional behaviours, whereas compassion and caring are seen as undesirable. The possibility of detachment, however, may well be one of the greatest myths humans have adopted in their working lives. For we are very subjective creatures, and our perceptions of reality are strongly influenced by the paradigms, myths, and metaphors that find their way into both personal and professional contexts. We are not value free, and, paradoxically, we may achieve greater degrees of objectivity only when we can appreciate our subjectivity.

Values emerged as key to my research in a number of ways. First, my co-researchers in the electronic collaborative inquiry that was the platform for my work unanimously agreed on the centrality of values in their own lives and work as well as on the importance of values in any study of sustainable development. Second, my own work is passionately informed by my fundamental belief that we live in a world of false dualities and pathological separations that powerfully shape how we view our world, our place in the world, and our relationships with one another as well as with other species. Because I firmly believe that there is no real difference between my life and the life of "others," my core value is a deep respect for all living beings.

And this core value affects the depth and nature of my grief when "other" creatures die, never mind members of my own species. My story, therefore, has been deeply affected by my context, and, perhaps, has become richer as a result of my internal journey. All stories, mine included, are greatly influenced by the prevailing cultural myths, metaphors, and paradigms that affect how we organize our activities at all levels of society.

Reconciliation became critical, for many, many reasons, while I was researching and writing this book. I lost four beloved animal companions and my only child. In my attempts to reconcile my grief and to continue my "professional" commitments, the only way through despair was to flow with my emotions. The one way I found to reconcile their loss was through the reintegration of my emotions with my intellect. Their deaths, paradoxically, freed me from an emotional straitjacket by opening up different pathways through despair. Just as life is a process, so is grief (and, I suspect, so is death). Most people survive grief, but to transcend the tragedy of premature death requires one to integrate the heart, the mind, and the soul. My personal experiences with grief have deepened my belief that the widespread denial of ecological reality is related to modern society's denial of mortality and bereavement. We deny the existence of limits because recognizing biophysical limits means facing our own mortality. Recognizing that there are limits to the earth means accepting that there are limits to our being and to human activities. And because we perceive our human activity systems to be apart from natural systems, few of us really believe that what we do to the biosphere we also do to ourselves.

I have tried to tell my story as clearly and as simply as possible. Hopefully, the narrative is powerful enough to convince you of the need for reconciliation at all levels and of the central role of values, reconciliation, and dialogue in any framework for sustainable development.

There are always many ways to tell and read a story, and this book is designed to be read on multiple levels, through the interplay of boxes, text, and margins. The reader can choose to read only the boxes, or to read only the text, or, I would hope, to go between the text and the boxes so that each enriches and informs the other, enabling the centres and margins to shift (Hooks 1984). The text and boxes are not meant to substitute for one another but, rather, to complement one another. They are also a means of reconciling the emotional with the intellectual and the spiritual. I have used most of the boxes to highlight specific values and issues, providing quotes that attest to a diversity of knowledge.

My aim is to enlarge the boundaries of the text and the margins, thereby transcending the limits that both place upon each other. I believe that process and product are not separate from one another but, rather, that each is informed and influenced by the other. Thus, I have tried to mirror principles of sustainable development in my choice of tools and techniques. I offer a kind of mapping of multi-level contextual space, where reconciliation of the ecological, social, and economic imperatives of sustainable development becomes an emergent process, and

the discourse [becomes] not a closure but a trace in an endless passage that can only aspire to a temporary arrest, to a self-conscious drawing of a limit across the diverse possibilities of the world. As Gilles Deleuze puts it, sense is a surface-effect, an event, and not the sign or symptom of an absent origin, a lost totality, or a pure consciousness. It is precisely this lack of a fixed referent or stable foundation that produces meaning. For to produce it does not mean to touch a sacred stone or turn the right key that will reveal the nature of things, but involves tracing out a recognizable shape on the extensive complexity of the possible. Our interpretations of society, culture, history and our individual lives, hopes, dreams, passions and sensations, involve attempts to confer sense rather than to discover it. (Chambers 1990: 11)

Acknowledgments

When I first began this book, I naively thought that I had begun an entirely new journey, until one day I pulled out a very short paper I had written in 1974 on organizational behaviour as part of my studies at the Master's level. There were remarkable similarities between that paper and the thoughts that led to this book. Just as my learning about ecological system function, structure, and processes has taught me that systems are sometimes chaotic, random, stable, and discontinuous, there is, at the same time, some sort of remarkable continuity at play that transcends the individual. Thus, I have learned that my work is sometimes chaotic, random, and yet has an emergent integrity that is due, in large part, to my family and friends and the people with whom I have had the privilege of working.

I would like to first thank my mother, Catherine, from whom I inherited a strength of mind that has allowed me to continue on in spite of some terrible losses, and my father, who gave me the gift of myself, free from gender constraints. Secondly, my sister, Elaine, who has been a constant source of support and wise editing. And lastly, my husband, Bill, and my beloved child, Daniel James, whose love and support gave me the courage to persevere. Without doubt, my work has taken time from my family, and many times I put those relationships to the side, thinking that I could always get back to them later. Danny was my master literary wizard, my keeper of integrity.

In terms of my professional colleagues, I am honoured to count many people who are at once colleagues, friends, and mentors, and who have shared unstintingly of their intellect, time, and support through this incredible journey of reconciliation. I would first like to thank Stuart Hill, Professor, School of Social Ecology, University of Western Sydney at Hawkesbury, for his collaboration as well as his unfailing personal support during this book. He truly demonstrated the importance of the "personal imperative" and its integration into the professional sphere, and I could not have completed this journey without him. I would also like to thank

John Robinson, Director of the Sustainable Development Research Institute at the University of British Columbia, for always being there and sharing so generously of his culture and intellect. I would also like to thank Valerie Behan-Pelletier, Agriculture and Agri-Food Canada; John Henning, Faculty of Agricultural Economics, McGill University; David Johnston, President, University of Waterloo; Jim MacNeill, Ombudsman, World Bank; and Frances Westley, Faculty of Management, McGill University, for their comments and review of key chapters, as well as their infinitely compassionate professionalism.

And I would like to thank my co-researchers who participated in the electronic collaborative enquiry, in particular, Nina-Marie Lister, David Sims, Caterina Geuer, Christine Massey, and Shealagh Pope. Finally, I would like to express my appreciation to Isabelle Cordua-von Specht and Randy Schmidt, Editor, UBC Press, who believed in this manuscript and ensured it saw the light.

To all of the people above, and to some unnamed, mille fois merci.

Acronyms

CEPA	Canadian Environmental Protection Act
CFCs	Chlorofluoro carbons
DFO	Department of Fisheries and Oceans
EDF	Environmental Defense Fund
ENGO	Environmental non-governmental organization
EPA	Environmental Protection Agency
FAO	Food and Agriculture Agency
GATT	General Agreement on Tariffs and Trade
GDP	Gross Domestic Product
GHG	Greenhouse gases
GNP	Gross National Product
GPI	Gross Personal Income
HCFCs	Hydrochlorofluorocarbons
HDI	Human Development Index
HDR	Human Development Report
HFCs	Hydro-fluorocarbons
IMF	International Monetary Fund
IPCC	Intergovernmental Panel on Climate Change
IUCN	International Union for the Conservation of Nature and Natural Resources
MAI	Multilateral Agreement on Investment
MMT	Methylcyclopentadienyl manganese tricarbonyl
NAFTA	North American Free Trade Agreement
NGO	Non-governmental organization
NPP	Net Primary Production
NRTEE	National Round Table on the Environment and the Economy
SSM	Soft systems methodology
UNEP	United Nations Environment Programme
WHO	World Health Organization
WRI	World Resources Institute
WWF	World Wildlife Fund

At the Edge

1
The Context

The very word environment is an abstraction, one that is wrong
in this context. It abstracts the environment from the person and
the person from the environment. It treats the two as different.
But the so-called environment is the very source of the being of
the person. The human being couldn't exist without oxygen,
water, food, and so on. Therefore all this really shouldn't be
called an environment. It's the wrong kind of abstraction. It
separates things that are one.

– D. Bohm, *On Dialogue*

Although the concept of sustainable development has been around for a
number of years, it was first popularized in 1987 when the Brundtland
Commission published its report, *Our Common Future*. By widely promoting this concept, the commission wisely sidestepped the polarized debate
over growth that was initiated by the Club of Rome's seminal document,
Limits to Growth (Meadows et al. 1972). Since the introduction of sustainable
development into common parlance, numerous variations have emerged,
such as sustainability, sustainable growth, sustainable economic growth,
and sustainable environmental (or ecological) development. Indeed, our
attempts to generate more meaningful definitions speak to the strength of
the concept. All of these variations, however, implicitly push us back
into the old debate of no growth (or limits to growth) versus unlimited
growth. Although different sectors and communities disagree about the
usefulness of the concept of sustainable development, this concept is recognized internationally. And it does avoid most of the traditional left-right
polarization around growth versus no-growth by surrounding the terms
"sustainable" and "development" with a constructive ambiguity that has
stimulated greater dialogue between various sectors. Despite its ambiguity,
this term has succeeded in uniting widely divergent theoretical and ideological perspectives into a single conceptual framework (Estes 1993). More
fundamentally, the concept of sustainable development has brought a
wide diversity of industrialists, environmentalists, public policy practitioners, and politicians to round tables in their attempts to define, deal with,
and actualize it. In order to provide an appreciation of context, I now offer
a brief examination of some of the earlier definitions of sustainable development. Human societies, according to their ecological, social, and economic conditions, will place different emphases on "sustainable" and
"development."

Historical Context

In 1980, the World Conservation Strategy, International Union for the Conservation of Nature and Natural Resources (IUCN), United Nations Environment Programme (UNEP), World Wildlife Fund (WWF), and others offered the following definitions relating to sustainable development.

- Development as the modification of the biosphere and the application of human, financial, and living and non-living resources to satisfy human needs and to improve the quality of human life. For development to be sustainable it must take account of social, ecological, and economic factors; of the living and non-living resource base; and of the long-term as well as the short-term advantages and disadvantages of alternative actions.
- Conservation as the management of human use of the biosphere so that it may yield the greatest sustainable benefit to present generations while maintaining its potential to meet the needs and aspirations of future generations. Thus, conservation is positive, embracing preservation, maintenance, sustainable utilization, restoration, and enhancement of the natural environment.
- Conservation, like development, is for people. While development aims to achieve human goals largely through use of the biosphere, conservation aims to achieve them by ensuring that such use can continue. Conservation's concern for maintenance and sustainability is a rational response to the nature of living resources (renewability and destructability) and also an ethical imperative, expressed in the belief that "we have not inherited the earth from our parents, we have borrowed it from our children."
- The integration of conservation and development is particularly important because, unless patterns of development that conserve living resources are widely adopted, it will become impossible to meet the needs of today without foreclosing the achievement of tomorrow.

In a 1986 statement to the World Commission on Environment and Development on behalf of Canadian environment, development, and peace organizations, Ralph Torrie defined sustainable development as development that is capable of meeting peoples' needs (as defined by them) in such a way that the potential for other people and future generations to meet their needs is not diminished.

Sustainable development implies decentralized development (which would ensure that people participate in decisions that affect them); appropriate changes in lifestyles and values; strong institutions devoted to protecting natural resources and the environment; efficient resource use;

reduced arms expenditures; and changes in aid, trade, and investment practices. The Brundtland Commission defines sustainable development as "development that meets the needs of the present without compromising the ability of future generations to meet their own needs" (Brundtland Commission 1987: 43). With respect to the operational objectives of sustainable development, *Our Common Future* (Brundtland Commission 1987: 49) lists the following strategic imperatives:

1 reviving growth;
2 changing the quality of growth;
3 meeting essential needs for jobs, food, energy, water, and sanitation;
4 ensuring a sustainable level of population;
5 conserving and enhancing the resource base;
6 reorienting technology and managing risk; and
7 merging environment and economics in decision making.

In 1987, Barbier argued that

as the primary objective is to provide lasting and secure livelihoods that minimize resource depletion, environmental degradation, cultural disruption, and social instability, sustainable development can be viewed as an interaction among three systems: the biological and resource system, the economic system, and the social system. The basic objective is to maximize the goals across all these systems through a dynamic and adaptive process of trade-offs. (1987: 109)

Repetto (1986: 17) expressed the idea of sustainable development as a tool for consensus.

Sustainable development has three bases ... scientific realities, consensus on ethical principles, and considerations of long-term self-interest. There is a broad consensus that pursuing policies that imperil the welfare of future generations ... is unfair. Most would agree that ... consign[ing] a large share of the world's population to deprivation and poverty is also unfair. Pragmatic self-interest reinforces that belief. Poverty ... underlies the deterioration of resources and the population growth in much of the world and affects everyone.

In 1988, the National Task Force on the Environment and Economy, a body established in Canada to examine the findings of the Brundtland Commission, generally defined sustainable economic development as development that ensures that the current use of resources and the environment does not damage prospects for future use. This means that our economic systems should be managed so as to maintain or improve our resource base, with the result that future generations will be able to live as well as, or better than, we do. Sustainable economic development does not require the preservation of the current stock of natural resources or any particular mix of human, physical, and natural resource assets. Nor does it place artificial limits on economic growth, provided that such growth is both economically and environmentally sustainable. Sustainable economic development implies that resources and the environment must be managed for the long term, taking into account both their future and current value.

By utilizing advanced and integrated planning, sustainable development would minimize environmental impacts and future clean-up costs. In a phrase, the current remedial-reactive approach to development would be replaced by an "anticipate-and-prevent" approach. The goal of sustainable economic development cannot be attained without making significant changes in how we plan and supervise our economic initiatives. This makes it a challenging goal, especially in Canada, because it will require different approaches in different economic sectors and political jurisdictions (although, of course, the same underlying principles should apply to every jurisdiction).

In 1989, Bill Rees offered the following definition of sustainable development:

> Sustainable development is positive socio-economic change that does not undermine the ecological and social systems upon which communities and society are dependent. Its successful implementation requires integrated policy, planning, and social learning processes; its political viability depends on the full support of the people it affects through their governments, their social institutions, and their private activities. Sustainable development:
>
> 1 is oriented to achieving explicit ecological, social, and economic objectives;
> 2 may impose ecological limits on material consumption, while fostering qualitative development at the community and individual levels;
> 3 requires government intervention, but also the leadership and cooperation of the private sector;
> 4 demands policy integration and coordination at all spatial scales and among relevant political jurisdictions, and depends on educational, planning, and political processes that are informed, open, and fair. (1989: 3)

The IUCN (1991) notes that sustainability refers to a process that can be maintained indefinitely. Pronk and Haq (1992) argue that sustainable development refers to the need for natural resources to be used in ways that do not create ecological debts by overexploiting the earth's carrying and productive capacity. Costanza (1991) further argues that a minimum necessary condition for sustainability is the maintenance of the total natural capital stock at or above the current level.

Meadows et al. (1992) define a sustainable society as one whose informational, social, and institutional mechanisms are able to keep in check the positive feedback loops that cause exponential population and capital growth. In other words, birth rates roughly equal death rates, and investment rates roughly equal depreciation rates, unless and until technical changes and social decisions justify a considered change in the levels of population or capital. In order to be socially sustainable, the combination of population, capital, and technology would have to be configured so that everyone's material living standard is adequate and secure. In order to be physically sustainable, a society's material and energy throughputs have to meet economist Herman Daly's (1991a) three conditions:

- its rates of use of renewable resources do not exceed their rates of regeneration;
- its rates of use of nonrenewable resources do not exceed the rate at which sustainable renewable substitutes are developed; and
- its rates of pollution emission do not exceed the assimilative capacity of the environment.

Thus, the concept of sustainable development has been constantly evolving (although all its definitions are decidedly anthropogenic). There is growing consensus that the term "sustainable development" implies the integration of the environment and the economy, but there is little consensus with regard to what it implies in terms of social dimensions.

A conserver society is a society which promotes economy of design, favours re-use, recycling, and reduction of resource use, questions the ever-growing per capita demand for consumer goods, and recognizes that a diversity of solutions in many systems, such as energy and transportation, might in effect increase their overall economy, stability and resiliency.

(Science Council of Canada 1977: 14)

The term "sustainable development" has provoked much criticism from a wide variety of scholars. Lele (1991) points out that the mainstream formulation suffers from an incomplete perception of the problems of poverty and environmental degradation as well as from confusion about the role of economic growth and the concepts of sustainability and participation. O'Riordan (1988) notes that current visions of sustainable development are messy and politically treacherous. Others (Redclift 1988; Norgaard 1988) argue that part of the definitional confusion surrounding the concept is not really about its meaning, but rather about which values should take precedence. The ongoing debate over language and definitions may have contributed to the politics of sustainable development being notable by its absence. Indeed, the nature of sustainable development, both conceptually and in practice, also contributes to a fragmented constituency and a lack of coalitions, in a country characterized by solitudes, silos, and stovepipes (see Chapter 7).

Qualitative research is an interdisciplinary, transdisciplinary, and sometimes counterdisciplinary field. It crosscuts the humanities and the social and physical sciences. Its focus is multiparadigmatic and its practitioners are sensitive to the value of the multimethod approach. They are committed to the naturalistic perspective, and to the interpretative understanding of human experience. At the same time, the field is inherently political and shaped by multiple ethical and political positions.

(Denzin and Lincoln 1994: 3-4)

Research Context

Just as there are many ways of viewing sustainable development, so there are many ways of doing research. Research methodology is context-dependent, in that the issue being studied informs the choice of methodology, just as the choice of methodology influences research outcomes. It is important to me that, wherever possible, my work mirrors the changes that I experience and write and talk about. Both the process and the product must have integrity, as both are informed by and inform one another. My choice of methodology is, therefore, dependent upon the overall contexts within which I am working as well as upon the context of the particular domain under study – in this case, sustainable development. Critical to my thinking are new process models of continuous learning and action, processes that contribute to critical consciousness, collective action, and common meaning (DeMello et al. 1994) as well as exposing the assumptions underlying our dominant paradigms. I recognize the value-laden nature of inquiry, and I believe that all forms of knowledge are important – not only propositional knowledge, but also practical knowledge and experiential knowledge (Heron 1996; Reason and Rowan 1981b). It is important to me, therefore, that my own experience as an executive within the federal public service be integrated into my research. Hence my concern with praxis; that is, with "theory both relevant to the world and nurtured by action in it, and an action component in its own theorizing process that grows out of practical political grounding" (Buker forthcoming, cited in Lather 1991: 11).

The principles of sustainable development described in this book were developed by bringing together a number of diverse methodologies – namely, participatory action research, soft systems methodology (SSM), systems thinking, and strategic questioning – through an electronic collaborative inquiry.

Inherent to SSM are the concepts of *Weltanschauung* (or worldview) and holon (Koestler 1978). Human activity is meaningful in terms of a particular image of the world, which, in general is taken for granted (Michael 1993). The methodology teases out various world-images and examines their implications (Checkland 1981). Systems thinking attempts to expose our underlying subconscious frameworks, making us self-conscious about our intellectual pigeonholes (ibid.). Thus, systems research is concerned with wholes and their properties. Indeed, the research methodology itself is regarded as a holon. SSM is concerned with both the natural and human spheres, and it is the interaction between the two that is of interest. In my chairing of the electronic dialogue, my objective was to ensure that any potential changes identified for the implementation of sustainable development be defined to meet two criteria: that these changes be both desirable and feasible (i.e., systematically desirable and organizationally feasible).

Collaborative inquiry is often grounded in dialectical thinking, as this is an effective means of dealing with contradictions and paradoxes. Dialectical theories are always looking for contradictions and paradoxes (within both people and situations) in order to determine what is likely to happen on three levels: the interdependence of opposites, the interpenetration of opposites, and the unity of opposites (Rowan 1981). Dialectic thinking informs us that any value, if held to in a one-sided way, will eventually be shown to be an illusion. Contradictions are never "resolved"; rather, an ongoing movement between opposites is an inevitable part of the human condition. We can no longer talk about simple "growth" as the basic need of the human being, for growth always exists within a dialectical relationship, which is itself part of a dilemma that can never be fully resolved (May 1974). The final aim of a dialectal dialogue is to distill a consensus construction that is more informed and sophisticated than any of the predecessor constructions, including, of course, the etic construction of the investigator (Guba and Lincoln 1994).

Electronic Inquiry

I chose electronic collaborative inquiry as a research tool because it satisfied four sustainability criteria. First, it saved on transportation costs, both economic and biophysical, by accommodating participation from across the country, allowing for the factoring in of diverse geographical perspectives. Second, it eliminated unnecessary transcription costs, as the electronic record was the immediate product, and allowed participants to have a direct voice. Third, it allowed for voices to be directly recorded as citations in this book, thus removing the filter of the researcher. Fourth, it addressed aspects of equity by considering such factors of inclusion as age, regional representation, gender, and sectoral representation (with the exception of the business and labour communities). It cannot be denied, however, that our research group was comprised of elite, White, middle-class experts.

Dialogue has the potential to alter the meaning each individual holds and, by so doing, is capable of transforming the group, organization, and society. The relationship between the individual and the collective is reciprocal and is mediated through talk. People are both recipients of tacit assumptions and the creators of them. In this way dialogue results in the co-creation of meaning. The meaning that is created is shared across group members; a common understanding is developed.

(Dixon 1996: 24)

Prior to starting the electronic collaborative inquiry in September 1997, I led two workshops in order to test the robustness of the models I had developed in my research proposal – one in Vancouver, British Columbia, at the David Suzuki Foundation and the other at the Centre for Policy Alternatives in Oslo, Norway.

The electronic medium allowed for continuous cycles of inward and outward contemplation, analysis, and reflection on the part of all participants. It also allowed for alternating spirals of strategic questioning, critical reflection, and action inquiry, followed by information consolidation and then further rounds of critical reflection, strategic questioning, and action inquiry through a peer review process. This led to establishing a common framework for governance. My choice of research methodology allowed me to examine both the product (i.e., the eventual framework) and the process; was it possible to have a long-term substantive dialogue? In some ways, an electronic collaborative inquiry is a form of extended interview survey, although it probes on multiple levels. My methodology was designed to facilitate meaningful social action and change by influencing the co-researchers both individually and collectively, and, through a peer review process, by influencing the systems under study.

The electronic means of communication explode the space-time limits of messages, permit the surveillance of messages and actions, complete the process of automation of production, despatialize certain kinds of work, enable signifiers to float in relation to refer ads, become a substitute for certain forms of social relations, provide a new relation between author and text, expand infinitely human memory, and undermine the Cartesian ontology of subject and object.

(Postel 1987: 121)

The three sectors from which I drew my co-researchers – public policy, academe, and non-governmental organizations (NGOs) – were deliberately chosen to enable me to identify emerging leaders who would be committed to the process of framework development and who would work as advocates for change in each of their respective domains. I cannot overestimate the importance of effective facilitation and leadership in chairing electronic collaborations. It took all of my management skills, paradoxically calling upon most of the interpersonal skills I have developed through my twenty-three years of management experience and expertise in multi-stakeholder processes. It was critical to know when to prompt the group and when to hold back. The silence was sometimes deafening; yet, as chair, I often sensed lurking active, albeit unexpressed, interest. I found that a variety of communication styles seemed to facilitate motion and that alternating professional and personal messages often eased "sticky" points. Although I had known everyone previously, I neglected to take into account the need for more interpersonal meetings. In hindsight, I should have scheduled the first face-to-face meeting after the first month of dialogue instead of mid-way through the process. I also should have held at least two other workshops, one half-way through the dialogue and one at the end, to facilitate the development of a more synthetic framework.

Another technique I employed involved asking one of my colleagues to play the role of agent provocateur. Occasionally, when the dialogue appeared to be flagging, he would come in with some provocative statements in order to stimulate or at times re-activate discussion. Although I generally avoided going off-line, upon occasion I did so in order to remind people of their commitment to the collective research process. One surprising barrier to effective dialogue was the tendency of a minority of my academic colleagues to go off-line to make individual comments (although, in many cases, I was sent a blind copy of these comments). There would appear to be a gender dimension to off-line communication, although my sample is so limited it is not meaningful to draw conclusions: all of the off-line communication was by male participants. This behaviour is not surprising, however, given the academic culture and its emphasis on individuality and individual research. Another barrier to free-flowing engagement was differing levels of seniority. As one academic co-researcher commented, "Given the level and quality of the other co-researchers, many of whom are in a position to hire me, there is a level of intimidation."

Aside from off-line communication and intimidation, there were at least five significant barriers to effective dialogue: literacy, language, trust, intersectoral communication, and disciplinary structure. With regard to literacy, in two cases people had self-identified and asked to be part of the dialogue but ended up being inactive participants. In one case I suspect the barrier may have had to do with age and typing ability – a major impediment to engaging in a deep, information-rich computer dialogue. In the other two cases, although both individuals were very literate verbally, I subsequently learned that they did not have a corresponding written literacy. In terms of written literacy, another interesting phenomenon emerged: academics place inordinate importance on the written word, and I frequently exhorted the group to allow the spontaneity of the medium, rather than the written word, to take over. This was one of the major sticking points when we lost the immediacy of the medium, a critically important compensatory mechanism for the emergent spontaneity and synergy that often develops in face-to-face interaction.

What does dialogue require of people? Those who engage in dialogue must come to it with humility, love, faith, and hope – a formidable list of characteristics, but one that exemplifies a relational, rather than technical perspective.

(Dixon 1996)

Freire (1970: 77-78) envisioned dialogue as the creation and re-creation of meaning and saw creation as an act of love. Love is at the same time the basis of dialogue and dialogue itself.

Language was another major barrier to participation, particularly between the three sectors. Many of the public policy participants found the level and tone of debate too academic, whereas the NGO participants were intimidated by the jargon (one of them withdrew). Even the use of the word "sector" shows the importance of language, as it is both divisive (connoting hard and demarcated differences between groups) and, yet, given its widespread acceptance, easy to use. The culture of vertical stovepipes is very much a macro-problem, and communication between sectors appears to be problematic. The academic sector, as was often reiterated by one of the co-researchers, must simplify its language in order to communicate with the wider public. The inability to take complex concepts and communicate them in clear and simple language proved to be a strong barrier to effective communication between the three sectors. Of course, in order to overcome this barrier, we need to overcome our beliefs that complex language and intelligence are somehow causally linked. This would require nothing less than a paradigm shift.

2
Paradigms, Myths, and Metaphors

Once we allow ourselves to see that there are alternatives to
traditional ways of thinking and being in [the] world, we may
permit ourselves to search for, explore, and practice them. This is
enormously difficult, since the principles of traditional logic are
entwined with ordinary states of consciousness so that our
"mindscape" (Maruyama 1979) seems to represent the only
possible world view.

– J. Rowan, *Human Inquiry*

A common symbol in young children's drawings is the sun. Young people
appear to have an innate sensitivity to their place in the world and the
importance of their environment to their well-being. Mentally disturbed
children often colour the sun black.

As we mature, our intuitive sense of our environment is influenced by
our family; the education we receive; the neighbourhoods in which we
grow up; our experiences with nature and other creatures; our culture and
religion; and, finally, our experiences as adults. All of these influences, in
turn, determine the nature of the lens we use to view the world around us
and our sense of place within it. The nature of our perceptual lens is
strongly shaped and coloured by the prevailing paradigms of the times in
which we live. A society can be characterized by its myths, metaphors, and
dominant paradigms – those phenomena by which its members make
sense of the world in which they live and of their place within that world.

Briggs and Peat (1985) describe paradigms as like "spectacles," which scientists put
on. Once donned, the spectacles mediate and condition the scientists' worldview: they
filter in some things and filter out others. The spectacles are made from particular
theories (e.g., quantum theory, relativity), together with the presuppositions
surrounding the theories. They constitute a lens through which scientists discover
what is worthwhile studying about nature, an object of scientific study.

(Pepper 1996: 261)

Myths lie at the basis of human society because they offer general statements about the world and its parts, and in particular about nations and
other in-groups. They are believed to be true and are acted upon whenever
circumstances suggest or require a common response. Myths are what
humankind has in place of instinct: they enable our characteristic way of
acting together (Michael 1993). Mythology, therefore, can be defined as

the unquestioned beliefs shared by a society about the purposes and ways of life that are right and natural and worth maintaining (ibid. 1993). More importantly, modes of governing and the expectancies held by constituencies derive from the prevailing mythologies.

"Paradigm" literally means "pattern," from the Greek root "paradigma" – "to show side by side." "Paradigm, in its established usage is an accepted model or pattern ... In a science, a paradigm is rarely an object for further articulation and specification under new or more stringent conditions ... Paradigms gain their status because they are more successful than their competitors in solving a few problems that a group of practitioners has come to recognize as acute" (Kuhn 1962: 23). From this established usage, however, the term has broadened to encompass a wider social definition. Capra (1991) defines a social paradigm as a constellation of concepts, values, perceptions, and practices shared by a community that forms a particular vision of reality that functions as the basis for how the community organizes itself. According to Henderson (1991: x), on the other hand: "In spite of Thomas Kuhn's many cautions not to over-generalize or to use his definition of paradigm in a social context, I believe a paradigm is a pair of different spectacles which can reveal a new view of reality, allowing us to re-conceive our situation, re-frame old problems, and find new pathways for evolutionary change."

Paradigms are the "logics," or "mental models," that underlie the missions, systems of governance, strategies, and organizational character and structures that form the parameters of the social architecture of institutions (Perlmutter and Trist 1986). Moreover, they have their place in the normative context of sustainable development problems: they are part of the social causes working against our being unable to effect necessary changes. These mental models underlie the "policy paradigms" of the normative observer, co-determining what comes to be seen as environmental problems and their appropriate solutions (de Groot 1992).

Dualism

Myths and metaphors, therefore, complement and reinforce dominant societal paradigms. A dominant myth in modern Euro-American thought is dualism – an "ism" that shapes the thickness and determines the colour and flexibility of the lens we use to understand the world in which we live. As well, it influences our relationships with other species and our sense of place. The *Concise Oxford Dictionary*, 8th edition, defines dualism as follows: "1. being twofold; duality. 2. Philos. the theory that in any domain of reality there are two independent underlying principles, e.g., mind and matter, form and content. 3. Theol. a. the theory that the forces of good and evil are equally balanced in the universe b. the theory of the dual (human and divine) personality of Christ."

Modern notions of duality are usually attributed to the eighteenth-century philosopher René Descartes. For Descartes, the pursuit of knowledge was the ultimate end; therefore, the defining characteristic of human beings was the mind. And he saw mind and matter as being fundamentally different from one another. For Descartes, the material universe was a machine and nothing but a machine. "Matter" had no purpose, life, or spirituality. Nature worked according to mechanical laws, and everything in the material world could be explained in terms of the arrangement and movement of its parts. Since Descartes, this mechanical picture of nature has been a central plank within the paradigm of science, at least until recently, when some have started to question it (Funtowicz and Ravetz 1993; Hill 1993; Holling 1989/90; Jantsch 1980; and Merchant 1980). But even though Descartes led us to venerate dualism as the highest God, with his fundamental distinction between mental and material substance, he was simply reflecting a theme that had long influenced Western thought. Indeed, a reliance on dualistic thought can be traced back to the Zoroastrians, as well as to the early Christians and the ancient Greeks.

Regardless of its origins, dualism has been, and continues to be, an underlying determinant of the West's relationship with the world. We tend to separate everything into polar opposites: sacred and profane; essential and existential; good and evil; and male and female. And, of course, these oppositions are loaded with assumptions. Dualisms emphasize only extremes or caricatures of entities (or attributes) that exist along a continuum. This emphasis, in turn, leads to an over-emphasis on opposites and a disregard for the infinite range of possibilities that exist in between. The non-dualist, by contrast, is concerned with both unity and multiplicity. Yes and no are regarded as part of one systemic, unified whole and, as such, are concerned with an infinite multiplicity of degrees of affirmation and denial.

All the basic dualities – the alienation of the mind from the body; the alienation of the self from the objective world; the subjective retreat of the individual, alienated from the social community; the domination or rejection of nature by spirit – these all have roots in the apocalyptic-Platonic religious heritage of classical Christianity. But the alienation of the masculine from the feminine is the primary sexual symbolism that sums up these alienations.

(Ruether 1979: 44)

Following directly from dualism are the values placed on the mind as opposed to the material, the dichotomy between the subjective and the objective, and the assignment of masculine and feminine attributes to one or the other. From the time of Plato and Aristotle, males have been described as rational and objective, while females have been described as nurturing and subjective. As early as the nineteenth century, some feminists warned passionately about the dangers of such classification. As Claire Demar (1976) exclaimed:

> You proclaim two natures! Indeed tomorrow, depending on how many declare themselves to belong to the one or the other ... [y]ou'll make one, perhaps involuntarily, predominate over the other; and soon we'll have a bad and a good nature, an original sin; ... you shall be the God and I shall be the Devil.

Unlike most other nineteenth-century feminists such as Goldwin, Pankard, Perkins-Gilman, and Woolf, who venerated difference and argued for the moral value of two natures, Demar feared the authoritarian dynamics of what she referred to as "classifications" – the subtle, metaphysical distinctions by which humanity divides itself into a series of orders, classes, and types. Congruent with Lakoff's (1987) postmodern theories on categories, Demar believed that classifications in and of themselves could be oppressive, and she saw that categorization held real dangers for women. Dualism and Judaism-Christianity mutually reinforce one another in that they both accept notions of the immanent and the transcendent, and both value notions of male and female difference.

The myth that describes everything in the material world in terms of the arrangement and movement of its parts, thus reducing nature to a linear mechanism, has led to the making of numerous artificial separations. For humans do not perceive themselves to exist only in deterministic mechanical relationships. It follows that, if humans are not mere machines, then perhaps there are other species that are also not mere machines. Indeed, the construction of any boundary between the machine-like and the not machine-like is a product of dualistic thinking. Another result of Cartesian philosophy is the separation of the heart from the mind (Head 1992). This separation has led to the decoupling of human society from its environment – a process of disembeddedness that has contributed to the destruction of nature (Rogers 1994).

Unless we think about fundamentals, our specific measures may produce new backlashes more serious than those they are designed to remedy ... The issue is whether a democratized world can survive its own implications. Presumably we cannot unless we rethink our axioms.

(White 1967: 1205)

Dualisms can lead to false dichotomies; that is, they can be constructed in order to maintain a power structure and a false conception of what constitutes essential reality. They help set up systems of binary oppositions that often become the bases of systems of dominance and subordination. One cannot overestimate the influence that dualism has on intellectual thought and research, the design of organizational structures, gender relations, our interaction with the material world, and our relations with other species. Until recently, many scientists maintained and vigorously defended the myth that researchers are objectively separate from their research: the researcher and the object under observation were regarded as context independent. Postmodern science, however, recognizes context as an important determinant of behaviours and beliefs. It acknowledges that no one can ever be separate from his or her context. Indeed, researchers are an integral part of the context. Just as objects and subjects influence and interact with one another, so, too, does the environment influence and interact with all who observe and conduct research (Denzin and Lincoln 1994; Guba 1990; Haraway 1991; Lather 1991; Miles and Huberman 1993; Reason 1993; Rosaldo 1989; Rowan 1981; Van Manen 1990).

Notions of objectivism, essentialism, empirical realism, and objective truth have been deeply challenged by constructivists, who argue that what we take to be objective knowledge and truth is a matter of perspective. Knowledge and truth are human constructs. In human societies, knowledge is pluralistic and plastic – pluralistic because reality is expressible in a variety of symbol and language systems; plastic because reality is stretched and shaped to fit purposeful acts of intentional human agents. Thus, we invent concepts, models, and schemes to make sense of experience, and reality is the result of social processes accepted as normal in a specific context, and knowledge claims are intelligible and debatable only within a particular context or community (Fish 1988).

Influential Paradigms

The dominant paradigms in our society exert considerable influence on how we structure our science, how we conduct our economic affairs, how we view our environment, how we build our settlements, and how we organize our institutions of governance. Often, the dominant paradigm is implicitly embedded in our daily decisions; how we receive or reject new information; and, most important, our receptivity to new ideas. All of our paradigms, or worldviews, have embedded within them implicit values and assumptions. They affect our concept of what is worth striving for and what will or will not work (Brewer and de Leon 1983).

The current prevalent socio-economic paradigm may be characterized by the following model (see Figure 2.1).

Figure 2.1

Exploitist model

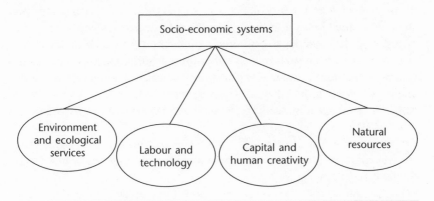

Source: Adapted from Folke 1991.

This "exploitist" model assumes that growth is inherently good; there should be no limits to that growth, and, if there are, then they can be transcended by human knowledge and technology. There is an infinite capacity for substitution between human and natural capital. The exploitist model is a model of dominance and hierarchy: it presumes the dominance of the human species over all others and its right to subjugate the natural world. Its science can be characterized by a belief in the certainty of knowledge and control over the natural world. It is reductionist, analytical, and curiosity-driven. Neutrality is revered as scientific rigour, which, in turn, is based on linear predictability and replicability along with duality (characterized by an either/or approach to explanation and research). Although some kind of cybernetic interactions may be regarded as occurring between human and ecological systems, these systems are still perceived as inherently separate.

In this model, the "environment" includes "nature," to which machine-like behaviour is often attributed. The paradigm of the well-oiled machine is reflected in the industrial philosophy of mass production (Taylor 1911), with workers being considered as parts of the machine. The fundamental characteristics of this model are its compartmentalization of complex systems and its reliance on models of direct, linear cause and effect. It leads to a hierarchic, classically bureaucratic philosophy of both management and regulation (Burrell and Morgan 1979; Parsons 1947). Human systems are dominant over natural systems, which exist as sources of resources and sinks for wastes, their purpose being to support production and consumption within the dominant socio-economic system. The environment and its ecological services are taken for granted and, because they are not valued, are seen as external to the market. Essentially, nature is seen as a free good and an unlimited factor of production. Natural resources are regarded as inexhaustible and substitutable. The socio-economic system is unconstrained by any biophysical limits, and if limits are acknowledged, they are regarded as transcendable by human innovation and technology. Policies that derive from such models suffer from rigidity; over-simplification; lack of adaptability; resource exploitation aimed at maximum sustainable yields; inefficiency; inability to recognize negative feedback; and ecologically damaging, economically perverse, outcomes (Holling 1978; MacNeill et al. 1991).

A utilist alternative to the above paradigm of nature as the "other" is a model being promoted by the International Institute for Sustainable Development (IISD) (see Figure 2.2).

The assumptions and values implicit in the utilist model (currently under discussion in federal and quasi-government organizations, where it is referred to as ecosystem management) include the notion of some limits to growth (imposed by the carrying capacity of the planet) as well as some recognition of human responsibility towards other species. By keeping the model open, by not mapping the figure as constrained by biophysical limits, it assumes that these limits are plastic and that, ultimately, human creativity may well find alternatives and substitutes with which to push

Figure 2.2

Utilist model

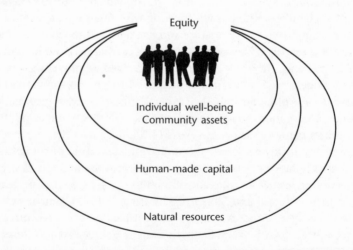

Equity

Individual well-being
Community assets

Human-made capital

Natural resources

Source: International Institute for Sustainable Development.

The concept of holism and holons has been proposed by a number of scholars. Smuts (1926: 342) suggested that "behind the evolutionary movement and the holistic field of nature is the inner-shaping directive activity of Holism itself, working through the wholes and in the variations which creatively arise from them ... these variations are not accidental or haphazard, but the controlled, regulated expression of the inner holistic development of organisms as wholes." Koestler (1978) states the concept of the holon is meant to supply the missing link between atomism and holism, and to supplant the dualistic way of thinking in terms of "parts" and "wholes," which is so deeply ingrained in our mental habits, by a multi-level, stratified approach. Jantsch (1980) proposes a paradigm of self-organization based on the interconnectedness of natural dynamics at all levels of evolving micro- and macrosystems. From such an interconnectedness of the human world with overall evolution springs a new sense of meaning.

the limits farther. There is a firm belief in the ability of human beings to manage the environment through ecosystem management. Policies underpinned by this model still include conquest and control of what are now recognized as dynamic, interactive natural systems, adherence to the myth that there is one (right) point of view, and the pursuit of stability. Policies underpinned by this paradigm still include conquest and control of dynamic, interactive living systems, and an adherence to the myth of one (right) point of view and the pursuit of stability. As well, policies are developed within a limited decision-making context, and the emphasis is on maximum sustained yields and the separation of human systems from natural systems. An alternative to this model is the integrist model (see Figure 2.3).

Within this integrist model, which is characterized by both/and thinking rather than either/or thinking, there is a growing appreciation for qualitative versus quantitative growth, and natural and human resources are regarded as complements to, rather than substitutes for, one another. Its science is characterized by systems that are seen as self-organizing, holarchic, open systems (SOHO) (Koestler 1978).

In this model, the global human system is seen as a "holon," or "whole-part," of reality, which is nested within a larger biosphere holon. Any holon with SOHO features has, inherent within it, a creative evolving capability. The holarchic model implies that there are absolute limits to growth imposed by the biosphere, to which human systems are subject. Any holon persists because of reciprocal relationships between it and the other holons with which it interacts. For the human holon, the biospheric holon is indispensable. These limits exist in both natural and human systems, although the nature of the biophysical limits are more fixed than are

Figure 2.3

___

Integrist model

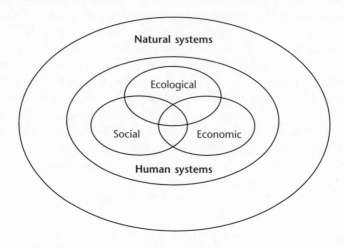

___

those of human systems. Different limits exist in all three spheres (ecological, social, and economic) within human systems, and the space for policy options decreases the closer human systems move towards the natural limits.

In the integrist model there is an interdependence between human species and other species, and a different sense of "relationality" with the world. There is an emphasis on co-evolving processes between human and natural systems, and a value is placed on designing and managing human impacts with the environment rather than on managing the environment itself. Other values include integration rather than separation, with a focus on reorganizing and valuing both commonalties and differences. This model emphasizes a plurality of hierarchies that respond to a shifting network of natural constraints and interactive influences (Lincoln and Guba 1985; Morgan 1986; and Weick 1985). The integrist model assumes a much more extended peer community than exists within traditional science (Funtowicz and Ravetz 1993, 1991).

Because the integrist model also embraces uncertainty and unpredictability – because it places human activity systems within the finite biosphere – it values long-term perspectives and courses of action that ensure survival, satisfying optimal rather than maximal requirements. This being the case, a multi-faceted flow of information is needed to support adaptive flexibility at all levels of an organization or system (Sahl and Bernstein

1995). The ability and capacity of human systems to respond to negative feedback is also critical to understanding the limits of the biosphere. Policy development, therefore, has to be a dynamic, interactive process, growing over time through a recursive process (Bateson 1979; Weick 1985), and it must have a greatly expanded decision-making context – one capable of respecting the plurality of "stakes" in the issues.

Changing the Lens

The illusion that human societies can use technology to transcend the time, place, and scale constraints of the biophysical world, and that they can continually expand their ecological footprint (their appropriation of resources from other geographical areas) well beyond finite limits follows from the exploitist model (Figure 2.1). This illusion is underpinned by dualism, as are all of the subsequent separations it engenders. It is only a short step from Descartes' radical separation of self and object, to the human-nature dichotomy, to separations based on gender, to the separation of the human species from "other" species. Our separation from nature, our making of it an "other," leads to attitudes that support dominance based on difference. Our emphasis on difference leads to differential valuations of what constitutes good and bad, of what constitutes integrity, and to polarities such as productive/non-productive, efficient/inefficient, and friend/enemy. Changing the way we view our environment and our place in it as well as our sense of relatedness is a crucial first step to changing our impact(s) in our individual communities, as nations and globally. We need to focus on "both/and" rather than "either/or." As we change our assumptions and associated definitions concerning relatedness, we are likely to challenge our current ways of viewing nature and our relationship with it.

The subject who excludes the other has been a white male subject and his exclusion of the other has been placed in the same logical class as the exclusion of "not a": this meant that "the other" was defined not in terms of its own properties, but in purely negative terms.

(Brennan 1997: 189)

Ornstein and Ehrlich (1989) recognize the challenge that this presents, given the limitations of what they call the "old mind," which evolved in a pre-modern habitat that is no longer the dominant environmental context of industrialized nations. Human capacity to create built environments and to develop technological innovations far exceeds our mental abilities to deal with the consequences of modern-day creations. Thus there is a fundamental mismatch between the "perceived" needs of humans and the natural world. Cultural responses are too slow to keep pace with the degree of change in rapidly co-evolving human/natural systems or, in many cases, to even perceive the reality of these changes before it is too late.

As I discuss in Chapter 3, human beings are highly influenced by their environmental contexts, and early in their development certain perceptual rules are hardwired into their genes and culture. Those rules help to shape the subjective world we inhabit. And many people remain unaware of the extent to which their worldviews are derived from their early experiences (Ornstein and Ehrlich 1989). Perceptual rules allow humans to absorb a vast variety of information and stimuli, and they act as a filter for a multitude of responses. One of the most important rules, or "defaults," is to ignore what is routine and to respond quickly to sudden shifts, to emergencies, to scarcity, to the immediate and personal, to "news" (ibid.).

But the increasing interdependence of biophysical phenomena, combined with the globalization of trade and commerce along with large-scale movements of people, move systems (both human and natural) in ways that are non-linear, interactive, and often unexpected (Holling 1993b). Given our old mind patterns, we do not have the mental capacity to appreciate or to respond to these slower, interacting biophysical phenomena. In addition, these effects tend to manifest themselves in human activity systems as a result of the increasing co-evolution of human and natural systems. Although the human species has developed cognitive strategies in response to the kinds of day-to-day conditions that challenged its ancestors, these same strategies, as well as the illusion that humans are mainly rational thinkers, often underlie personal, social, and political problems (Ornstein and Ehrlich 1989). For human reality is the product of selective perceptions, beliefs, and interests, which are always strongly influenced by personal contexts and feelings (Michael 1995). Thus, many of the current challenges to modern societies are, to a very large extent, due to the inadequacies and the immaturity of contemporary thinking that underpins the values, motivations, behaviours, and institutions that keep modern societies lagging behind the realities of a constantly changing world (Peccei 1978).

Human societies are clearly living in a period of fluctuating myths. The positivist modernist myth claims that we can understand nature with science, control it with science, and prosper through material abundance (the value of which is assessed on the marketplace). Human societies, however, are only now beginning to realize the naiveté of this, and they are now witnessing the numerous unexpected negative side-effects (Norgaard 1994). The postmodern myth recognizes that systems are complex, interactive, co-evolving, and, to some extent, self-organizing, and that they exhibit unique properties within different contexts. This latter myth builds on the insights of quantum mechanics, irreversible thermodynamics, information theory, and organic evolution, as well as constructivism and pluralism, rather than on the limited mechanistic insights of Descartes and Newton. Thus, our current array of critical problems, ranging from local toxic dumps to the disruption of the global climate, is a product of the drastic mismatch between the cyclical and self-consistent processes of the biosphere and the linear, innovative, but ecologically disharmonious processes of the technosphere (Commoner 1975). What this implies for our species is that we must conduct our affairs so that we conserve both cultural and natural capital, and facilitate their positive co-evolution by means of suitable institutional structures and processes.

What is needed is a large-scale program for a rapid change of mind (Ornstein and Ehrlich 1989) along with new forms of discourse. This will require changes in our educational systems, our values, our systems of governance, and both private and public decision making. The necessary changes will only occur, however, through transformation of civil societies into communities that are ecologically knowledgeable; that is, communities that are capable of learning equally from natural systems and human systems.

One of the greatest challenges, then, will be to change the dominant paradigms and prevailing mythologies, especially since the modes of governing and the expectancies held by constituencies derive from them (Michael 1993). They can be challenged in at least five ways: first, by making them explicit in everyday discourse; second, by showing the interaction between language and domination; third, by questioning the underlying values; fourth, by creating new narratives, myths, and metaphors for social change; and fifth, by changing the boundaries of decision making. Since mythologies are mostly unconscious social constructions of reality, the process of making them explicit exposes them to questioning and re-examination. The onus, therefore, is not always on those proposing "alternatives" to justify their viewpoints or to compete to be heard, but rather, on those adhering to the dominant modes to re-examine and explain their patterns of thinking and action in the light of the current realities.

These structures arise out of history and our own thinking. First there is the paradigm – the mind-set from which it arises. Then there is the organizational structure which is built upon a certain world-view. If the mind-set is patriarchal, then the externally-imposed structure will tend towards the hierarchical. If the mind-set is that of community building, then the structures put into place will tend to the co-operative or collective.

(Kaufman Hall 1995: 19)

Systems of governance will eventually have to change to acknowledge and support the notion of civil societies as communities of learning and knowledge. Their structures of signification, of legitimization and domination (Westley 1995), will also have to fundamentally change. With respect to the latter, it can be argued that governments must move to take initiatives to strengthen local communities because highly centralized national bureaucracies, multinational mining and logging corporations, and international resource management agencies are incapable of responding to (and, indeed, may actually suppress) important local ecological feedback signals. Diffuse feedback processes in the natural world need to be matched by much more diffuse decision-making processes in human societies (Dryzek 1990).

Governments can play a key role in enabling communities to acquire ecologically sensitive knowledge. This, however, would mean abandoning current forms of dominance and power, of controlling and monitoring, and moving to a model of civil dialogues by leading and catalyzing strategic partnerships between government, NGOs, and the private sector. These strategic partnerships must be inclusive, allow for broadened notions of "expertise," and be representative of the Canadian plurality. Public disenchantment with the political system will not abate if the new fora emerging in response to citizen demands are simply manifestations of entrenched vested interests. In addition, if their procedures are flawed, then they will only serve to further increase public alienation and disrespect for elected officials. Both levels of government – elected and non-elected – need to recognize the legitimacy of this pressure and begin to address public concerns for greater participatory democracy. This will require the provision of analytical space for the development of policy alternatives and the creation of new narratives for social change, which, in turn, will require the ability to acknowledge and accommodate diverse perspectives within a community (Boland and Tenkasi 1995) or a domain such as sustainable development.

Governments can also play a key role in facilitating the necessary changes in the nature and quality of these discourses. In order to accommodate change, it is important to expose and challenge the implicit assumptions and paradigms that underlie diverse arguments, so as to allow for new emergent thinking. Narrative modes of cognition provide access to those implicit assumptions and interpretive structures that characterize a self-conscious learning society (ibid.). In order to challenge the old mind and its default mechanisms, governments must support the inclusion of continuous updates in the media concerning the slower ecological problems, as well as information on how to solve the problems (Ornstein and Ehrlich 1989). Strengthening the infrastructure within the NGO community may help to develop the ability to challenge old mind ideas. In any case, mounting such challenges will require some sort of government partnership and leadership, as it is not within the self-interest of the many vested interests manifest in modern society to change the status quo. The capacity of governments to play this role is dependent on the existence of ethical and responsible leadership based on well articulated values that are shared by a majority of their constituents.

Another artificial construct of our dualistic, rational, expert-driven model is the notion that values may be excluded from paid work and scientific research. Values, however, are part of the human condition and do, in fact, determine day-to-day decision making. By reintegrating values into human systems, we make them explicit, subject to debate, and, therefore, we are able to respond to current realities through creative destruction and reorganization. It is only through creative destruction of the old mind patterns, historical paradigms, myths, and metaphors that we are able to see whether or not they still apply to the real world as we have changed it. Values are central to how we organize, to how we see our place in the biosphere and the space we believe we are entitled to, to how we see our knowledge systems, and to the technologies we design and use.

Another key role in encouraging the development of new narratives for social change involves fostering the production of useful knowledge and information that makes explicit our dominant myths and metaphors, thereby creating space for the discussion of alternatives. In particular, this requires that the influence of language on human beliefs and actions be exposed. For example, researchers need to know to what extent using the term "living organism" rather than "living being" allows them to continue experimenting on animals without questioning this (largely unnecessary) practice. As well, our dominant language is not matched to the reality of systemic interactions, circular feedback processes, non-linearity, or multiple causations and outcomes (Michael 1995). Increasing awareness of the power of language is crucial to exposing the often hidden influence of dominant paradigms.

The mere act of exposing these dominant paradigms may function as a powerful catalyst for opening up space for new or emerging paradigms that are more reflective of changing realities. When combined with transdisciplinary networks of collaboration (see Chapter 9), this awareness could lead to the development of new perspectives and the emergence of myths and metaphors that support new appreciations of our role in the universe and our relationships with other species. It could also lead to a new understanding of the value of diversity and beauty in our world, perhaps ultimately to the realization that there is really no separate "other," that we are all part of a still largely mysteriously integrated universe.

3
Sustainable Development Imperatives

The implementation of sustainable development is the human imperative of the 21st century, requiring strong leadership by local, regional and national governments. A framework across governments is critical to their ability to provide consistent and effective leadership to other sectors of Canadian society, in order to diffuse its concepts and practices in the next decade, before irreversible thresholds are reached.

In this period between myths, old belief systems are beginning to fragment (Lincoln and Guba 1985). We are living with dissatisfaction, a kind of quiet despair over the old solutions that no longer seem to be working quite so effectively in the face of the crises that are occurring everywhere. Human societies are obviously in tremendous states of flux, and current decision-making contexts are complex, plural, and paradoxical.

Decision-making contexts that are multiple and overlapping often make it difficult to obtain needed information, even if individuals are predisposed to question their present beliefs (Dyckman 1981). The new myths and solutions we seek for moving towards more sustainable societies worldwide may well lie in learning to reconcile the tensions within the paradoxes of sustainable development rather than denying their existence and carrying on with business as usual.

Human societies are obviously living in massive denial of their current ecological reality, for they continue to degrade their current and, some analysts would argue, future ecological capital at an unprecedented rate and scale (Daily and Ehrlich 1996b; Rees 1996) in order to support the dominant Eurocentric economic system. Chapter 4 further describes the nature and extent of this degradation.

Just as postmodernism recognizes the importance of social context for human thought, the structure and processes of natural systems illustrate equally important contexts for sustainable development. Evolution, for example, did not take place in an already created physical environment that remained static and to which life then adapted; rather, life created the physical environment we know today, gradually transforming an extremely inhospitable environment into one favouring the extension of life (Ophuls 1977). Diverse organisms live together in an orderly fashion, interacting with their environment; and the maxim, "as the community goes, so goes the organism" expresses a fundamental law of life (Odum 1971). In spite of the sophistication of postmodern societies, current socio-political institutions in Canada (and elsewhere) appear incapable of acknowledging this fundamental law, of recognizing the severity of the impacts of human growth on the biosphere, and of accepting the importance of taking into account the diverse interrelationships and complexity of ecological interactions.

Chaos theory predicts that undampened oscillations, which our human activity systems now appear to be experiencing, will proceed to extinction as a function of increasing rates of growth.

(May 1974; Schaffer and Kot 1985)

As is discussed in Chapter 6, the paradox of growth may well be the most critical issue facing human societies in the twenty-first century. The acceptance of growth is partly rooted in two related (although not always explicitly recognized) tenets of mainstream neoclassical economics: (1) resources are infinite; and (2) a satisfactory substitute can always be found for the role of any one of them (Ehrlich 1982), the (false) law of "infinite substitutability." All indicators point to continued growth in population, in the space we occupy, and in our consumption. Their subsequent impacts on our life support systems will cause changes of expanding severity, including global warming, stratospheric ozone depletion, acid deposition, loss of biodiversity, and cultural breakdown.

Impacts of Human Activities
Humans now appropriate between one-third and one-half of the present net primary production (NPP) of the biosphere (Pauly and Christensen 1995; Vitousek et al. 1986). NPP is the amount of energy left after subtracting the respiration of primary producers (mostly plants) from the total amount of energy (mostly solar) that is fixed biologically. NPP provides the basis for the maintenance, growth, and reproduction of all consumers and decomposers on earth. It is the earth's total food resource. The paradigm that separates socio-economic systems from their environment has led to overestimations of the planet's capacity to absorb the impacts of human activity. It has also led us to ignore another fundamental law, the "law of the minimum," or Liebig's law. This law states that whatever necessity is least available (relative to per capita requirements) sets an environment's

carrying capacity. This is similar to the idea that the weakest link determines the strength of the chain. While it may appear that human systems are infinitely flexible and plastic, either through technological innovation or trade, it is now clear that the environment, enlarged through globalization, still has finite carrying capacity (Rees 1996).

Due to the difficulty in coming up with a measure of the relative scale, I feel that it is better to focus on the fact that we do live in a finite physical system and that as we approach important boundaries this system will send us "feedback." I picture this sort of as approaching a tree. As soon as we start running into some branches (e.g., ozone holes, changing climatic conditions, die-off of amphibians), we had best start paying attention before we slam into the trunk.

(Rothman, Electronic Dialogue, 12 November 1996)

Some analysts argue that human society is approaching, and perhaps has already exceeded, global ecological carrying capacity and that extension of present rates of industrialized consumption and production to the rest of the globe is simply not feasible (Costanza et al. 1995; Daily and Ehrlich 1996a; 1992 Meadows et al.; Odum 1972; Wackernagel and Rees 1996). If current population rates continue, it would appear that by the year 2030 the human species may be appropriating 80 percent of the earth's total carrying capacity (Regier, personal communication). Indeed, in spite of the vast amounts of information now circulating, it is difficult to determine exactly where we are on the following spectrum (see Figure 3.1), although most ecologists are clear that we are already well past the point of sustainable development.

Furthermore, civil societies have not been able to successfully engage in collective dialogues about which is the preferred state, since it raises the difficult issues of population, resources, consumption, and environmental health. This discussion also brings into play such complex issues as the nature of limits and their plasticity, values, human ingenuity, and the role of technology. In addition, there are differing assumptions, perceptions, and knowledge about the importance of environmental conditions and processes in supporting human well-being, and in the sensitivity of these

---

Present-day society is locked into four positive feedback loops which need to be broken: economic growth which feeds on itself, population growth which feeds on itself, technological change which feeds on itself, and a pattern of income inequality which seems to be self sustaining and which tends to spur growth in the other three areas.

(Furkiss 1974: 235)

Figure 3.1

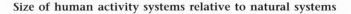

Size of human activity systems relative to natural systems

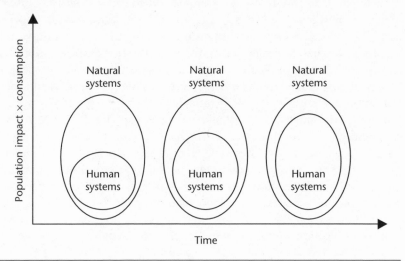

processes and conditions to disruption (Holdren et al. 1995). Hardin (1986) proposes abandoning the term "carrying capacity" when dealing with human problems in favour of the term "cultural capacity." In his definition, the cultural capacity of a territory is always smaller than its carrying capacity.

Regardless of the debate over definitions, it is clear that human appropriation of carrying capacity will continue to increase unless we make some immediate changes in our values and current levels of growth. Since 1900, the world's population has multiplied more than three times, and the world's economy has expanded twenty times. The consumption of fossil fuels has grown by a factor of thirty, and industrial production has increased by a factor of fifty. Most of this growth has taken place since 1950 (MacNeill et al. 1991). Estimates of the fraction of land on the planet transformed or degraded by humanity fall in the range of 39 to 50 percent; and, by the end of this century, the flow of about two-thirds of all of the earth's rivers will be regulated (Vitousek et al. 1997).

One of the resources most critical to an animal population's carrying capacity is food, and it may well prove to be the ultimate determining factor for human societies in the future. Brown (1995) predicts that food security and distribution will become the defining focus of the global environmental threat, as seafood catch and grain production per person continue to fall, coupled with rising food prices and increasing demand for grain. In addition, a doubling of the human population portends a more than doubling of human impacts because humanity has sequentially exploited the most accessible of its essential resources (Daily and Ehrlich 1996b).

There are quite simply no new frontiers left to exploit (McNeill 1992). Boom and bust resource cycles and environmental degradation have been part of our history since the beginning of civilization. In hunting and gathering societies, as the resources in one area were diminished, humans moved to another area. With the agricultural revolution, however, people became more place-bound, and new forces, such as privatization and centralization, were introduced into human production, rapidly expanding human activity impacts on ecological carrying capacity. Exploration and conquests of new worlds meant new markets and, with them, resource exploitation on an even greater scale. This appropriation of new frontiers gave humans the perception that they could engage in infinite expansion and growth. As scale, time, and place appeared to be transcended by human ingenuity, and as human population began to expand exponentially, there was an imperative to intensify production, particularly agricultural production, by means of enhanced technology.

Human culture has removed the constraints that result in dampened oscillations characteristic of most other species. Human systems are presently incapable of responding to negative feedback loops even though they loom before us. The result is unregulated growth and potentially lethal population instability that degenerates to figurative, literal and mathematical chaos.

(Hern 1990: 33)

Not only the scale, but also the nature of this growth is having profound impacts on the ecological carrying capacity of the planet. For example, if every Chinese person were to purchase a car and a refrigerator using chlorofluoro carbons (CFCs), then although as a nation they would be better off, the result in terms of global warming and ozone depletion would be catastrophic. It would appear, therefore, that the closer we come to these ecological limits, the less we can assume that economic welfare, as generally defined today, and total welfare are moving in the same direction. Nevertheless, as Gwynne Dwyer's (1997) four-part CBC series, "The Population Bomb," dramatically demonstrates, the increasing demand from less developed countries (LDC) for access to the same products that are currently consumed in so-called developed countries is inevitable. Clearly, to achieve sustainable development, the material nature of these products, along with our production processes, must change dramatically or be fundamentally redesigned.

Economically, the world is undergoing both massive and rapid change. Coupled with the rapid worldwide disappearance of centrally planned economies, there is a tidal wave of development and expanded reliance on market forces and market-based policies. There are powerful trends towards global economic integration through trade liberalization and the emergence of an international capital market, which is characterized by flows of capital in search of ever higher rates of return. The growth of newly industrializing countries in Asia (now including China, Indonesia, Malaysia, and Thailand), and the rapid expansion of world trade, will continue to challenge the ability of all systems to maintain their integrity. Indeed, the current crises in the economies of the Asia-Pacific Rim probably indicate that the global trading system as a whole is following the boom and bust cycles of resource exploitation. Fundamentally, social and economic imperatives can be supported only with as equal an emphasis on rehabilitation and maintenance as on production, and, I would further argue, worldwide enhancement of ecological systems.

Socially, we appear to be witnessing a psychopathological and simultaneous uncoupling and coupling. Examples of the former include the uncoupling of money and production as well as employment and profit in many sectors. Thus, as companies become more profitable, they lay off more and more workers. This can be seen most clearly in the banking sector. As more and more industries move into the global marketplace, there is an uncoupling of work and place. As resources are depleted in one community, companies simply move to another, leaving local governments to deal with the subsequent unemployment, social dislocation, and ecological degradation. These processes continue to create a social trap (Costanza 1987) within which population growth is coupled with increasing inequity, reduced carrying capacity, and unsustainable development. Catton (1993) further argues that most of today's less developed nations will never become developed and that this will have serious repercussions for civil societies everywhere.

The foregoing leads us to the overwhelming conclusion that we are approaching, and in some realms may have already exceeded, the global carrying capacity of the planet. It is clear that, whereas loads can grow exponentially, carrying capacity cannot (Arrow et al. 1995; Catton 1993; Rees 1996). As will be shown in the following chapters, there is already ample evidence of system breakdowns, global climate change, ozone depletion, unprecedented rates of biodiversity loss, and inequity both within and between countries. Our species has clearly moved from a self-perpetuating way of life that relied on the circularity of natural biogeochemical processes to a way of life that is ultimately self-terminating because it relies on linear chemical transformations (Catton 1993). Current practices are clearly not sustainable, and business as usual is not an option. Sustainable development is, therefore, a strategic imperative for all nations at every level of human activity.

Contextual Appreciation

Critics have argued that the term "sustainable development" is an oxymoron and that development is being emphasized at the expense of sustainability (Jickling 1994; Lele 1991). Much of this criticism stems, in part, from the fact that sustainable development touches on every sphere of human activity – technological, economic, political, and cultural – thus bringing into play many of the dominant paradigms, myths, and metaphors. In addition, the current structure of academe and government ensures that practitioners in the various relevant fields have access only to a small part of the picture. They typically think in terms of different time scales and often use the same words to mean different things (Holdren et al. 1995). Jacobs (1994) argues that any sustainable development formulation must be able to meet the metatheoretical criteria that determine the ability of a framework to effectively guide research and, ultimately, the development of policies to achieve a given set of objectives. Lele (1991) further suggests that the definitional confusion surrounding the concept is not really about meaning so much as it is about whose values should take precedence. Some analysts argue that sustainable development is not possible without massive cultural change (i.e., a paradigm shift) and that such change would be a form of feminization in that it would emphasize connectedness, relationships, cyclicity, and non-linearity (Malley and Lawrence 1994).

The concept of optimal allocation among alternative uses of the total resource flow (throughput) must be clearly distinguished from the concept of an optimal scale of total resource flow relative to the environment. Under ideal conditions, the market can find an optimal allocation in the sense of Pareto. But the market cannot find an optimal scale any more than it can find an optimal distribution. The latter requires the addition of ethical criteria; the former requires the further addition of ecological criteria.

(Daly 1991a: 241-242)

Nevertheless, I believe that the strength of the concept lies in its constructive ambiguity and that this has kept people – people who normally would not talk to one another – at the table. I believe the term does, inherently, raise the issue of growth. Its greatest strength may lie in its ability to transcend the old left/right dichotomy, the no-growth/full-growth polarization, and to stimulate new discussions about the nature and meaning of growth in a sustainable society. As well, putting "sustainable" in front of "development" implies that development cannot be continued indefinitely – that how we proceed with development must be compatible with indefinitely maintaining livable conditions. A sustainable process is one that can be maintained indefinitely without progressive diminution of valued qualities, both inside and outside the system in which the process operates and the condition prevails (Holdren et al. 1995).

Sustainable development, since its widespread promulgation through the 1987 Brundtland Commission Report, has brought together new coalitions (albeit that some of them are rather fragile). Nonetheless, if these coalitions can now strengthen and begin to work together in more synergistic ways in the third sector (Rifkin 1995), then we may be able to accelerate positive social changes.

Earlier I defined sustainable development as a process involving the reconciliation of three imperatives: (1) the ecological imperative to live within global biophysical carrying capacity and to maintain biodiversity; (2) the social imperative to ensure the development of democratic systems of governance that can effectively propagate and sustain the values that people wish to live by; and (3) the economic imperative to ensure that basic needs are met worldwide (adapted from Dale et al. 1995). And equitable access to resources – ecological, economic, and social – is fundamental to its implementation. Meeting all three imperatives is both necessary and sufficient; it is counter-productive to debate which is more fundamental. Without satisfying ecological imperatives, we poison ourselves, deplete our resources, and destroy the basic life support systems essential to human and nonhuman survival. Without satisfying the economic imperative, we cannot provide the necessities of life, let alone meaningful work. And without satisfying the social imperative, our societies will collapse into chaos. Given the interconnected nature of sustainable development, failure in any one area will result in failure in the other two, particularly over the long term.

Like many things, the value of the sustainability journey seems to be in the journey itself rather than the destination. Even though the goal is elusive, and perhaps impossible, the challenge of responding creatively is what motivates many of us. Aiming for sustainability necessitates the re-examination of fundamental assumptions about the business we are in, the objectives we set and the way we organize ourselves. It places everything we do directly into an ecological context.

(Torrie 1996: 25)

But what are the characteristics of sustainable development? When considering the specific issues of global warming, ozone depletion, biodiversity loss, overpopulation, and consumption, it quickly becomes clear that they are more complex and interactive than is generally assumed. These problems are more and more frequently caused by local and global human impacts on air, land, and oceans – impacts that slowly accumulate to trigger sudden abrupt changes that directly affect the health and innovative capacities of people, the productivity of renewable resources (Holling 1996), and the well-being of human societies everywhere. And this increasing globalization of biophysical phenomena is interacting with the globalization of trade and the large-scale movements of people (Holling 1993b). These problems are emerging suddenly in several places, albeit rather slowly and locally. For example, the hole in the ozone layer had to reach a critical level before it could be detected by scientists; then it quickly became a major problem affecting many nations and communities, including many that have not contributed to the problem. Consequently, the solutions must involve all nations. The problems and the potential responses to them move both human and natural systems into such novel and unfamiliar territory that many aspects of the future are not only uncertain, but also inherently unpredictable (Holling 1993b). We shall never attain scientific consensus concerning the systems that are being examined, and our knowledge of any system with which we deal will always be incomplete (Walters 1986: 1990). Moreover, there is an inherent unknowability, as well as unpredictability, surrounding evolving managed ecosystems and the societies with which they are linked (Holling 1993b). Because of uncertainty, sustainable development issues can often be manipulated by political and economic interest groups (Costanza 1987). And because everything in ecological systems is in a constant state of change, sustainable development is a moving target (Salwasser 1993).

We must recognize that the assault on the environment cannot be effectively controlled, but must be prevented; that prevention requires the transformation of the present structure of the technosphere, bringing it into harmony with the ecosphere; that this means massively redesigning the major industrial, agricultural, energy, and transportation systems; that such a transformation of the systems of production conflicts with the short-term profit-maximizing goals that now govern investment decisions; and that, accordingly, politically suitable means must be developed that bring the public interest in long-term environmental quality to bear on these decisions.

(Commoner 1975: 192-193)

Sustainable development issues are scale, place, and time dependent, and they must be defined according to the type, intensity, and frequency of use – subject to maxims defined locally, regionally, and nationally (Regier and Baskerville 1986). Concerns about precise definitions and frameworks may be spurious, given the diversity of regions, both socially and geographically. Appropriate forestry practices for the West Coast of Canada, for example, are very different from those needed on the East Coast. These communities, therefore, must define the specifics of sustainable development according to their unique ecological, social, and economic imperatives. In some cases, there may well be greater emphasis on development than sustainability, whereas in others the reverse may be true. By extension, these imperatives will also vary greatly from nation to nation, and from region to region, as cultural factors affect the decision-making process. That is why I have collapsed all the many ecological, social, and economic imperatives into three relatively simple statements that I believe are the minimum requirements for effectively implementing sustainable development. This implementation will require fundamental changes in human activity systems, particularly with regard to government decision making. Given the above description of the characteristics of sustainable development, each socio-politically bounded region will have to further elaborate its own imperatives. Although those three imperatives appear deceptively simple, I believe they are sufficiently robust to ensure a more sustainable pathway. All three are, therefore, necessary and sufficient conditions. They involve difficult questions of valuation, however, such as defining "basic needs."

Defining Characteristics
Another key question involves specifying what is to be sustained. Sustainable development is a normative concept, and it evokes strong values at both societal and individual levels. Knowledge related to sustainable development is more value-driven as well as more curiosity-driven, and this necessitates an unprecedented interface between research and public policy – a kind of civic research. Moreover, Ludwig et al. (1993) make an important criticism of the idea of sustainable exploitation of resources: without an adequate grasp of the human dynamics that drive exploitation, there can be no adequate understanding of how sustainable exploitation can be achieved or maintained. It is important to realize that in democratic, postmodern societies there are no single, right answers to the many complex, interacting problems; rather, we must always be willing to work with multiple emergent realities, and these can be decided upon only by the plurality of interests affected. Sustainable development, therefore, has both highly political and social contexts.

Figure 3.2 puts values at the centre of human organization. In this model, values are put at the centre of the decision-making process rather than denying that they can be "objectively" submerged. By making values explicit to the decision-making process, Keeney (1996) believes that a meaningful consensus may be achieved. This model provides for a richer picture of human activity systems by uncovering the dominant values that act as barriers to the emergence of new paradigms, thus allowing them analytical space. I maintain that, since values are inherent to human behaviour, the separation of values from organizational life is artificial. Values determine how we structure our organizations; the nature of our science; and

Figure 3.2

Values-based thinking

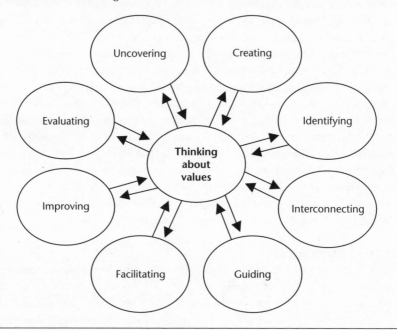

Source: Keeney 1996.

the paradigms, myths, and metaphors with which we make sense of our world, our interpersonal relationships, and our relationships with the environment. Putting values at the forefront, then, results in exposing our dominant paradigms because it encourages debate about their applicability vis-à-vis current realities. Since sustainable development is a normative concept, values and their articulation are key to any discussions about common frameworks.

Because of the complexity and interlocking nature of the systems involved, interdisciplinarity is fundamental for both decision making and finding sustainable development solutions to problems such as global warming. Indeed, a major element in the lack of progress in implementing sustainable development may well be the historical separation of the biological and social sciences, and the resultant distrust that social scientists tend to have of biological analogies (Caldwell 1969).

A critical distinction, however, must be made between multidisciplinary and interdisciplinary and transdisciplinary research. The former usually consists of different disciplines investigating the same topic but still adhering to their traditional disciplinary languages and concepts. If integration is attempted, it is frequently an add-on to a traditional separate discipli-nary approach. In contrast, interdisciplinary and transdisciplinary research implies a common conceptual framework. This type of research requires the conscious searching for unifying and holistic concepts that foster and reinforce understanding across disciplines. Integration among disciplines occurs in the design and conduct of the study.

Formal research, experimentation, and testing (i.e., systematic observa-tion, theory forming, and experimentation as a scientific activity) are needed to produce generic knowledge, but they are not always needed for problem solving. The challenge of sustainable development increasingly presents itself as a problem-solving activity. It is also about the production of useful knowledge; that is, it is inherently applied research. The nature of sustainable development issues requires, at all levels, expanded decision and research contexts.

> It seems that, in an adaptive and resilient management and decision-making model for sustainable development, we need expertise that has co-evolved out of place, culture, and tradition, which is every bit as important as the acquisition of new knowledge in disciplinary expertise. In this sensibility, "expertise" that is adaptive and resilient is diverse: it incorporates local wisdom, traditional knowledge, understanding of history, context, place, and scale.
>
> *(Lister, Electronic Dialogue, 11 July 1997)*

A systems perspective is also critical, since sustainable development issues require us to deal with complex personal, social, and ecological sys-tems. Systems thinking provides a framework for interrelationships rather than things, for seeing patterns rather than static snapshots. Some of the principles governing natural systems are holism, interdependence, and inter-relationship. Just as all the properties of water are not predictable from the properties of oxygen and hydrogen, so all the properties of ecological systems are not predictable from studying the properties of the living entities and non-living matter of which they are composed. The classical duality between the living and the non-living (as I argue in Chapter 5) is one of the pervasive old myths that must be changed. As I discussed earlier, habits of thought tend to be extremely persistent, and mainstream thought, by definition, excludes consideration of alternatives. This and other related barriers to sustainable development will be examined in Chapter 7.

Most important, knowledge experts from every domain have to realize, accept, and plan for the fact that knowledge of the systems with which they deal is, and always will be, incomplete. Surprise is inevitable, and, thus, there will rarely be unanimity of agreement among peers, only an increasingly credible line of tested argument (Holling 1996). Indeed, this lack of unanimity can be used by competing vested interests as an argument for maintaining the status quo. Moreover, not only is the science for sustainable development incomplete, the system itself is a moving target, continually evolving because of the impacts of management and the progressive expansion of the scale of human influence on the biosphere (ibid.). This incomplete knowledge is partly the result of the uniqueness of interactions in space and time, and partly a result of the evolving nature of the relationships between natural and human activity systems, given the dominance of the human species in ecosystems everywhere.

The most basic idea of ecology is that of a "system." The practical implication of an ecological system is just this: we can never do merely one thing. Living things are all a part of a "web of life," and we cannot touch a single species without tugging at relational strands extending in all directions.

(Hardin 1969: 152)

In addition to the need for interdisciplinarity and transdisciplinarity is the need for human activity systems to recognize and understand the interdependence of ecological systems. Everything within any ecosystem can be shown to be related, mostly indirectly, to everything else. Moreover, there are no linear relationships; every effect is also a cause in the web of natural interdependency. Of course, not all relationships are equally important or equally sensitive, and most operate slowly, indirectly, over the long term and in non-linear ways. In general, however, interdependence is total. Thus, the biosphere is a unity and can be understood only in terms of itself (Daly 1994; Ophuls 1977; and Odum 1971). Systems thinking requires, therefore, the ability to work with both the parts and the whole, for they are nested realities, as is shown by Koestler's work (1978) on holons and Smuts' (1926) work on holism.

Systems thinking is about relationships and interrelationships between the parts and the whole. Studying structure is one method of approaching a system so that many other things can be seen in relation to one another and so understood. Another method involves the transfer of principles and attitudes, and a third involves examining underlying principles and ideas. As I will argue in the following chapters, understanding structure, the transfer of principles and attitudes, and the underlying principles of natural and ecological systems is critical to developing more sustainable human activity systems.

Sustainable development is as much a revolution, at the redesign stage (Hill 1985, 1996, 1998), as was the Industrial Revolution of the eighteenth century. Modern society, however, is much more sophisticated, complex, and institutionally organized than was eighteenth-century society. Many barriers at the individual, intra-organizational, inter-organizational, and societal levels work against major change. If change occurs, it is often, at best, piecemeal and incremental. Innovation, defined by Kanter (1983) as the generation, acceptance, and implementation of new ideas, processes, products, or services, and by others (Commoner 1975; Dale and Regier 1995; Hill 1998) as a process of political and social change, is key to ensuring the transition to sustainable development. Clearly, integrative innovation-stimulating cultures (Kanter 1983) in industry and governments are a prerequisite for realizing change of the magnitude required if sustainable development is to be integrated into all levels of Canadian society.

Robinson (1988, 1992b) has argued that the "dragnet" view of science should be replaced by a model relationship in which researchers, policy makers, and the public form "mutual learning systems" that use modelling tools to explore alternative futures (backcasting) rather than trying to predict the future (forecasting). Elements of this model include the explicit recognition that policy questions are not essentially questions of fact but value and that both a "physical-flows" perspective and an "actor-system" perspective are needed to provide a usefully integrated approach to policy questions.

It is only when we open our minds to paradoxes and the possibilities of new paradigms, myths, and metaphors that we will be able to implement sustainable development. Some of these paradoxes are concerned with how to develop: local self-reliance in the face of increasing globalization, equity between present and future generations, equity between the North and the South, balance between the competing forces of centralization and decentralization, balance between diversity and the potential for increasing homogenization as a result of globalization, and balance between the space we occupy and the space we leave for other species. These paradoxes will not be resolved without an explication of differing individual and cultural values, preferences, and beliefs about a highly uncertain and unknowable future, and the resolution of such differences through supportive social processes (Holdren et al. 1995). This resolution, I will argue in succeeding chapters, must include expanded decision-making contexts, especially on the part of governments.

Let us now look at the global context of each of the three sustainable development imperatives – ecological, social, and economic – in order to determine the nature and the magnitude of the changes necessary to ensure the effective implementation of sustainable development, beginning with the ecological imperatives.

4
Ecological Imperatives

The greatness of a nation and its moral progress can be judged by the way its animals are treated.

– Mahatma Gandhi

The health, well-being, and ultimate survival of our own species is linked to, and dependent upon, the health and sustainability of ecological systems (Ehrlich et al. 1977; Francis 1994; Holling 1986; Odum 1989). These systems provide the basic elements essential to life: fixation of solar energy; protection against harmful cosmic influences; regulation of the chemical composition of the atmosphere; operation of the hydrological cycle; water catchment and groundwater recharge; regulation of local and global climate and energy balance; formation of topsoil and maintenance of soil fertility; prevention of soil erosion and sediment control; food production by food webs; biomass production; storage and recycling of nutrients and organic matter; assimilation, storage, and recycling of waste; maintenance of habitats for migration and nursery; maintenance of the scenery of the landscape and recreational sites; and provision of historic, spiritual, religious, aesthetic, educational, and scientific information and cultural and artistic inspiration (Costanza and Folke 1996). The details of these essential "natural" services remain poorly understood in terms of their systemic processes, their interlocutory effects, and the co-evolutionary relationship between human activity systems and natural systems. Most ecological services are unpriced, and there is a near total lack of public awareness that our societies are dependent upon natural ecosystems (Daily 1997).

Their [i.e., educated people] inadvertent ignorance of the services that natural ecosystems supply to the human enterprise – of the reasons that the economy is a wholly owned subsidiary of those systems – amounts to a condemnation of schools, colleges, universities, and the print and electronic media. It also highlights the failure of professional ecologists to communicate their findings to the general public.

(Mooney and Ehrlich 1997: 17)

Biological Diversity

What is the state of current global ecological capital? With respect to biological diversity, expert assessments vary greatly concerning the scale and temporality of its decline, although as early as 1980 it was predicted that 500,000 to 2,000,000 species would become extinct worldwide by the year 2000 (Lovejoy 1980) and that the rate of decline would increase from one per day in 1970 to one per hour by the end of the twentieth century (Myers 1979). Within tropical rain forests, we may already be exceeding these estimates. Moist tropical forests, which are the most species-rich environments on earth, extend over some 8 percent of the world's land surface but contain more than 90 percent of its species (UNEP 2000). These biological treasures are disappearing at the rate of about seventeen million hectares per year (WRI et al. 1992). Large blocks of forest habitat are crucial to maintaining biodiversity, yet 80 percent of the natural forests that originally covered the earth have been cleared, fragmented, or degraded. And logging, mining, and other large developments threaten 39 percent of the remaining natural forests (WRI et al. 1996; UNEP 2000). During 1980-90, Latin America suffered the largest reductions in the world, losing sixty-two million hectares (6 percent) of its tropical forests; and then it lost another twenty-nine million hectares between 1990 and 1995 (FAOSTAT 1997). Estimates of potential species extinction in the tropics in general vary from 20 to 50 percent over the next thirty years. It is predicted that these species will either die out or be reduced to such small populations that extinction will be inevitable (Ehrlich 1982; Wilson 1988).

Most threatened species are land-based, and more than half are forest-based, but mounting evidence points to the growing vulnerability of freshwater habitats and marine habitats such as coral reefs. In the United States, nearly 70 percent of mussels, 50 percent of crayfish, and 37 percent of fishes are threatened (Master et al. 1998, in UNEP 2000). Coral reefs, which make up only 0.3 percent of total ocean area, are second only to tropical rain forests in terms of biodiversity richness. One in four ocean species are reef-dwellers. Unfortunately, coral is extremely vulnerable to rising sea surface temperatures, and it reacts to such stress by "bleaching" (i.e., turning white). Prolonged stress can be fatal. With atmosperic concentrations of CO_2 levels being higher now than at any time in the past 420,000 years, and with global temperatures being warmer than they have been in 1,200 years, the past two decades have badly damaged the reef biome. Beginning in the 1980s, mass bleaching has been occurring in every coral reef region in the world. And in the Indian Ocean, 70 percent of the coral appears to have died. In addition, sedimentation, nutrient pollution, and the demise of seagrass and mangrove ecosystems as a result of human development have caused, at least in part, a series of disease epidemics that are also seriously threatening coral communities (Brown et al. 2000).

Losses of this magnitude are clearly undesirable. Ehrlich (1988) estimated that, in the closing decades of the twentieth century, the rate of
species extinction would be some forty to 400 times the rate that has pre-
vailed through most of geological time. Much of this accelerated loss is
occurring before we have had a chance to even name these taxa, much less
to appreciate the unique services they provide within ecosystems. Because
so few habitats have been adequately investigated, estimates of the total
number of species on the planet vary by orders of magnitude from three
million to over thirty million. Only 1.7 million of about 12.5 million
species are known, and just a fraction of these have been studied in any
detail (Wilson 1988; WCMC 1992 in UNEP 2000). Our knowledge of most
invertebrates, primitive plants, and micro-organisms remains particularly
fragmentary.

Three-fourths of the world's bird species are declining, and nearly one-
fourth of the 4,600 species of mammals are now threatened with extinction (Brown et al. 1997). Radar images of flights of migratory birds across
the Gulf of Mexico over a twenty-year period reveal that the frequency of
trans-Gulf flights has declined by almost 50 percent (Costanza and Folke
1996). In spite of the 1992 Convention on Biological Diversity, in two of the
most important countries with regard to biodiversity (i.e., Brazil and Indonesia), the loss of species has continued to increase. More forest is being
lost in the Amazon Basin, arguably the world's greatest single concentration of biodiversity, than anywhere else on earth. In 1997 and 1998, fires
set to clear land claimed more than 5.2 million hectares of Brazilian forest,
brush, and savanna (Brown et al. 2000). Indonesian wildlife is uniquely
threatened: with little more than 1 percent of the earth's land area, it has
roughly 12 percent of the world's mammals, 16 percent of its reptiles and
amphibians, and 17 percent of its birds. Driven by a large and politically
influential logging industry as well as a human population that is expanding by some three million people each year, Indonesia is currently losing
species at a rate of one per day (Costanza and Folke 1996). Loss of primary
forest affects all components of biodiversity, but it especially affects our
closest relatives – orangutans and the other great apes – who have lost 80
percent of their forest habitat in the last twenty years (Kuznik 1997).

The ever-expanding use of environmental goods by human activity systems, which ignore the negative impacts on ecological services, has severe
ramifications for the loss of biological diversity everywhere. Since human
estimates of carrying capacity are dependent upon the value we place on the
needs of other species within human systems (and the subsequent place
we allow them), all approaches to carrying capacity are species-dependent.
In general, human carrying capacity can be increased only at the expense
of other species (Dale et al. 1995). The scale and nature of the resources and
space that human activity systems appropriate, therefore, will determine

the relative space and resources available for other species. Because of its irreversibility, the conservation of biodiversity is undoubtedly one of the most important issues now facing our society.

If we learn to measure our activities in terms of biodiversity impacts and if we reconceptualize our socioecosystem in a way that biodiversity losses are seen to matter to us as much as a shift in balance of trade or inflation rates, then we will begin to get signals back from the systems we are part of that will provide stabilizing feedback.

(Meredith 1999: 270)

The rates of loss and degradation of terrestrial and aquatic habitats are continuing to increase, and the existing mechanisms to ameliorate this are inadequate. The main cause of biodiversity loss is habitat destruction through resource exploitation, increasing population growth, and technological expansion (Ehrlich 1988; McNeely et al. 1990; Reid and Miller 1989). In fact, population may be the key driver, as projected population growth for the next half-century is expected to exacerbate nearly all other environmental and social problems. Between 1950 and 2000, world population increased from 2.5 billion to 6.1 billion, and it is projected to reach 8.9 billion by 2050 (Brown et al. 2000). And whereas past growth occurred in both developing and industrial countries, virtually all future growth is to occur in the developing world, where overpopulation, hunger, and ecological decline are already major concerns. Shrinking per capita supplies of natural resources threaten not only the quality of life, but also life itself (ibid.).

But what is happening to the hundreds of non-commercial species taken incidentally or by poaching or ghost fishing by lost or abandoned gear? There is virtually no information.

One irreparable consequence of this widespread damage is the loss of the opportunity to study and understand intact communities. The damage is so pervasive that it may be impossible even to know or reconstruct the ecosystem. In fact, each succeeding generation of biologists has markedly different expectations of what is natural, because they study increasingly altered systems that bear less and less resemblance to the former, preexploitation versions.

(Dayton 1998: 821)

As our numbers increase, we inevitably displace other species. In the process of designing and managing human habitats, human activity systems also tend to create conditions in which pest and disease species, and species with requirements similar to our own (such as rats, cockroaches, and houseflies), are favoured. And efforts to control them inevitably result in further negative effects. Even in those countries where burgeoning human numbers do not appear to be a problem, we are continuing to displace other species from the highest quality space through deforestation, agricultural expansion and intensification, and urbanization. Moreover, all of the world's great industrial cities are located on coasts, large estuaries, large rivers, or fertile deltas where the life-support capacity of the natural environment is high, and where we compete with other species for the same high quality space.

It follows that, without exception, every sustainable development issue affects and is affected by biodiversity. Biodiversity may be viewed as a library of historical and emergent information, and, as such, it provides not only a multiplicity of evolutionary and adaptive pathways for future development of life on earth, but also the essential regenerative capacity for all living systems (Ehrlich 1988; Regier 1995a). Put simply, human societies need high biodiversity to ensure their own survival. Wilson (1988) estimates, for example, that the full information contained in the DNA of the common house mouse is equivalent to the text in the fifteen editions of the *Encyclopaedia Britannica* published since 1768 (assuming they were translated into ordinary printed letters). Schneider and Kay (1994: 36) have pushed this idea further. They describe the gene as "a record of successful self-organization. Given that living systems go through a constant cycle of birth, growth, death and renewal, at many temporal and spatial scales, a way of preserving information about what works and what doesn't so as to constrain the self-organization process is crucial for the continuance of life. This is the role of the gene. At the larger scale, it is the role of biodiversity."

The lessons animals bring us as a community lie in our willingness first to acknowledge, then to question, our historic and current attitudes towards them. Why have certain animals been defined as "varmints"? Why have we collectively decided it is acceptable to kill nuisance animals? Why do we accept extinction for certain animals, yet protect others? If myths tell us that all predatory animals are cruel and merciless, how do we feel about ourselves, the supreme predators? ... We need myths that can speak to our children of love, compassion, mercy and courage.

(McElroy 1997: 222)

Because certain species are known to play a keystone role within ecosystems, they, especially, ought to be conserved because they have a disproportionate effect on the persistence of all other species (Bond 1993). Such species include large predators that "manage" competitor populations, mutualists such as pollinators and dispersers that facilitate reproduction, and nitrogen fixers and mycorrhizae (a kind of fungus) that affect rates of nutrient transfer (Boucher 1985). As well as affecting the survival of other species, keystone species play a major role in maintaining community integrity and environmental quality. Thus, the loss of a keystone species will eventually lead to a multitude of linked extinctions through a ripple effect that spreads throughout the ecosystem (Myers 1990).

Climatic Changes

With respect to ecological services, human activity systems are seriously affecting these critical life-sustaining processes. The thinning of the ozone layer is occurring much faster than was thought possible several years ago, and, in addition, we are now beginning to appreciate that this process may have significant biological effects. In response to the 1987 Montreal Protocol on Substances that Deplete the Ozone Layer, global production of the most significant ozone-depleting substance – the chlorine containing chlorofluoro carbons (CFCs) – was down 76 percent from its peak in 1988. Unfortunately, two alternative compounds, hydrochlorofluorocarbons (HCFCs) and hydro-fluorocarbons (HFCs), are both potent greenhouse gases, even though the latter is ozone benign and the former significantly less hazardous than CFCs (Brown et al. 1997). Each year, the chemical industry produces more than 100 million tons of organic chemicals, representing some 70,000 different compounds, with about 10,000 new ones being added annually (Postel 1987). According to the projections of the Intergovernmental Panel on Climate Change (IPCC), annual HFC emissions could reach 148,000 tons by 2000 and 1.5 million tons by 2050. This is roughly equivalent in global warming impact to the current fossil fuel-based carbon emissions of France, Germany, Italy, and the United Kingdom combined. Ultimately, a sustainable society may be one that minimizes its dependency on synthetic chemical production systems.

There has been a general upward trend in average annual global temperature, from about 14.5 degrees Celsius in 1866 to around 15.4 degrees Celsius in 1995, the warmest year on record. This trend correlates closely with an increase in atmospheric levels of heat-trapping greenhouse gases (GHGs), principally carbon dioxide (CO_2). Since the Industrial Revolution, atmospheric concentrations of CO_2, methane, and nitrous oxide have increased by 30 percent, 145 percent, and 15 percent, respectively (Hengeveld 2000). And, since 1970, fossil fuel use has released 160 billion tons of carbon into the atmosphere compared to 1,110 billion tons in the previous 230 years (UNEP 2000). More important, emission rates continue to rise. In spite of the 1992 Framework Convention on Climate Change signed in Rio, annual fossil fuel-related emissions of carbon rose by 113 million tons, reaching six billion tons in 1995. As mentioned in the Preface, even the revised figures under the 1997 Kyoto Protocol are highly unlikely to be met. By 1996, American carbon emissions were already 6 percent above the 1990 level, and, without major new policy initiatives, they were expected to exceed 1990 levels by a full 11 percent by 2000. Canada's emissions have been rising faster than expected. By 1997, Canadian GHG emissions were already 13.5 percent higher than they were in 1990, and, without significant policy actions, they are projected to be 35 percent higher than 1990 levels by the 2008-12 Kyoto commitment period (Canada's National Climate Change Process 1999). Moreover, carbon emissions from developing countries soared dramatically in the first half of the 1990s. In China, already the world's second largest carbon emitter, emissions grew at 5 percent per year in the early 1990s, while economic growth averaged 10 percent. The International Energy Agency predicts that global emissions of carbon from fossil fuels will exceed 1990 levels by 17 percent in 2000 and by 49 percent in 2010, when they are estimated to reach nearly nine billion tons annually. More important, there is a significant time delay in the reduction of emissions and effects on the atmosphere, and some further warming is already "in the pipe." For example, an immediate decline of 68 percent in greenhouse gas emissions is required to cause atmospheric concentrations of these gases to stabilize by about 2050 (Robinson 1996). Experts suggest that a doubling of pre-industrial CO_2 levels within the next century is likely, and even a tripling is possible (Hengeveld 2000).

Globally, cars are responsible for more than 15 percent of greenhouse gas emissions (Natural Resources Defense Council 1996), and yet we continue to produce more of the same technology. Global production of automobiles grew to 36.1 million in 1996, with the most dramatic increases occurring in Asia, where the fleet size rose 15 percent to 19.5 million (Brown et al. 1997). While human population has doubled since 1950, the number of cars has increased nearly tenfold. If countries such as India and China adopt the car practices and habits of the North American consumer, then there will be serious repercussions for global emissions. Unfortunately, any emission standards and increases in gasoline efficiencies are more than offset by the increase in car usage, as analysts project a doubling of the world fleet over the next twenty-five years. What is most unfortunate is the lack of progress on overall vehicle fleet fuel efficiency in North America since the early 1980s. This is due to the growing popularity of minivans and sport utility vehicles, which are heavier and have more lenient standards than do cars.

Ecological Services
In the early 1960s, most nations were self-sufficient with regard to food: now only a few are self-sufficient, in spite of the Green Revolution (high-yield crops and energy-intensive agriculture), which was introduced during the period between 1950 and 1984. Twenty years ago, Africa produced food equal to what it consumed; today it produces only 80 percent of what it consumes (Cherfas 1990). Less than half of the world's land area is

suitable for agriculture, including grazing (Lal 1990). Nearly all of the world's productive land, flat and with water, is already exploited (Kendall and Pimentel 1994). Meanwhile, population and urban pressures continue to contribute to a decline in agricultural land (Meadows et al. 1992).

There has been a gradual decline in grainland area since 1981, with little or no growth in irrigation water supplies since 1990. Irrigation underpins modern food systems, yet one out of five hectares of irrigated land is damaged by salt. At the same time, pressure to leave more water in streams, rivers, and lakes for fish and aquatic habitats is mounting. Depletion of groundwater resources is perhaps the most alarming phenomenon to emerge from recent research (Postel in Brown et al. 2000). Aquifer depletion is now widespread in central and northern China, northwest and southern India, parts of Pakistan, much of the western United States, North Africa, the Middle East, and the Arabian Peninsula. For example, in the state of Gujarat, India, eighty-seven out of ninety-six wells observed had declining groundwater levels during the 1980s, and aquifers in the Mehsana District are reportedly empty (ibid.). In China, groundwater levels are falling much faster than is the average recharge rate in major wheat- and corn-growing regions in the North (Postel 1992). And more than 10 percent of the world's irrigated area appears to suffer from a salt build-up that is serious enough to lower crop yields.

The human race now appears to be getting close to the limits of global food production capacity based on present technologies (Postel 1992). Global population, at some 6.1 billion today (Brown et al. 2000), is projected to top eight billion by the year 2020; nearly all the increase will occur in the developing world, where the constraints on increased production are even more keen than they are in industrialized countries. Experts anticipate that, over the next twenty-five years, food demand will increase by some 64 percent globally and by almost 100 percent in developing nations (Brown, Flavin, and Starke 1996). They further estimate that, with the world population at 5.5 billion, food production is adequate to feed seven billion people on a vegetarian diet, with ideal distribution and no grain being fed to livestock (ibid.).

Pressures from growing populations are also straining water resources worldwide (Postel 1992). Globally, 214 rivers and lake basins, around which 40 percent of the world's population is located, now compete for water (Gleick 1993; WRI 1992-93). There are strong arguments that the issue most likely to perpetuate interstate resource wars is access to river water (Homer-Dixon et al. 1993). Fisheries stocks are collapsing everywhere. Coho salmon are now extinct in 55 percent of their range and declining in 39 percent. In only 7 percent of their range are they considered to be stable. Of approximately 1,000 historic fisheries stocks, only 100 are considered somewhat healthy (Brown et al. 1997). Mussels are very important indicators of the health of freshwater ecosystems, both because of their filtration and cleansing abilities (which help to maintain water quality for other species) and because their intricate connection to particular fish can warn us of shifts in ecosystem dynamics. Fish transport mussel larvae to new habitat for reproduction. Thus, if the host fish disappears, the mussel species dependent upon it cannot reproduce. Since 1900, 10 percent of North American mussels have become extinct, and 67 percent of the remaining 297 species and subspecies are at risk. Only 25 percent are considered stable (Abramovitz 1996).

It is clear that the current decline in ecological capital, and the projected future rates of draw-down on natural capital and ecological services based on population figures, is not sustainable. Ecological systems provide the most critical infrastructure for humanity and its activities (Behan-Pelletier, personal communication). If we accept that our survival is linked to the sustainability of our ecological capital, then the latter's persistent accelerated decline cannot continue. Human activity systems are a part of ecological systems. It is only our distorted worldviews that enable us to maintain the perception that human beings are separate from the rest of nature. It may well be that, if human activity systems redesign themselves according to analogs in natural systems, then they may begin to restore degraded ecosystems.

Ecosystem Dynamics

Ecosystems are unique, often highly dynamic open systems characterized by complex, non-linear relationships between the parts and the whole. They exhibit self-organizing maintenance, regulatory, and co-evolutionary processes. Some of these may be fairly resilient, while others may be highly susceptible to disruption (Holling and Sanderson 1996). The task involved in working with ecosystems is to support these processes – thereby building negentropy (i.e., negative entropy) – and to understand that our knowledge of them is fragmentary and often not sufficient to provide a solid foundation for decision making. All species are the product of co-evolutionary processes; a few species are highly adaptable, but most are highly specialized, having narrow environmental requirements and tolerances. Appropriate decisions must be based on an understanding of this complexity; priorities must be assigned based on the implications of irreversible crises (i.e., those related to biodiversity) versus reversible crises (i.e., those related to economics).

Ecosystems are composed of communities that are made up of definable and interdependent assemblages of populations of different species. These populations tend to be structured in chains and webs from producers to primary, secondary, and tertiary consumers to scavengers to decomposers. Ecosystems are open systems (i.e., things are constantly entering and leaving them), and they are characterized by material and energy flows. These materials, which include carbon, phosphorous, oxygen, and nitrogen, flow in cycles of varying complexity and scope. Energy flows through ecosystems according to the laws of thermodynamics. The first law of thermodynamics states that energy may be transformed from one form (such as light) into another (such as food) but that it is never created or destroyed. The second law of thermodynamics states that no process involving an energy transformation will occur unless there is a degradation of energy from a concentrated form (such as food or gasoline) into a dispersed form (such as heat and carbon dioxide). This is known as entropy, which is a measure of disorder based on the amount of unavailable energy within a closed thermodynamic system. To survive and prosper, both natural and human systems require a continuous input of high-quality energy, storage capacity, and the means to dissipate energy. These three attributes are part of the maximum power principle, which states that the systems most likely to survive in this competitive world are those that efficiently transform the most energy into useful work for themselves and for the surrounding systems with which they are linked for mutual benefit (Odum and Odum 1981). Successful systems also use these entropic processes to create order and mechanisms for maintenance, renewal, and evolution (negentropy).

The wisdom of many contributors to the Club of Rome reports, as well as the output of global models, conforms rather well to basic ecosystem theory, especially three paradigms: a holistic approach is necessary when dealing with complex systems; cooperation has greater survival value than competition when limits (resources or otherwise) are approached; orderly, sustainable development of human communities requires negative as well as positive feedback.

(Odum 1989: 262)

Fundamental characteristics of ecosystems are scale and limits, notions that apply equally to human activity systems (although we may postpone the day of reckoning by taking from others, especially those yet to be born). As we move closer and closer to these limits, we reduce our resilience, thereby limiting our options to respond to further stressors on both human and natural systems. Another integral part of ecosystem functioning is feedback loops that maintain a balance between inputs and outputs. In ecosystems, individual parts are as important as is the whole, and both are involved in a type of dynamic connectedness. An ecosystem is a set of coherent evolving and interactive processes, an open system that co-evolves with its larger environment, just as human systems function as a part of the larger natural system – the biosphere.

Diversity, through the provision of options, enables a system to restore functions after it has undergone stress. This is limited by the system's inertia; that is, its ability to resist change, its resiliency, and its capacity to absorb a certain amount of stress. Without functional diversity, over time all systems, both natural and human, become increasingly rigid and less responsive to external signals, ultimately finishing in total collapse (Holling 1993a). It appears to be a near universal truth that, whereas functional diversity is the foundation of developmental progress within complex systems, uniformity (and dysfunctional diversity) leads to stagnation and decay (Korten 1995).

Ecosystems can also be described as self-determining, self-organizing, and self-renewing. They exert a systemic interconnectedness among all natural processes over space and time; they are open, and their unpredictable evolution renders them creative (Jantsch 1980). They are dynamic living systems, within which uncertainty and surprise are the norm. The belief of the 1970s – that, for management purposes, one can assume that ecosystems are stable, closed, internally regulated, and behave in a deterministic manner – is at last being replaced by a growing recognition that ecosystems are open, in a constant state of flux, usually without long-term stability, and affected by many factors outside of the system (Mangel et al. 1996). "Self-supporting" and "self-maintaining" are key terms characterizing the natural environment, which operates without energetic (or even economic) flows being fully controllable (Odum and Odum 1972).

Are there essential ecological principles, ways of organizing, and processes that may prove to be important analogs for enabling human activity systems to implement sustainable development? For example, is it important to be aware that young ecosystems are characterized by production, growth, and quantity? And that mature ecosystems are characterized by protection, stability, and quality (Odum 1969)? Let's look at what happens as an ecosystem, of the autogenic, autotrophic type, moves through ecological succession (see Table 4.1).

This successional framework may have important analogs for the future development of human society, since both natural ecosystems and human activity systems are complex and adaptive. For example, the species (or other component) matrix appears to adapt to the strength and variety of energy and material inputs. A dominant strategy within nature, then, is to diversify, but not to the extent of reducing energetic efficiency (Odum 1975). This principle of "maximum protection" (i.e., trying to achieve maximum support of complex biomass structure) appears contrary to the current human strategy, which usually emphasizes "maximum production" (trying to obtain the highest possible yield, often regardless of costs) (Odum 1969).

The relationship between gross production (P) and total community respiration (R) is important for gaining an understanding of the total function of the ecosystem and predicting its resistance in the event of perturbation

Table 4.1

Typical successional ecosystem changes

Ecosystem characteristic	Trend in ecological development early stage to climax or youth to maturity or growth stage to steady state
Community structure	
Total biomass (B)	increases
Organic matter	increases
Energy flow (community metabolism)	
Gross primary production (P)	increases during early phase of succession little or no increase during secondary succession
Net community production (yield)	decreases
Community respiration (R)	increases
P/R ratio	P > R to P = R
P/B ratio	decreases
B/P and B/R ratios (biomass supported/ unit energy)	increases
Connectedness	from linear food chains to complex food webs
Biogeochemical cycles	
Mineral cycles	become more closed
Turnover time and storage of essential elements	increase
Role of detritus	increases
Nutrient conservation	increases
Natural selection and regulation	
Growth form	from r-selection (rapid growth) to k-selection (feedback control)
Quality of biotic components	increases
Niches	increasing specialization
Life cycles	length and complexity increase
Symbiosis (living together)	increasingly mutualistic
Entropy	decreases
Information	increases
Overall efficiency of energy and nutrient utilization	increases

(outside forces). One kind of ecological "steady-state" exists when the annual production of organic matter equals total consumption (P/R = 1) and when exports and imports of organic matter are either nonexistent or equal (Odum 1975). When primary production and heterotrophic use are not equal (i.e., when P/R is greater or less than 1), and when organic matter either accumulates or is depleted, then the community changes by a process of ecological succession. Succession may proceed towards a steady-state condition (P = R) either from an extremely autotrophic (producers) condition (P > R) or from an extremely heterotrophic condition (consumers) (P < R).

The rate of biomass energy production to rate of energy flow is another important property of ecosystems. Biomass and the standing crop of organic matter increase with succession. In both aquatic and terrestrial environments the total amount of living matter (biomass) and decomposing organic materials (detritus and humus) tends to increase with time. The larger the biomass (B), the larger the respiration (R). However, if the biomass is large and the structure diverse and well ordered, then the respiratory maintenance cost per unit of biomass can be decreased (Odum 1975). Whereas the strategy of natural systems seems to be to reduce the R/B ratio, our strategy has tended to the opposite – to harvest as much as possible and to leave as little structure and diversity within the landscape as possible. It may well be that human activity systems should model their management and planning on the characteristics of mature ecosystems, especially given the current interpenetration and interdependence of natural and human systems.

Ecosystem Lessons
Holling's (1986) ecosystem model may provide another possible analog for the necessary reconciliation of maintenance (and regeneration) and production processes as well as for the elimination of artificial separations that permeate our current institutional systems.

Holling proposes four basic phases that are common to all complex systems, along with a spiralling evolutionary path that cuts through them (see Figure 4.1). According to this model, systems evolve from the rapid colonization and exploitation phase (1), during which they capture easily accessible resources, to the conservation phase (2) of building and storing increasingly complex structures. Examples of the exploitation phase are early successional ecosystems colonizing disturbed sites and pioneer societies colonizing new territories. Examples of the conservation phase are climax ecosystems and large, mature bureaucracies.

The release that occurs within the "creative destruction" phases (3, 4) involves the breakdown of mature structures via aperiodic events such as fire, storms, pests, or political upheavals. The released structure is then

Figure 4.1

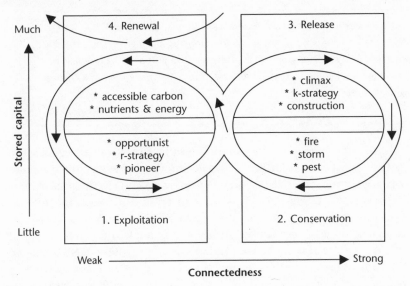

The four ecosystem functions

Source: Holling 1986.

available for reorganization and uptake in the next exploitation phase. The amount of ongoing creative destruction that takes place in a system is thus critical to its behaviour.

The conservation phase within bureaucracies often builds elaborate and tightly bound structures by severely limiting creative destruction, but these structures predictably become increasingly brittle and susceptible to massive and widespread destruction. This is evident in the former Soviet Union and, currently, in Canada, with its widespread federal/provincial gridlock (Phase 3). If some moderate level of release were allowed to occur on a routine basis, then the destruction would occur on a much smaller scale (thanks to co-evolutionary renewal [Phase 4]), and the structure would be able to support a more resilient system. It would appear that our current institutions are locked in a spiralling pattern of exploitation and conservation, and we have lost our capacity for release and renewal. We must now actively integrate these latter processes into government policy development and program design.

If we now turn to human activity systems, as they have developed from hunting-gathering societies to the postmodern information age, and examine how they have evolved, we get a totally different scenario. In its short history, relative to other species, humankind has experienced a succession of growth states with ever-increasing levels of population density, resource and energy utilization, and environmental impact.

The real difference in these two classes of systems [human and natural] is in the distribution of the energy flow; man works to channel as much energy as possible into food he can immediately use, while nature tends to distribute the products of photosynthesis among many species and products and to store energy as a "hedge" against bad times.

(Odum 1975: 19)

Furthermore, none of the essential "public services of the global eco-system" (Ehrlich and Ehrlich 1997) is currently valued by the dominant socio-economic system. No nation on the planet subtracts the costs of biotic impoverishment, soil erosion, poisons in the air or water, and resource depletion from its gross national product (GNP); rather, such impacts are, paradoxically, regarded positively. For example, the *Exxon Valdez* oil spill off the coast of Alaska was depicted as an increase in GNP because of the costs of labour and raw materials required to clean it up. Nowhere in national accounts do we find the costs of long-term pollution and the loss of marine life. Nor can we even accurately assess these costs, given the interactive effects and complex functioning of ecosystems.

There have been some preliminary attempts to put a value on these key ecological services. Costanza and Folke (1997) have estimated that the current economic value of seventeen ecosystem services for sixteen biomes is in the range of US$16-54 trillion per year, with an average of US$36 trillion per year. This approaches annual gross world product of about US$39 trillion (Hawken et al. 1999) and is more than the global GNP at around US$25 trillion a year. Assuming that global natural assets yield "interest" of $36 trillion annually, total natural capital would be somewhere between $400 and $500 trillion, equal to tens of thousands of dollars for every person on the planet. Pimentel et al. (1996) estimate that, whereas the value of over-the-counter, plant-based drugs is $84 billion annually, the value of ecotourism is $500 billion. Coastal tourism is valued at $161 billion in 1995 dollars, and ocean-based fisheries are valued at $80 billion dollars (while employing 200 million people) (Platt McGinn 1999). On a smaller scale, the water storage and aquifer recharging services of a 223,000-hectare swamp in Florida have been calculated at $25 million per year. Yet at least half of the original wetlands in the United States have been drained for development at an astonishing rate of twenty-four hectares per hour for every hour between the 1780s and the 1990s (Abramovitz 1996).

Thus, there is a fundamental imbalance in both the way we record our financial affairs and the way we think about what is valuable. Valuation involves resolving fundamental philosophical issues (such as the underlying bases for value), being aware of the context, and defining objectives and preferences, all of which are inherently uncertain (Daily 1997). This quantification becomes even more problematic with ecological systems because ecosystem-level experiments are difficult to conduct, their outcomes can be costly, and they need to be pursued over long periods of time (Carpenter et al. 1995).

It must be recognized, however, that not all of nature can be quantified. How, for example, does one assess the significance to Canadian society of the loss of the common loon? This involves, in addition to traditional valuation, complex aesthetic, spiritual, and ethical considerations. What value do polar bears have to Canadians? How will our society be affected by their disappearance or their decline? Do we think that we would be worse off or are we indifferent to their extinction? Do we save only the attractive birds and mammals, or do we consider the trade-offs between those species that provide keystone functions essential for the maintenance of ecosystems? There are no easy answers to any of these questions.

It is important to realize, therefore, that, although economic valuation of ecological services and benefits must be confined to use values, the sometimes larger qualitative values simply cannot be measured. And these values are based on both use and non-use. Use value includes direct value (e.g., harvesting for food), indirect value (e.g., contributing genetic diversity), and option value (e.g., the potential for future contribution). Non-use value derives from a resource's existence and aesthetics: its value as a bequest to future generations and as a contributor to a general feeling about the environment (Norton 1987; Pearce 1993). We cannot afford to wait for such valuations to be formed before initiating programs of conservation, rehabilitation, and policy reform.

As I was writing this chapter in the summer of 1997, a golden retriever puppy died in the Ottawa market area while locked in a car with the windows rolled up in over 30-degree-Celsius heat. About twenty concerned bystanders stood helplessly watching, while waiting for the humane society officer to arrive (unfortunately, this person was caught in traffic). If it had been a child inside the car visibly suffocating to death, would the bystanders have hesitated to break the windows?

The failure of modern human activity systems to understand, value, and take into account this critical ecological capital has resulted in a significant decline in our natural assets and the ability of the earth's ecosystems to continually absorb the impacts of human activities. In terms of the scale of all human endeavours – our population size, our waste products, our use of renewable and non-renewable resources, our economic practices, and (most important) our appropriation of the net primary productivity of the biosphere – we are now clearly approaching critical thresholds.

Ecosystem structures, functions, and processes are primarily concerned with the maintenance of systems, whereas human systems are primarily concerned with production. We have been far more efficient in designing incentives to capture the flow of ecosystem goods than in protecting either the capital stock or the flow of ecosystem services (Hanna and Jentoft 1996). An important feature of ecosystems is that they are, for the most part, sustainable and self-organizing. They have virtually no waste. It would, therefore, appear to be prudent for human activity systems to reconcile methods of production with the rehabilitation and maintenance of ecosystems that provide the essential services for all life. We need a common language and an adequate conceptual framework within which to work (Costanza and Folke 1996), institutional reform based on a convergence of human and natural system cycles (Holling and Sanderson 1996), and an emphasis on fundamental system design rather than on simple substitution (Hill 1998).

Throughout the twentieth century, human societies have had ample warning about the dangers of non-sustainable development from a wide variety of experts as well as from the experience of boom and bust resource cycles. One has to ask why mainstream agendas have not involved more debate around these issues. Avoiding boom and bust cycles will depend upon recognizing key ecological imperatives and proactively addressing them. Five key ecological imperatives that, I believe, are necessary if human activity systems are to realize sustainable development imperatives are: (1) worldwide movement away from r-strategy behaviour (many offspring) to k-strategy behaviour (limited reproduction); (2) redesign of all human production systems so that they produce virtually no waste; (3) societal determination of the appropriate scale of human activity systems relative to the maintenance (and enhancement) of ecological systems; (4) maintenance of functional biological diversity worldwide; and (5) reduction of human-induced impacts on climate systems.

Let us now turn to examining the nature and magnitude of social imperatives and some of the societal changes that are essential to the implementation of sustainable development.

5
Social Imperatives

Complex societies in fast-changing environments give rise to
sets or systems of problems (meta-problems) rather than discrete
problems. These are beyond the capacity of single organizations
to meet. Inter-organizational collaboration is required by groups
of organizations at what is called the "domain" level.

– E. Trist, "Referent Organizations and the Development
of Interorganizational Domains"

The preceding chapter has shown how, for many reasons, ecological capital
is seriously declining. Social capital is dependent upon ecological capital,
just as it is dependent on economic capital. All countries now face enormous social pressures from the interactive effects of over-population and
associated environmental degradation, both of which are linked to and
underpinned by poverty and inequity. Despite the unprecedented global
economic wealth and food surpluses of the twentieth century, malnutrition has spread more widely than at any other time in history. Fully half
of the human family suffers from some form of malnutrition, and at least
1.2 billion people suffer from hunger. At the same time, another 1.2 billion
consume too much food and become overweight, with detrimental health
consequences. Obesity-related health costs in the United States total more
than $100 billion annually, or more than 10 percent of the national health-
care bill (Gardner and Halweil 2000).

World population grew from about 200 million people at the time of Christ to
about 500 million by the mid-seventeenth century. It doubled to one billion by the
mid-nineteenth century, with another doubling, to two billion, by 1930. It now
currently stands at over six billion. Hern (1990) has characterized this growth as a
planetary ecopathological process.

Meanwhile, one-quarter of the world's people remain in severe poverty in
a global economy of $25 trillion (United Nations Development Programme
1997). An estimated 1.3 billion people survive on less than the equivalent
of one dollar per day. Well over a billion lack access to safe water. And
nearly one-third of the people in the least developed countries – most of
which are in Sub-Saharan Africa – are not expected to reach the age of
forty. A 1999 World Bank study of India found that hunger-induced productivity losses cost the economy $10 to $28 billion per year, which is

equal to between 3 and 9 percent of India's 1996 gross domestic product (GDP) (Gardner and Halweil 2000).

Consequences for women have the added dimension of affecting future generations. For example, hungry women are less able to provide for their families and for their own bodies during pregnancy. This often leads to life-long impairment for their children, accompanied by loss of personal and community potential (Gardner and Halweil 2000). Half a million women die each year in childbirth. The rates of such deaths are ten to 100 times greater in developing countries than they are in industrial countries. World-wide, women face worse threats of violence than do men. It is estimated that one-third of married women in developing countries are battered by their husbands during their lifetimes (United Nations Development Programme 1997).

Poverty

Developed countries, despite their greater material well-being, face poverty of a different kind from that faced by developing countries. Rising unemployment, declining disposable income, and cuts in social services are driving many people into poverty. And they are driving some from relative poverty to absolute poverty. In the midst of increasing wealth among the upper classes of the North, hundreds of thousands of people are without housing on any given day, and several million are so poor and vulnerable that homelessness is a daily threat (Erikson 1994). In industrialized countries more than 100 million people live below the poverty line, which is set at half the individual median income; and thirty-seven million people are jobless (United Nations Development Programme 1997).

In addition, poverty among the elderly and children has increased dramatically. In Australia, the United Kingdom, and the United States more than 20 percent of the aged are income poor. With respect to income, a person is absolutely poor if her income is less than the defined income poverty line, while she is relatively poor if she belongs to a bottom income group (such as the poorest 10 percent). One in every four children in the United States is income poor – one in six in Australia, Canada, and the United States. In the United States every year nearly three million children are reported to be victims of abuse and neglect. In Canada, although 20 percent of Canadians aged sixteen and older are at the highest levels of literacy scales, 22 percent have very limited literacy skills, and an additional 26 percent have some difficulty reading and writing (Canada 1997).

In developing countries, the situation for women and children is much worse. According to the 1997 Human Development Report (United Nations Development Programme 1997), in developing countries, about seventy-five million children aged ten to fourteen – forty-five million of them in Asia, twenty-four million in Africa – are often working in slavery, prostitution, and hazardous conditions. And each year, an estimated one million children, mostly girls in Asia, are forced into prostitution (ibid.). More recent estimates show that the number of children living and working on the streets in the Third World is closer to 100 million. In Guatemala, 100 percent of 143 street children surveyed had been sexually abused, 64 percent of girls on the street had their first sexual experience with one of their parents, 93 percent admitted contracting a sexually transmitted disease, and none used contraceptives (Casa Alianza 2000). In Bangladesh, 56 percent of children are underweight; in India, 53 percent; in Ethiopia, 48 percent; and in Vietnam, 40 percent (FACO 1999, in Brown et al. 2000). Paradoxically, the condition of being overweight or obese is no longer restricted to industrialized countries. A 1999 United Nations survey found obesity in all developing regions. In the short time between 1989 and 1992, the share of obese adults in China almost doubled. In Brazil and Colombia, the prevalence of overweight people – at 31 percent and 43 percent, respectively – approaches levels in Europe (Brown et al. 2000). These statistics point to growing disparities between the rich and poor within both developed and developing countries.

According to the 1997 Human Development Report, the Human Development Index (HDI), a measure created by the United Nations Development Programme to gauge the degree to which people have access to the resources needed to attain a decent standard of living, has declined in thirty countries. This is a steeper decline than has occurred in any year since the Human Development Report was first issued in 1990. Meanwhile, in many of these countries the GDP continues to grow. This is because the GDP regards every expenditure as an addition to well-being, regardless of why it was made. The perversity is that this measurement, which is currently used to define "progress," is a more accurate indicator of social decay. Indeed, primary indicators of social decline – such as crime, divorce, and mass-media addiction – actually increase the GDP. Divorce, for example, makes a significant contribution to the GDP through legal bills; the establishment of second households; and increased transportation costs, therapy, and counselling. Similarly, crime positively adds to the GDP through a growing crime-prevention and security industry that has revenues of more than $65 billion per year (Cobb et al. 1999). The GDP also excludes the value of unpaid housework, child care, volunteer work, and leisure time – all of which are important to civil society. Many salaried professionals feel pressured to work overtime, often without compensation, but the GDP does not reflect this erosion in leisure time. Yet leisure time is very important to overall well-being and, thus, the overall productivity of a country. For example, on average, 37 percent of salaried Americans work fifty or more hours per week and receive only thirteen days of vacation per year. Japanese workers receive twenty-five days of vacation per year, yet, annually, 10,000 deaths in Japan are attributed to overwork (Lardner 1999). A similar perversity occurs with respect to resources and the environment. The more a nation depletes its natural resources and degrades its environment, the more the GDP increases. This violates basic accounting principles, as it portrays the depletion of capital as current income. Most pollution, for example, shows up twice as a gain. Take toxic chemicals: they show up once when the factory produces them and liberates them into the environment and once more when the nation spends billions of dollars to clean up the resultant toxic site (Cobb et al. 1999). The GDP is biased against the future, which goes against one of the important fundamentals of sustainable development: intergenerational justice. By not accounting for natural resources that are required to sustain current and future economic development, the implication of the GDP is that the future has no value. The GDP does not value natural resource capital, environmental resources/services, human resources, or research and development. All that matters to the GDP is the present (Anielski 2000).

The increasing globalization of the world's economies is having negative effects on civil societies everywhere. Many communities are facing profound social disruptions as they struggle to diversify in this post-NAFTA, postindustrial age. There is an accelerating economic interdependence and decreasing national sovereignty with the emergence of a truly global set of corporations and financial institutions and increasing pressure to maintain international competitiveness. As well, in many industrialized economies there are pressures to reduce public-sector spending (including spending on social programs) coupled with growing problems of structural unemployment. There is a growing international debt and, along with it, the imposition of International Monetary Fund (IMF) structural adjustment policies on developing countries.

Concurrent with this globalization, three particularly disturbing trends are emerging. First, there appear to be increasing income disparities, both among and within countries, coupled with rising levels of absolute poverty. A review of global economic growth since the mid-twentieth century shows growth peaking during the 1960s at an annual rate of 5.2 percent and dropping in each of the next two decades (Brown 1995). There is much debate about whether increasing income disparities and rising levels of absolute poverty are made worse or better by the trend towards global economic integration (Henderson 1991; Rees and Wackernagel 1994; Waring 1995). But regardless of one's views, it is clear that current socio-economic conditions are unsustainable for a large and growing proportion of the world's population in both so-called developed and developing countries. Although the ratio of global trade to GDP has been rising over the past decade, it has been falling for forty-four developing countries that have a combined population of more than a billion people. The least developed countries, with 10 percent of the world's people, have only 0.3 percent of world trade – half of what they had two decades ago (Brown 1995).

Second, there is a worldwide trend towards an increasing feminization of poverty, and women continue to be victims of social exclusion. Although women make up just over half of the world's population (50.4 percent in Canada) and contribute to over two-thirds of all human labour hours, they are disproportionately poor (Waring 1995).

Social Costs

Estimates indicate that women are the sole breadwinners in one-fourth to one-third of the world's households; and at least one-fourth of all other households rely on female earnings for more than 50 percent of their total income (ibid.). In Canada, in 1993, 56 percent of all people below the poverty line were women. This increased to 72 percent among those over age sixty-five. Children bear the brunt of women's economic inequality. Of the 601,000 children in Canadian single-parent families headed by women in 1993, 65 percent were below the poverty line, compared to 18 percent of all children in two-parent families. Clearly, gender bias contributes to the increasing global feminization of poverty; in its various forms it prevents hundreds of millions of women from obtaining the education, training, health services, child care, and legal status they need in order to escape from persistent poverty.

About one in five Canadian children – more than 1.4 million – live in poverty. Studies show that poor children are more likely than well off children to lead a life of poor health, poor education, trouble with the law, and dead-end jobs. Children born into poverty usually remain in poverty for the rest of their lives, thus perpetuating a cycle of winners and losers. Clearly, over the long term, this is an unsustainable path. A society that tolerates 20 percent of its children growing up in poverty is not a healthy society. This, in its turn, leads to a rotten economy (Paul Martin, *Ottawa Citizen*, 10 January 1997) and increasing unsustainability.

Gender analysis is based on the belief that policy cannot be separated from social context and that social issues are an integral part of economic issues. Social impact analysis, including gender analysis, is not just an "add-on" to be considered after costs and benefits have been assessed, but an integral part of good policy analysis.

Despite the importance of women's role in society and the advances they have made towards securing equality, according to the 1992 Human Development Index, women have lagged behind men in every country for which data are available. In 1995, the United Nations made gender analysis integral to the overall annual reporting process by adding two measures: the

Gender Development Index (GDI) and the Gender Empowerment Index (GEM). The latter measures the extent to which women and men are able to actively participate in economic and political life and to take part in decision making. It is clear that, although the pace of development has been robust, it has been accompanied by rising gender-related disparities both within and between nations. Women still constitute 70 percent of the world's poor and two-thirds of the world's illiterates. They occupy only 14 percent of managerial and administrative jobs, 10 percent of parliamentary seats, and 6 percent of Cabinet positions in Canada. According to the most recent United Nations report, Canada is the number one country in which to live, unless you are a woman. For women, Canada ranked eighth compared to other countries (MacDonald 1995).

Ultimately, the continued exclusion of women from ecological, economic, and social opportunities is not sustainable. If sustainable development, through the reconciliation of all three sustainable development imperatives (the ecological, the social, and the economic), is to be realized, then both short- and long-term equitable access to the fundamentals of life by women as well as by men would appear to be a basic precondition.

Gender inequity is particularly significant in certain sectors. For example, women represent only 17 percent of Canadian university faculty and continue to be significantly underrepresented in disciplines that have direct environmental significance, such as ecology, biology, economics, and geography. In corporate decision making, only 2 percent of chief executive officers in Canada, and 2 to 3 percent of top executives in the United States, are women (ibid.). This underrepresentation of women in decision-making positions pertaining to sustainable development and the primary-sector labour force ensures that women's concerns are likely to be neglected with regard to generating policy. The participation of women in environmental industries, and in businesses promoting Agenda 21, is poor; almost 90 percent of employees in environmental industries are male (ibid.).

Because strengthening the power of women to choose and act is congruent with reconciling the three imperatives, it is an essential condition for achieving sustainable development. For example, a recent World Bank study conducted in four countries in Africa showed that a 15 percent increase in food production could be achieved, without consuming more resources, if women had better access to land, production inputs (e.g., credit, fertilizer, and improved seed), and markets. Additional data from the World Bank (1997) indicate that, if the education of girls and women had been raised thirty years ago to the level of that of boys and men, then today's fertility levels would be nearing the target of global population stabilization. Furthermore, household welfare among the poorest would be higher, and local management of natural resources less problematic than it is now.

The social costs of gender inequity and gender-related exclusion from decision making – of societies divided into winners and losers – must be addressed if we are to achieve sustainable societies. Indeed, gender equality may well be the most important tool for attaining a more rapid diffusion of sustainable development practices, policies, and programs.

In promoting sustainable development, we are in fact talking about upgrading the value of feminist "values," both in men and women. A dualistic approach will never do – the "balance" in the middle does not exist as a solution: that would be stagnation. The human dimension in sustainable development is, according to a non-dualistic approach, to make spirit and matter meet. In order to do that, we have to develop as a whole (bi- or non-polar as opposed to uni-polar), independent, conscious, and responsible individuals. It requires that we move from gendered men and women to men that accept the feminine dimensions within themselves, and women that also accept their masculine dimensions.

(Eie, Electronic Dialogue, 21 January 1997)

A third global trend is the rising concentration of income, both within and between countries. The ratio of the income of the top 20 percent to that of the poorest 20 percent rose from thirty to one in 1960, to sixty-one to one in 1991, and to a startling new high of seventy-eight to one in 1994 (United Nations Development Programme 1997). This income gap has been increasing in spite of structural adjustment programs and financial assistance from the international monetary agencies. Income disparities are also rising within developed nations; paradoxically, as wealth increases it is not being dispersed but, rather, is becoming more and more concentrated. In 1994, in twenty-nine of the sixty-eight developing countries for which data were available, the ratio of incomes of the richest 20 percent to those of the poorest 20 percent was over ten to one; in sixteen countries, it was fifteen to one; and in nine countries it was twenty to one (ibid.). During the present decade overall income per person has actually declined slightly (Brown 1995).

Such inequalities undermine human development locally, nationally, and globally. Disparities in income produce disparities in impacts. The per capita contribution to atmospheric pollution and global climate change is often orders of magnitudes higher for citizens of the industrialized countries than it is for those in poorer nations (Ehrlich and Ehrlich 1991). Per capita North American carbon dioxide emissions in 1995 were 19.83 tonnes per year, compared to 7.35 tonnes in West Asia, 2.55 tonnes in Latin America, 2.23 tonnes in Asia and the Pacific, and just 1.24 tonnes in Africa (UNEP 2000). The dominant Euro-American socio-economic paradigm, now being promoted throughout the developing world, is a main cause of increasing poverty. The conversion of staple crops to cash crops has contributed to increasing malnutrition and a decrease in the ability to meet basic needs, while, at the same time, it has concentrated wealth in the hands of a few and deprived many from achieving sustainable livelihoods. About one billion people still do not have access to diets that can support normal daily activity, and nearly 500 million are slowly starving to death (Daily and Ehrlich 1996b). The earth could support more than the present population, but the distribution of good soils and favourable growing conditions does not match the population distribution; and this is being exacerbated by increasing land degradation, which is particularly severe in areas where local food production is already unable to provide adequate dietary needs for bare survival. In Africa, 65 percent of the region's agricultural land was lost to soil degradation; this is equal to about 500 million hectares since 1950 (UNEP 2000). Chronic under-nutrition is expected to affect 11 percent of the population (637 million people) in Sub-Saharan Africa and South Asia by 2011 (FACO 1996, in UNEP 2000).

Paradoxically, with increasing global population has come homogenization. Just as we are losing biological diversity, it appears that we are losing cultural diversity as well. Brazil, for example, has lost eighty-seven tribes in the first half of this century, and one-third of North American languages and two-thirds of Australian languages have disappeared since 1800 (Durning 1992). Over one-half of the world's 6,700 languages are now moribund and are spoken only by people who are middle-aged or older (Harmon 1995). As humanity's linguistic heritage disappears, so too does much of our knowledge, wisdom, and history.

All but about 200 of the modern world's 6,000 languages are likely to be extinct or moribound [sic] by the end of the next century. The analogy that occurs to me is the final destruction, in A.D. 391, of the largest library of the ancient world, at Alexandria. That library housed all the literature of Greece, plus much literature of other cultures. As a result of that library's burning, later generations lost all but the *Iliad* and *Odyssey* among Greek epics, most of the poetry of Pindar and Sappho, and dozens of plays by Aeschylus and Euripides – to mention just a few examples.

(Diamond 1993: 251-271)

Human health is also directly linked to loss of cultural and biological diversity. According to the World Health Organization, over 80 percent of people rely for their primary health care on traditional plant medicines (Dobson 1995). Most villages in the world are no longer surrounded by the natural habitat that formerly provided most of their indigenous medicines; and bodies of folk knowledge are disappearing at an unprecedented rate. It is estimated that, annually, one indigenous culture becomes extinct in the Amazon Basin alone (ibid.). Plant-based pharmaceuticals are inextricably linked to biological diversity. In the United States, nine of the ten top prescription drugs are based on natural plant compounds (Farnsworth 1988), and 118 out of 150 top prescription drugs are based on chemical compounds taken from other organisms (three-quarters of them being derived from plants) (Daily and Ehrlich 1996a). High population density may also affect human health by facilitating the spread of contagious diseases such as dysentery and influenza (Ewald 1994).

Within the next decade, more than half the world's population, an estimated 3.3 billion people, will be living in urban areas – a demographic shift with far-reaching negative implications for the environment. It is estimated that, by 2025, two-thirds of the world's people will be living in urban areas (United Nations Population Division 1995). Although cities provide tremendous benefits in some cases, such as increased infrastructure services (particularly with respect to access to improved health care) and many cultural amenities, once again, scale appears to be critical. Some cities appear to be reaching unmanageable sizes – Tokyo, 27 million; São Paulo, 16.4 million; Bombay, 11.5 million – placing enormous strains on the institutional and natural resources that support them (ibid.). Most cities now have health-threatening levels of a range of pollutants – particularly air pollutants. For example, air pollution in Mexico City is among the world's worst, with health impacts estimated at about $200 billion per year. And these burgeoning cities are forever expanding into fragile ecosystems – nearly 40 percent of cities larger than 500,000 are located on the

---

An important concept in population biology is that populations tend to maintain themselves in a series of dampened oscillations. Digression from this pattern results in severe instability and even extinctions. Part of this instability and vulnerability to extinction appears to be related to stresses that develop under conditions of high population density and severe crowding. Crowding leads to social and biological pathology, which results in high mortality and diminished group survivability.

(Cassel 1971; Aaby et al. 1983)

---

coast (WRI et al. 1996). In addition, their ecological footprint extends far beyond their geographical boundaries (Wackernagel and Rees 1996). For example, London's ecological footprint for food, forest products, and carbon assimilation is 120 times the geographic area of the city proper (ibid.). Similarly, Folke (1991) found that the aggregate consumption of wood, paper, and food (including seafood) by the inhabitants of twenty-nine cities in the Baltic Sea drainage basin appropriates an ecosystem area 200 times larger than the area of the cities themselves. Nationally, the total land required to support present consumption levels by the average Canadian is at least 4.3 hectares, including 2.3 hectares for carbon dioxide assimilation alone. Thus, the per capita ecological footprint of Canadians is almost three times their "fair earthshare" of 1.5 hectares (Woollard and Rees 1999). Socially, governments and communities around the world are under unprecedented stress. In many industrialized countries there is an emerging alienation between populations and their systems of governance. Conflict exists between the desire to cut taxes and reduce debt and the desire to maintain social and environmental programs. The increasing alienation and distrust of government is resulting in significant losses in "social capital" (Cox 1995) and, in some inner cities, unprecedented increases in violence and crime. Coupled with this violence, in the United States there is an increasing civic disengagement of approximately 40 percent (Putnam 1993b), and voting patterns in Canada tend to support the same trend. In the former Communist Bloc countries, fragile structures of governance are often barely surviving the stresses of converting to market economies. In developing countries, the strains of poverty, rapid population growth, and rapidly industrializing economies (with their massive environmental impacts) often overwhelm the ability to maintain viable cultural systems.

There is growing evidence that the competing forces of centralization and decentralization are leading to various forms of nationalism; tribalism; ethnic strife; separatist movements; and, arguably, greater susceptibility to demagoguery and political authoritarianism (Homer-Dixon et al. 1993). These sentiments are undoubtedly linked to the growing sense of alienation, fear, and loss of community in many parts of the world. Traditional notions of global security are under threat, and this is exacerbated by the increase in global arms expenditure. In the post-Second World War period (1945-89), according to a 1989 United Nations study (Head 1992), the level of this trade increased, in real terms, four or five times. Even more disturbing, much of this arms trade involves developing countries and results in their diverting money from critical social infrastructure to military expenditures.

In developing country after developing country, not least in Africa, expenditures in the defence sector exceed those in the social sectors. Often, defence expenditures equal more than health and education expenditures combined (ibid.). The face of conflict is also changing: it is moving from conflict between major nation states to inter-state warfare and civil strife. Only six out of 101 conflicts in the period between 1989 and 1996 were international. An estimated quarter of a million children are soldiers, and children under eighteen years of age were among the combatants in thirty-three current or recent conflicts (Brown et al. 1998). In addition to major weapons systems, hundreds of millions of low-tech, inexpensive, and easy-to-use weapons make up the new tools for most killing – causing as much as 90 percent of battle-related deaths. An estimated $3 billion worth of small arms and light weapons is shipped across borders each year (ibid.). Such an arming of the world, combined with the decline of social capital, has clearly exceeded the "carrying capacity" of many countries and has adversely affected their ability to govern.

The preceding data illustrate the psychopathology that occurs when a civil society designs and operates its systems without adequate reference to reconciling the ecological, social, and economic imperatives of sustainable development. There are numerous pervasive and systemic barriers to such a reconciliation, and changes of the magnitude required to move towards more sustainable societies in both the North and the South are socially problematic. The measures required may at first appear paradoxical, but they may actually converge through the reconciliation and integration of the three imperatives. Whether social transformation of this kind is possible globally will be determined over the next decade. If we are to implement sustainable development and so safeguard the future of successive generations, then we will have to make fundamental changes in how we make decisions, how we do business, how we socially construct the world, and how we perceive our place in the biosphere.

Modern humans, though, do introduce a troubling novelty. They have uncoupled decisions about reproduction from production. The ability to make decisions about future ecosystems-carrying capacity does not lie with reproducing units, and rapid feedback regulation could hardly be expected.

(Haraway 1991: 103)

Changing the Lens

It is clear that the increasing globalization of human activities and large-scale movements of people mean that humankind is in an era marked by the co-evolution of ecological and socio-economic systems at both regional and planetary levels (Holling 1994). In biology, co-evolution refers to the pattern of evolutionary change of two closely interacting species, where the fitness of genetic traits within each species is largely governed by the dominant genetic traits of the other. Co-evolutionary explanations, therefore, invoke relationships between entities that affect their evolution. Everything is interlocked, yet everything is changing in accordance with that interlockedness. Co-evolution is organic and unpredictable because of the interactive effects and synergies between human and natural systems.

Norgaard (1994) uses the co-evolution of pests, pesticides, and policy in the twentieth century as an example of the co-evolutionary process. With the discovery of DDT in 1939, and other organochlorine insecticides soon after, the use of insecticides expanded dramatically after the Second World War. Their initial effectiveness set off a spiralling co-evolutionary process between pesticides and pests. The few insects that survived were the ones most resistant to the pesticide, and a high proportion of their offspring carried genetic traits that favoured resistance. Given the number of insect generations in a season, the selective pressure of insecticides on the evolution of resistance was dramatic. Coupled with the problem of more and more species of pests developing resistance, thereby necessitating greater and greater use of insecticides, was the opening of niches for secondary pests that, for a variety of reasons, were less susceptible to spraying. Their resurgence was even greater than it would have been if left to natural processes due to the competitive niche opened up by the demise of their cohorts. Because the sprays are invariably more lethal to the predators than to the pests, the pest populations return even faster. Ironically, in spite of this pesticide treadmill, crop losses to insects are about the same as they were before the use of modern insecticides (ibid.).

We now use about 2.5 million tons of synthetic pesticides worldwide each year, and pesticide production is a multi-billion dollar industry. Yet pests and spoilage still destroy about 25 to 50 percent of crops before and after harvest. That proportion, if anything, is higher than average crop losses before synthetic pesticides were widely introduced after World War II.

(Ehrlich and Ehrlich 1997: 44)

Keeping in mind Norgaard's co-evolutionary process and Holling's ecosystem model (see Figure 4.1), how can the dominant paradigms and prevailing myths and metaphors be changed and used for the social reconstructions so necessary for sustainable development? Since the 1930s, we have seen the rise of a vast literature that argues for alternative paradigms and ways of viewing the world and human relationships. Yet there appears to be a systematic refusal on the part of mainstream agendas to include debate on these alternative paradigms. Institutional and political structures, in conjunction with business, educational, and research institutions, exert powerful influences on our values, goals, priorities, and polices; our information, knowledge, and skills; our environment, natural resources, wildlife, human health and well-being; and on our technologies (Norgaard 1994). In some ways, these structures and institutions colonize the other areas in order to maintain their influence and power; for example, technology can become a powerful "shaper" of the other four areas. As I discuss further in Chapter 8, the larger the scale of human activity, the greater the rate of change, and the greater the dependence on increasing technology.

Astounding shifts in vision have occurred before – most recently, we have seen the collapse of the Berlin Wall and the breakup of the Soviet Union. What we should avoid doing is simply trying to fix the existing dominant socio-economic paradigm, as it has systematically degraded both ecological and social capital and is in the process of distorting economic capital.

Deeper ways exist, however, to challenge and, I would hope, change these pervasive influences. One of the questions we have to ask ourselves is whether strengthening civil society means hiring more police officers or encouraging more people to know their next-door neighbour's name (Putnam 1996).

Williamson and Pearse's (1980) concept of mutual synthesis, derived from years of study and research pertaining to the Peckham Experiment, provides another lens on our relationships with the world. The experiment, designed to discover the root causes of health, was conducted at the Pioneer Health Centre in a part of London called Peckham, over a period just before and just after WWII (1926-1950). Over the 25-year research period, all of its findings coalesced around the central concept that health is a process (not a product) that requires the freedom and opportunity to experience being in a relationship of mutual synthesis with the environment. Health thus emerges from acts of spontaneity. What the Centre provided was a context and an approach to health management that supported and facilitated such freedom, experience, and spontaneity. Indeed, in such an environment, the researchers found that health became 'contagious.' Thus, instead of adopting the planner's view of the environment as innately hostile, passive, or dead, Williamson and Pearse viewed the environment as a field of function where individual and environment work in strict mutuality. This mutuality is characteristic of even the simplest cell, and is common to all living beings. Thus, the amoeba encountering a particle of food engulfs and digests it. "Once within the body the morsel is picked to pieces, chemically analyzed, sorted out and separated. Certain selected portions are then as it were reshaped and woven into its very substance according to its specific order, thereby adding to and developing its unique basic design" (27). This is a process that Williamson and Pearse describe as "synthesis," meaning "[the] living power to build up a basic organic design from the substance of the environment" (ibid.). This process of synthesis is identical whatever the interaction involves, be it food, light, or social relationships. It is mutual – an unending process between living organisms and their environment. The healthy individual, therefore, is one who enjoys a buoyant and creative mutuality with the environment.

At the individual level, education plays a critical role in changing our consciousness concerning dominant paradigms and mythologies. An important first step towards accepting the need for sustainable development will involve integrating ecological literacy (Orr 1994) into every school curriculum by the third grade. Another step, in addition to teaching ecosystem principles, involves (where applicable) modelling these principles by redesigning schools based on the structure, processing, and functioning of ecosystems. In addition to inculcating an ethos of lifelong learning, teaching young students to be self-conscious learners by illustrating cognitive complexity can make them aware of how their worldviews are strongly shaped by the physical environments and cultures in which they live. By what and how they teach, teachers affect whether children see themselves as apart from or as part of the natural world. Getting students to suspend their assumption that they can see the world as it is may be the most important step in developing the analytical dexterity they need in order to think critically. Critical thinking, however, is not easily taught because it requires students to question what Ornstein and Ehrlich (1989) refer to as the "old mind." For the "new mind" to emerge, the relationships between the inner world and the external world will need to be brought into consciousness.

Optical illusions illustrate how easy it is to make snap judgments and to fall into the trap of believing that there is really only one way to see a phenomenon when, in reality, there are many. Children could learn how to develop a set of lessons or stories that flow from their experiences within multiple valid contexts. In addition, appreciating the importance of context and of the uniqueness of each situation is crucial to self-conscious learning. When students see that they can arrive at erroneous conclusions because their contextual appreciation of the image distorted their perceptions of reality, then they can appreciate how cultural and value frames serve as filters (and distorters) of the information that we process daily (Ornstein and Ehrlich 1989).

Another important tool for self-conscious learning involves making explicit the old mind default mechanisms through which we tend to oversimplify our day-to-day decision making. We all need to learn how we cut mental corners in order to make decisions and how these cognitive shortcuts lead to systematic caricatures that prevent us from being objective in making certain kinds of judgments (Ornstein and Ehrlich 1989). New competencies in decision making that involve high levels of uncertainty, imprecise information, and rapidly and slowly changing contexts will also have to be taught. As well, we must be able to accept errors in order to learn (Michael 1993), in order to implement changes at the system level. We need to make fundamental changes in our institutions and policy frameworks; and developing appropriate institutions depends, among other things, on understanding ecosystem dynamics and relying upon appropriate indicators of change (Arrow et al. 1995). We also need to make changes in how human activity systems structure knowledge and use information for decision making; in the choice and design of our technologies; in our social constructions of the world; in institutional relationships based on gender equity; and most, fundamental of all, in value systems.

A key social imperative, therefore, is to develop principles for human activity systems that provide a basis for a more sustainable co-evolution with natural systems over the long term. This task is extremely challenging, especially given the influence of the expert-driven, rational decision-making model. Brewer (1986: 467) argues that "prevailing attitudes and styles of knowledge creation and uses have too often done precisely the opposite – by denying the legitimacy of different perspectives and preferences, by adhering narrowly to intellectual paradigms ill-suited to the challenges (and then dissolving into brittle squabbles when the limitations of each are exposed), and by favoring tools and methods used to solve problems only remotely like those facing us (and continuing to use them despite lack of success)." Another essential condition for the realization of sustainable development is the decoupling of what has been traditionally defined as human progress from the traditional belief that growth is the basic engine for improving human welfare (Pierce 1999).

> Specifically, if theory and common sense locate our humanness outside of, or transcendent to ecological fields and considerations, we will continue to reproduce alienation and problematic cultural dualisms. Running counter to this ecological alienation, greening is a reaction against many of the prevailing paradigms of modernity. For deeper green theorists, the development of new discourses involves paradigm shifts and decenterings across human spheres. Ecological vision locates humanity in an extended community of other life forces and their ecologies. In working toward the preservation of ecologies and the cultivation of ecological awareness, dichotomies are transgressed, identities shifted, and the self becomes extended and inclusive.
>
> *(Jagtenberg and McKie 1997: 125)*

Although over-population and over-consumption are key drivers for unsustainability, I believe that, in the long run, the problem is the structure of the polity and of human societies. If one looks at population and consumption as cultural systems, then it is clear that the cultural systems of both the North and the South are not sustainable and have to change. There is a political economy of fertility and consumption, and we need to look at decoupling decisions pertaining to fertility and consumption from their cultural context. If sustainable development is to be realized in the next century, then some of the key social imperatives will be the world-wide education of women; the worldwide elimination of poverty; massive public education programs to increase ecological literacy, including a targeted program for political decision makers; gender equity in political parties; and the reconciliation of the ecological, social, and economic imperatives.

Chapter 6 examines the nature of economic imperatives. As previously discussed, sustainable development is a normative concept: it is all about what we value. I have deliberately ordered the three imperatives of sustainable development according to what I believe are the most critical imperatives for sustaining human life as we currently know it. In the twenty-first century, ecological and social imperatives must assume the same political priority as economic imperatives. If they do not, then we will face the consequences of living in an increasingly inequitable world made up of winners and losers, and the chaos that will result.

6
Economic Imperatives

Poverty is a human construct. The way economic resources are
distributed is not a function of unchangeable economic laws, but
of political – that is, human – choices.

– Sign outside St. Anthony's Church, Ottawa

The preceding chapters have illustrated the widening social disparities and
growing inequities among nations. One-fifth of humanity now consumes
four-fifths of all the earth's resources (Independent Commission on Future
Population and Quality of Life [ICFPQL] 1996). Whether or not we can
grow our way out of this dilemma is one of the crucial issues currently facing both developed and developing countries. Growth in all its dimensions
represents one of the greatest paradoxes facing human societies in the
twenty-first century. On the one hand, it appears to provide for human
material well-being; on the other, it contributes to decreasing ecological
and social capital. Even its ability to provide well-being is being refuted, as
the link between growth in production and the creation of human welfare
has begun to weaken, and we are now faced with the curious phenomenon
of growth in production leading to a decline in welfare (Common and Perrings 1992; Daly, Cobb, and Cobb 1989; Dasgupta 1995).

A world economy that thrives on relentless exploitation of natural resources,
depending perilously on fossil fuels, causing limitless waste, and remaining oblivious
to the precepts of equality and equity among different societies, is neither sustainable
nor tolerable.

(Independent Commission on Future Population and Quality of Life 1966: 50)

Economic Paradigms

When the Club of Rome published *Limits to Growth* in 1972 (Meadows et al.
1972), it sparked intense international debate by fundamentally challenging
the widely held belief that growth is inherently good. This dualistic argument – growth versus no-growth – continues today and is strongly reinforced by the dominant socio-economic paradigm depicted in Figure 2.1.
As well, since the 1970s there have been major debates about the degree to

Figure 6.1

Open economic systems

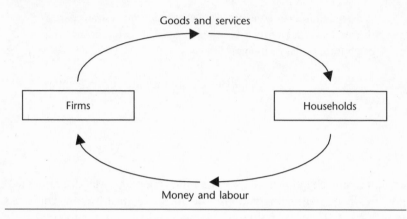

which the economy is an open or closed system and, more recently, about the nature of limits, both biophysical and human. Dominant economic paradigms, however, have influenced the nature of that debate: are these limits fixed or plastic? is the economy a closed or an open system? The current prevalent economic paradigm sees the economy as an isolated system, a circular flow of exchange value between firms and households (see Figure 6.1).

The economy is the political system of interest, and natural systems are simply regarded as either sources of resources or sinks for wastes. Nature may be finite, but many economists believe that these natural sources and sinks can be indefinitely substituted for by human ingenuity without limiting overall growth in any significant way. In this paradigm, instead of economic theory acknowledging its embeddedness in the real world of physical reality and contexts, it seeks to expand so as to *include* its context (O'Hara 1995). Not land (i.e., nature), but human labour and capital creation are seen as the source of economic progress. Such a perception involves a fundamental and artificial separation of human and natural systems.

An alternative view, known as steady-state economics, sees the economy, in its physical dimensions, as an open subsystem within a finite, non-growing, and materially closed total system – the earth, ecosystem, or biosphere – as depicted in Figure 6.2.

The growth of the economy is, therefore, constrained by the physical carrying capacity of the larger biosphere. In this view, human and natural capital are regarded not as substitutes for one another but, rather, as complements to one another. In fact, Daly (1995) cautions that we may be facing a historic juncture in which, for the first time, the limits to increased

Figure 6.2

Closed economic systems

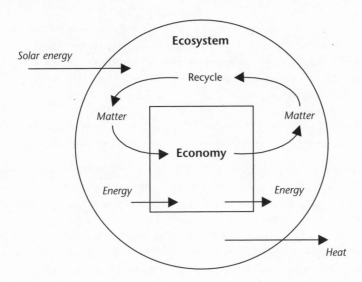

Source: Daly 1995.

prosperity are not the lack of human-made capital but the lack of natural capital. Debates on growth continue, however, with no greater resolution than in the early 1970s.

I believe that one of our principal mistakes has been to view ourselves as separate from our environment and not part of it. Moreover, we have not accepted the notion of biospheric limits (Commoner 1975; Meadows et al. 1972; Odum 1975). Thus, we perceive the environment and the economy as separate cycles connected by a one-way movement of resources from nature to humankind. Paradoxically, ecological and economic systems actually have very similar needs in terms of maintaining essential structures and ensuring performance. They each require energy, elemental diversity, and free-flowing circulation in order to function. As described in Chapter 3, ecosystems can be characterized as primarily concerned with maintenance of a system. Human activity systems have become mainly concerned with production and consumption, placing little or no emphasis on maintenance and rehabilitation; and growth is regarded as central to fuelling the production processes of human activity systems. Unfortunately, there are no new frontiers left for virgin exploitation, although, as discussed in Chapter 5, we are doing our best to open up new possibilities by imposing monetarized economic systems on the developing world. The preceding two chapters showed that, somehow, human activity systems must begin to reconcile methods of production and consumption with the essential maintenance of ecosystems.

Conventional economic theories will not guide our future for a simple reason. They have never placed "natural capital" on the balance sheet. When it is included, not as a free amenity or as a putative infinite supply, but as an integral and valuable part of the production process, everything changes. Prices, costs, and what is and isn't economically sound change dramatically.

(Hawken 1997: 42)

Achieving such a reconciliation, without growth in human systems, will be impossible without a paradigm shift in economic thought. On the one hand, some argue, economic growth has the ability to raise the material standards of a large number of people around the world and, indeed, represents the only way the needs of the planet's growing human population can be met (Brundtland Commission 1987). On the other hand, some claim that it is impossible for the world economy to grow its way out of poverty and environmental degradation. Proponents of the Genuine Progress Indicator (GPI), a more comprehensive measure of human well-being, Cobb, Goodman, and Wackernagel (1999) argue compellingly that economic growth alone does not equal progress. As the economic subsystem grows it incorporates an even greater proportion of the total ecosystem into itself and thus reaches a limit of 100 percent, before ecosystem limits are approached (Daly 1990; see also Rees and Wackernagel 1994).

This debate is both psychopathological and counter-productive, as biophysical evidence continues to mount and make clear that the products of our growth and consequent consumption patterns are slowly destroying the very habitat on which we depend. This discussion is further complicated by the schizophrenic refusal of both the North and the South to recognize and respect limits on their own behaviour. Whereas the former is finding it hard to accept limits and to take responsibility for its increasing consumption, the latter is finding it equally difficult to recognize limits and to take responsibility for its increasing population growth.

In fact, there is a hyperactive rhythm of consumption that underpins the dominant socio-economic system in North American society. For example, modernizing agriculture has increased the speed and diversity of acquisition through increasing scale, which then depends on whole networks of processing, distribution, and storage – as does industrial production; and whereas agriculture could be a net producer of energy (through carbon fixation in photosynthesis), it is now an energy sink. Achieving faster rates of production means distributing more and consuming more natural substances. This then puts pressure on agriculture to produce at a rate comparable to those involved in other aspects of production and distribution. As available local sources of energy (in either agricultural or industrial production) are diminished, capital either has to create routes to enable old sources of energy to come from farther away or it has to create new sources of energy altogether (ranging from chemical inputs to nuclear power) (Brennan 1997). To the extent that capital's continued profit must be based more and more on speed of acquisition, it must centralize and command more distance; in this respect, short-term profit takes precedence over the generational time of natural reproduction (ibid.). Thus, more and more space is appropriated by socio-economic systems predicated on growth and perceived as isolated systems. Perhaps even more important are the impacts of this economic system on social cohesion and quality of life, specifically in terms of crime, depression, addiction of all forms, violence, mental illness, and spiritual emptiness (Trainer 1996).

Take the giant, airy American strawberry. Genetically recombined for improved size, and growth in degraded soil, it looks great and tastes like nothing. In the medium term, even its comparative price has fallen. It is a symptomatic industrial product: seemingly wonderful, yet it has literally less substance, and hence less value.

(Brennan 1997: 182-183)

The crux of the issue, then, is whether to continue to regard the economy as an isolated system or whether to regard it as an open subsystem of a finite system. If we choose the former, then there is no environment to constrain the continual growth of the economic system. If, however, we choose the latter, then growth is limited by its finiteness. The economy may continue to develop qualitatively, but it cannot continue indefinitely to develop quantitatively: at some "sustainable" point it must approximate a steady state in its physical dimensions. And determining these sustainable points involves addressing complex socio-political questions and an unprecedented interface between the research community and the public policy community.

Another issue central to this debate concerns substitution – specifically, the degree of substitutability between produced capital and natural capital (Daly, Cobb, and Cobb 1989; Daly 1991a; Turner 1992). Some economists believe in fixed coefficients, the opposite of substitution at the margins. For example, during the 1970s, the Club of Rome, in its report *Limits to Growth*, used fixed technology and no substitution in its modelling (Meadows et al. 1972). As a result, it predicted an apocalyptic collapse sooner than would be likely. Some experts, however, believe that, with human ingenuity, the potential for flexibility and substitutability in the economic system is enormous. They argue that, because of the uncertain limits of human ingenuity, it is impossible to predetermine future trends and the limits of technological development. In addition, Lipsey (1995) maintains that most technological development has both economic and environmental benefits because it involves fewer inputs and technologies, thus becoming absolutely more efficient over time. He argues that we should do our best to manage sustainable growth and that growth, if it is to be maximized, must occur through technological change. Regardless of one's technological lens, however, it is now generally recognized that there are limits to the possibilities of substituting produced for natural capital, although there is considerable debate about the nature and degree of those limits (Meadows et al. 1992). The World Bank's 1995 Wealth Index valued human capital at up to three times greater than all of the financial and manufactured capital reflected on global balance sheets, and this estimate is conservatively based on only the market value of human employment. All technological growth, whether efficient or not, eventually increases both consumption and impacts on the environment. Technology can neither replace the earth's life support systems nor substitute for human intelligence, organizational ability, and culture (Hawken et al. 1999).

Plumwood defines five features that are typical of dualisms: backgrounding (denial); radical exclusions (hyperseparation); incorporation (relational definition); instrumentalism (objectification); and homogenization or stereotyping. Through backgrounding, economics establishes common "ways to deny dependency" through disempowering an other "by denying the importance of the other's contribution or even his or her reality."

(Plumwood 1983: 48)

As previously discussed, if we accept that we live in a closed system – the biosphere – then we must accept that there are important limits to its carrying capacity and that these are difficult to determine and predict. Therefore, the precautionary principle must prevail. Ecosystems are the key "factors of production," and, as a consequence of the growth of human activity systems, they are becoming increasingly impacted and diminished (Barbier et al. 1994; Jansson et al. 1994). Because many of the most important environmental effects of human activity systems are not recognized and valued in market prices, it is clear that current social institutions, including markets, are incapable of responding to environmental feedbacks (Berkes and Folke 1994). We should, therefore, deliberately attempt to keep our economic system well below critical ecological thresholds, especially given our imprecise information, incomplete knowledge, and the dynamic complexity of the interlocutory effects of ecological, social, and economic systems. Moreover, we can anticipate that our knowledge will never enable us to completely control and manage complex and dynamic living systems.

If one accepts the need for steady-state economies, then compelling and socially complex questions emerge for civil society and how it defines what constitutes sustainable development. What is the optimal scale of the subsystem relative to the entire system? If one accepts the reality and necessity of limits, should we live at the limits? or should we live below the limits to allow space for other species (or at least a safety margin for ourselves)?

Another key characteristic of our current human activity systems is change (Toffler 1970), and the rate of that change has been greatly influenced and hyper-stimulated over the past few years by globalization. Henderson (1991) has identified six driving forces behind globalization: (1) industrialism, technology; (2) finance, communication, information; (3) employment, work, migration; (4) human effects on biosphere pollution; (5) militarization; and (6) consumption, culture, and media-driven world citizenship movements. And there is a seventh driving force – interactions, responses, realignments, and restructurings.

Global Context

But what is the scale of this global economy? Global economic output expanded from $3.8 trillion in 1950 to $18.9 trillion in 1992 – a nearly fivefold increase. And world trade soared from total exports of $308 billion to $3,554 billion, an 11.5-fold increase (Korten 1995). Just as industrialization fostered the separation of land from production, consolidation combined with the twinning of computerization and globalization has created another new (artificial) separation, delinking money from production. For example, investment decisions once taken by many individuals are now increasingly consolidated in the hands of a few investment managers. As individuals increasingly placed their savings in professionally managed funds, the pool of investment funds controlled by mutual funds doubled in three years, totalling $2 trillion at the end of June 1994 (ibid.). As well, Joel Kurtzman, the editor of the *Harvard Business Review*, estimates that, for every one dollar circulating in the productive world economy, twenty to fifty dollars circulate in the economy of pure finance (i.e., the money markets); and these are also in the hands of individuals who, essentially, have no knowledge of the limits of ecological systems (cited in Korten 1995).

Linked to this consolidation of individual investors is a corresponding concentration of multinationals, with sweeping ramifications for national sovereignty. This "concentration without centralization" has four interesting elements of transformation; namely, downsizing; computerization and automation; mergers, acquisitions, and strategic alliances; and headquarters teamwork and morale (Korten 1995). The result, whether deliberate or not, is a dualistic employment system consisting of corporate headquarters staff who are very well compensated and temporary or part-time employees who are not well compensated.

Globalization is also underpinned by a variety of legal instruments, such as the North American Free Trade Agreement (NAFTA) and, most recently, the Multilateral Agreement on Investment (MAI). The MAI, developed by the twenty-nine member nations of the Organisation for Economic Co-operation and Development (OECD), and which was defeated by a unique consensus among civil society groups, had some very remarkable features. For example, it would have allowed investors the unrestricted right to buy, sell, and move businesses, resources, and other assets wherever and whenever they wanted; it would have overridden all "non-conforming" local, state, and national laws and regulations; it would have severely restricted the ability of governments to impose obligations on foreign corporations; and it would have allowed corporations to sue non-conforming cities, states, and national governments before an international tribunal composed of judges largely of the corporation's own choosing.

Advocates of the MAI argue that reducing restrictions on capital is the logical next step after treaties such as NAFTA and the General Agreement on Tariffs and Trade (GATT) reduced restrictions on the mobility of goods and services. Opponents of the MAI contended that capital, unlike other economic factors, brings with it power and control. In addition, the MAI codified and reinforced the increasing tendency of modern economies to separate those who make the decisions from those who feel their impact, to separate capital from physical space, and to separate the economy from ecology.

Hence, the MAI offered capital a right that even GATT does not. Under the agreement, investors and corporations could sue governments directly – a privilege that NAFTA already allows. On 17 April 1997, the United States-based Ethyl Corporation became the first corporation to exercise this right when it sued the Canadian government. The Ethyl Corporation/MMT case demonstrates the changing nature of state sovereignty under these international trade agreements. MMT is a manganese-based compound that is added to gasoline to enhance octane and to reduce engine knocking. The United States Environmental Protection Agency (EPA) has banned its use in formulated gasoline, which includes approximately one-third of the American gasoline market. An Environmental Defense Fund (EDF) survey of the remaining producers reports that none use the additive (Roe et al. 1997), and California has imposed a total ban on MMT.

Canadian legislators wanted to ban the use of MMT in order to protect the Canadian public. Because they could not do so under the Canadian Environmental Protection Act (CEPA) provisions, they chose the best available alternative: banning the import and transport of MMTs. Ethyl (the company that invented leaded gasoline) responded to the Canadian Parliament's act to ban the import and interprovincial transport of an Ethyl product by filing a lawsuit against the Canadian government under NAFTA. Ethyl claims that the Canadian ban on MMT violates various provisions of NAFTA, and it seeks restitution of $251 million to cover losses resulting from the "expropriation" of both its MMT production plan and its "good reputation." Consequently, the Canadian government withdrew its ban in July 1998.

As discussed in Chapter 5, there is also considerable debate about whether or not poverty and income disparities will be made worse or better by the trend towards global economic integration. In fact, it appears as though, in industrialized nations, the real incomes of the middle class are decreasing while poverty is increasing (Korten 1995). Along with this comes a disturbing acceleration of the feminization of poverty. In spite of growth in corporate profits, through technological innovation and the disappearance of any corporate responsibility to geographical place, the usual linkage between growth in the bottom line and employment has also been broken. Most industrialized countries are undergoing significant downsizing in both the corporate and government sectors. Indeed, in parts of the industrialized world for more than twenty-five years unemployment and underemployment have risen faster than employment (Hawken 1997).

How well does the current economic system support the welfare of people locally and globally? Korten (1995) and Mishan (1977) maintain that there is little basis for assuming that economic growth, as it is currently defined and measured, results in automatic increases in human welfare. Daly, Cobb, and Cobb (1989), after adjusting the national income accounts to count only increases in output that relate to improvements in well-being and adjusting for the depletion of human and environmental resources, show that, on average, individual welfare in the United States peaked in 1969. It remained on a plateau until the early to mid-1980s, when it fell. Yet from 1969 to 1986, GNP per person went up by 35 percent, and fossil fuel consumption increased by around 17 percent. Despite the economic growth in the Third World between 1960 and 1980, the gap in real income between rich nations and poor nations increased from a factor of twenty to a factor of forty-six. And that gap continues to increase (Hawken 1997).

Nor do markets appear to be as effective as in the past in their ability to distribute wealth and create employment. It could be argued that the economic system, despite its systemic problems, appeared to be effective in maintaining a civil society by creating a large middle class through the economic development of the 1950s and 1960s. The inflationary pressures of the 1970s, however, resulted in a slowing of this process. Part of the widening gap between rich and poor in the 1990s derived from the tremendous surge in the value of equities. From 1990 to 1997, the market value of American corporations almost tripled, rising from $3,452 billion to $10,293 billion (1992 dollars). The rising stock market exacerbated the already widening gap between those who have inherited or invested in stocks in recent decades and those who have barely managed to get by (Cobb et al. 1999). Thus the 1990s saw a growing gap between the income of rich nations and poor nations, an increasing gap between the rich and poor in developed countries, and a shrinking of the Canadian middle class (Rees, personal communication). While the GDP rose from $20,310 per capita in 1980 to $27,939 per capita in 1988, the GPI fell from $8,722 per capita in 1980 to $6,649 per capita in 1998 (1992 dollars). And while the GPI measures this change in monetary terms, corresponding social costs are difficult to quantify. They include increased alienation between rich and poor, heightened social conflict, resentment, and despair. Individual costs include increasing suicide rates, particularly among young men (Cobb et al. 1999). As industrial production is thus being transformed, and as transnational corporations redefine the world's labour markets to minimize their production costs, unemployment grows in the traditional industrial sectors of rich countries (McMichael 1995: 305). Nor does the global trading system value creating employment opportunities in communities. As always, it strives for competitive advantage, going to those markets where labour is cheapest and regulations minimal, regardless of the conditions. As the forces for globalization continue to accelerate, and corporate activity is no longer tied to a sense of place, there are few or no social obligations for communities and nations to create work for people or even to maintain a regional resource base.

There are two dimensions to materialism as a worldview: economic and scientific. The latter is absolutely essential to the former, and may even be the prerequisite for its existence. This other materialism is the philosophy that nature is nothing but physical matter organized under and obeying physical laws, matter rationally ordered but devoid of any spirit, soul, or in-dwelling, directing purpose. On this view of nature converge many of our modern university departments of learning along with our extra-academic institutions of research and development, governmental bureaucracies, and multinational corporations, all of which tend to approach nature as nothing more than dead matter.

(Worster 1993: 211)

Although this intense globalization of the economic system appears to be creating space for new avenues of economic growth, this is merely an illusion. Hawken (1997) points out that the American economy may not be growing at all and, if depletion of natural capital is factored into GNP measures of growth, may have actually ceased growing nearly twenty-five years ago. Thus, we may well be reaching our last frontiers, as absolute limits to growth are being imposed by the biosphere. There is considerable evidence (see Chapter 4), some in very critical areas, that most of our economic growth has been at the expense of natural capital. Given our current rates of natural capital depletion and continuing human appropriation of carrying capacity, it is clear that our current economic system is not ecologically sustainable. In other words, our economic system is destroying the essential inputs on which it depends and is also beginning to deplete "social capital" through its current inability to generate wealth and through rising income disparities and inequalities.

Psychopathologies
There are four driving forces behind the systemic decline in ecological capital. First, unrestricted access to a resource and unsustainable management of a common good reflects the imperfect allocation of property rights (e.g., water) (Hawken 1997). Second, mismatched rights and obligations and other market imperfections (externalities) can cause value and price to diverge (e.g., a tall building's shadow being cast over a previously sunlit park will not be captured in its price structure). Third, a myriad of neglected ecologically damaging and economically perverse side-effects result from most government subsidies to industry (MacNeill n.d.). Fourth, the measures of economic progress, such as the GNP and the GDP, are seriously flawed because, due to the preceding three forces, they are based on improper information.

One of the greatest mythologies of the dominant socio-economic paradigm is that we live and work in a free market system. In reality, this market system is significantly supported by public monies. Commercial fisheries, for example, cost much more than they contribute to the economies of the world. At present, the annual worldwide catch has a market value of about US$70 billion, yet it costs $124 billion to land. The difference – $54 billion – is made up in subsidies; that is, in tax dollars (Earle 1997). With respect to energy, most nations spend several times more taxpayer dollars on encouraging greater consumption of fossil fuels than they do on encouraging greater efficiencies (or the use of alternatives). In Canada, the ratio is more than three to one (MacNeill n.d.). There are subsidies to encourage the use of the automobile, including road construction and externalized costs, and to encourage the mining of minerals and the cutting of forests. For example, worldwide reductions in the use of hydrocarbon fuels are being impeded by an annual subsidy of about US$2,400 per year per automobile (Brown et al. 1988). Fiscal bias in the treatment of virgin versus recycled material amounts to almost $400 million annually – a significant barrier to the use of recycled material and one with clear environmental implications (Bregha et al. 1995). Thus, taxpayers are, mostly unknowingly, spending several times more to promote global warming and acid rain than to reduce it; and there are other negative effects associated with technological innovation and competitiveness (MacNeill n.d.).

International armaments remains one of the most heavily subsidized industries (Head 1992). Tax dollars are used to subsidize the disposal of waste in all its forms, from landfills to deep-well injection, to storage of nuclear waste. All of these subsidies continue to encourage the persistence of an economy in which 80 percent of what we consume gets thrown away after one use (Hawken 1997). According to Robert Ayres, a leading researcher in the area of industrial metabolism, about 94 percent of the materials extracted for use in manufacturing durable products become waste before the product is even manufactured (ibid.).

What is the global magnitude of this subsidy regime? A recent study undertaken by de Moor and Calamai (1997) for the Earth Council examined four areas: water consumption, transportation, energy use, and agriculture. In these combined areas alone, subsidies ranged between $700 billion and $900 billion per year. More recent work by Cambridge University researchers suggests that the total is now between $950 billion and $1,450 billion annually, including commercial fishing (Sapa 1999). Moreover, the study revealed that most of these subsidies no longer serve their original purposes and now actually harm economic prospects. In other words, in most cases subsidies had become socially perverse, environmentally destructive, and/or trade distorting; in most countries they became all three at the same time (MacNeill n.d.). The University of Cambridge researchers concluded that, if just $300 billion worth of these subsidies were diverted to environmental programs, biodiversity could be saved (Sapa 1999). MacNeill (n.d.) has further estimated that, based on his work with the Brundtland Commission, the global spending on subsidies that undermine sustainable development is approximately $1.5 trillion per year.

Taxes and subsidies are information that influence behaviour. The most fundamental policy implication, therefore, is simple to envision, but difficult to execute. We have to revise the tax system to stop subsidizing behaviours we don't want (resource depletion and pollution) and to stop taxing behaviours we do want (income and work). We need to transform, incrementally but firmly, the sticks and carrots that guide business.

(Hawken 1997: 53)

New Economic Paradigms
The most critical step in moving to more sustainable economies, therefore, is to identify and then systematically eliminate subsidies that encourage unsustainable extraction and consumption of resources and waste production.

The next step is to create incentives for people and economies to act more in harmony than in conflict with those processes that maintain the dynamics and structure of ecosystems (Folke et al. 1996).

Within the context of sustainable development there are possibilities of reconciling the economic and ecological imperatives, at least in open industrialized economies like Canada's. A traditional suggestion in response to the increasing global integration of the world's economies is to argue that high-wage, resource-based industrialized economies must increasingly move towards a future based on information-rich content goods and services. Indeed, such an economy will be required if we wish to continue to compete in an increasingly integrated and competitive global marketplace characterized by increasingly mobile capital and investment flows that face ever-decreasing barriers.

Moreover, the economic and social development needs of Southern countries, economies in transition, and rapidly industrializing economies are such that greatly expanded flows of investment capital, along with trade activity, may be required merely to maintain the present (although often inadequate) growth rates. This will remain the case unless the twin forces of globalization and consumption can be changed. At the same time, industrialized countries are increasingly dependent upon export revenues derived from trade with developing countries, as is reflected in the expanding size of their ecological footprints (Wackernagel and Rees 1996). This expansion of the economic needs of Northern countries into Southern countries has been particularly facilitated by the structural adjustments imposed on the latter by Northern aid programs and international monetary institutions such as the World Bank and the IMF. Clearly, it is predictable that, if one accepts the arguments for limits to the carrying capacity of the biosphere, then current patterns of globalization and consumption will cause worldwide ecological collapse within a short time frame.

While business teaches us effective forms of human organization, environmental science reveals that those forms do not necessarily preserve the natural resources that are the basis of our well being. While business teaches how to gain financial wealth, ecological understanding demonstrates wealth to be ultimately illusory unless it is based on the principles and cyclical processes of nature. The dialogue reconciling these dichotomies will be the fundamental basis for economic transformation.

(Hawken 1993: 10)

Sustainable development, because of the inevitability of ecological limits, will increasingly become an emergent force for industry and its practices; and the proactive adoption of more sustainable industrial processes and practices – politically, economically, and institutionally – will benefit our competitive world position in the twenty-first century. This lesson has already been learned by an increasing number of leading German, Japanese, North American, Scandinavian, and Swiss industries, which, when pressed by high world oil prices and tight emission standards, invented many of the industrial technologies of the 1980s and 1990s. These technologies were not only energy, resource, and environmentally efficient, but also internationally competitive, as was evidenced by their domination of the market share in almost every sector (from automobiles to pulp and paper, food processing, the service industries, and communications) (MacNeill et al. 1991). And they have only scratched the surface of such opportunities: those opportunities involving fundamental redesign – where the major advantages will be realized – have yet to be developed (Hill et al. 1994). Consider, for example, the Atlanta-based Interface Corporation, which has shifted away from selling carpeting to leasing floor-covering services. It is using a new material that requires 97 percent less material, is cheaper to produce, and is completely recyclable (Hawken et al. 1999).

There may well be strategic opportunities for Canadian society and business to go beyond thinking of environmental and economic agendas as necessarily in conflict, of economic activity as undermining sustainability, and of ecological sustainability as a constraint on economic activity. It may be that ecological and economic imperatives, if interpreted and acted upon imaginatively, can actually reinforce one another and be reconciled by supportive government interventions. The alternative is for their convergence to emerge as an eventual response to system collapse.

Indeed, the solution lies in changing the objective function of our activities, optimizing them, and then offering better forms of resource cycling (Henning, personal communication, 1998; Mallet 1991). Recent developments in industrial ecology can help this process over the short term, but fundamental system redesign will be required over the long term. Industrial ecology is evolving beyond mere efficiency changes and "end-of-the-pipe" solutions to eliminating waste by linking industrial systems to ecosystem principles. It is increasingly recognizing the crucial connections between the structure of ecosystems and the structure of other systems (both natural and human). Being involved in industrial ecology means designing for the environment, integrating the design of production systems technology with closed loop manufacturing. New processes and new products is what industrial ecology is all about: it merges ecological principles with industrial practices by taking the basic principles of nature and incorporating them into the front end of industrial production and processes. One such principle is that nature produces virtually no waste because waste is transformed and used by something else, either through symbiosis or mutualist relationships (Odum 1975).

Over the long term, ecological and economic imperatives converge and lead to competitive advantage. It is clear from industrialized countries that, as the costs of materials and of waste treatment continue to mount, it can become a competitive advantage to use less virgin material, to consume less energy, and to produce less waste. For example, Germany has legislated that its automobile manufacturers must now take back their product at the end of its life cycle, essentially mandating a simulated negative feedback loop. Canada's international competitiveness will be affected by its ability to move from basic efficiency measures to substitution measures (such as clean, green technologies and technological systems) to fundamental re-design (Hill and Henning 1992).

The efficiency-substitution-redesign framework provides another useful model for making a deeper transition to sustainable development (Hill 1998; 1985; MacRae et al. 1990). Through it, a firm gradually evolves from making minor "efficiency" changes to substituting activities, then to totally rethinking and redesigning its structures, processes, and procedures. Efficiency strategies involve making minor changes to current practices in order to increase output and to reduce waste per unit of input. A substitution strategy replaces an environmentally stressful product, practice, or process with a more benign one (e.g., using biotechnology to convert a waste disposal problem into a new product-producing process). Redesign is holistic in its approach, and its goal is to prevent environmental problems through the design and management of healthy systems based on ecological principles (Hill et al. 1994).

With the population doubling sometime in the next century, and resource availability per capita dropping by one-half to three-fourths over that same period, which factor of production do you think will go up in value – and which do you think will go down?

(Hawken 1997: 60)

In the efficiency stage, conventional systems are altered to reduce both consumption of resources and environmental impacts. In the substitution phase, finite and environmentally disruptive products are replaced by those that are more environmentally benign (e.g., non-organic fertilizers are replaced by organic fertilizers, non-specific pesticides are replaced by biological controls, and herbicides are replaced by appropriate systems of cultivation). In contrast, the redesign stage aims to avoid problems through adopting site- and time-specific design and management approaches. The farm is made more ecologically and economically diverse, self-reliant in terms of resources, and self-regulating. Problems are solved at the causal level by building self-regulating mechanisms into the structure and functioning of the agroecosystem. The redesign stage is similar to those aspects of industrial ecology that attempt to mimic ecosystem processes and incorporate them into human production systems. This means moving beyond waste management to waste elimination by redesigning industrial systems according to ecosystem principles. Industrial ecology integrates the design of production systems technology with closed loop manufacturing. It is also a total systems design that incorporates design for the environment at the product and process levels; practises disassembling, reuse, and recycling; and makes the best use of control and assessment technologies.

Another path to more sustainable economic systems may involve the dematerialization of the economy. A country's ability to dematerialize – to reduce its materials and energy inputs – directly affects its competitive advantage. For example, Canada, as a nation, already lags behind other countries, particularly Japan, which currently uses 38 percent less energy input per GDP output than do any of the other industrialized countries (MacNeill et al. 1991). Even when allowing for differences such as geography and climate, Canada remains significantly less efficient than do most other industrialized countries. Canada is now facing a competitive disadvantage in some resource sectors, as its previous relative abundance of natural resources has provided few, if any, incentives for energy efficiency, never mind substitution or redesign. For a whole set of interconnected economic and ecological reasons, it is becoming clearer and clearer to Canadians that cod fishing on the East Coast, assembling automobiles in Ontario, and clear-cut logging on the West Coast are not going to be the basis of continued prosperity in these three regions.

For both economic and ecological reasons, we need to decouple human welfare from the throughput of matter and energy, and human well-being from consumption. This will require the development of values and incentives that support such changes. But that can only happen through the creation of a national framework of sustainable development that will facilitate changing both the way we produce products and the material and energy inputs of those products. If we do this, then both the processes and the products will become sustainable; that is, they will fall within ecological carrying capacity locally, regionally, nationally, and internationally. Clearly, a creative balance between public policies and market forces will be needed, as will new ideas and an incentive structure.

Restructuring so as to incorporate industrial ecology practices into both large and small businesses is a first step towards the deeper level of fundamental redesign, and it will require appropriate government policies to provide a consistent framework of proactive incentives, for three reasons. First, structural adjustments of this magnitude cannot occur via reactive signals through markets or even through pricing signals. As discussed, most environmental amenities – indeed, all ecosystem services – are still regarded as market externalities and do not have a price. There is, therefore, little economic incentive to value them, and, as a result, any integrative strategies based on existing market forces will continue to ignore or undervalue environmental costs (in spite of some preliminary attempts by Costanza and Folke 1997). Second, there is a gridlock of perverse economic disincentives and ecologically destructive incentives that actively encourage continued exploitation of renewable and non-renewable resources and ecological services, and that run counter to sustainable development. Third, bureaucratic inertia and the current federal/provincial morass make the required changes unlikely unless we can develop radically new incentives and policies.

New Policy Directions

Three interrelated policies exist to redirect market forces towards sustainable development in the immediate term: withdrawal of ecologically damaging and economically perverse subsidies, green taxes, and a basic income scheme. All three are complementary and are not substitutable. Given the current climate of deficit reduction and downsizing, a significant reallocation of resources is necessary to free up the finances for changes of this magnitude. Quite often, sustainable development arguments and, particularly, discussions about a basic income scheme are arrested by the question: Where would the money come from to finance such programs? As well, there are powerful interests concerned with continuing business as usual. And polarized debates about the existence of limits versus no limits, and unrestrained growth versus no-growth, do little to increase the likelihood of innovative solutions to the problems surrounding ensuring sustainable development. This is why green taxes must be considered prior to the introduction of any guaranteed annual income scheme: the former would demonstrate one way in which the latter could be financed.

To create a policy that supports resource productivity will require a shift away from taxing the social "good" of labor, toward taxing the social "bads" of resource exploitation, pollution, fossil fuels, and waste. This tax shift should be "revenue neutral" – meaning that for every dollar of taxation added to resources or waste, one dollar would be removed from labor taxes.

(Hawken 1997: 59)

The main function of green taxes is not to raise additional revenues for governments but, rather, to redirect industrial production and practices away from unsustainable to sustainable development. Their purpose is to reflect the full environmental costs of doing business, thereby providing consumers with accurate information about the true costs of their choices in the marketplace. Their intent is to immediately correct the distortions created by the free ecosystems commons and the belief that nature can endlessly absorb human impacts without cost (Hardin 1993). Most important, they correct the distortions created by the relentless pursuit of lower prices and reveal true costs to purchasers (Korten 1995; Jacobs 1994). Environmental disasters such as the *Exxon Valdez* oil spill, therefore, would no longer contribute to an increase in GNP. Korten (1995) further recommends that such taxes be revenue-neutral; that is, every incremental dollar collected from green fees should reduce income and payroll taxes equally, starting with the lowest income brackets and moving to the highest. He estimates that the annual fees and taxes on virgin resources, emissions, fuels, products, wastes, rights, and services would equal about 1.2 percent of GDP. And by shifting the tax burden from income and entrepreneurial activity to those activities that we wish to discourage, we would be able to transform the economy. Several Swedish CEOs have already asked their prime minister to implement some form of ecological tax reform in order to gain an advantage over American and Japanese companies (Van Gelder 1995). In other words, Swedish industrialists believe that future international competitive advantage lies in increasing dematerialization and industrial ecology practices. Changes in incentives, such as ecological tax reform, that encourage industries to move in these directions will stimulate further necessary changes.

Numerous researchers and organizations are exploring the policy implications of reducing the energy/material throughput of so-called advanced economies. Conscious of the need for growth, particularly in the developing world, they conclude that the material intensity of consumption in industrial countries should be reduced by a factor of up to ten to accommodate it (BSCD 1993; Ekins and Jacobs 1994; Rees 1995; RMNO 1994; Schmidheiny, Bleek, Young, and Sachs 1994). Since markets do not reflect ecological reality, governments must create the necessary policy incentives to ensure that as consumption rises, the material and energy consumption falls apace.

(Woollard and Rees 1999: 36)

A guaranteed annual income scheme is needed in order to remove one of the biggest barriers to these kinds of structural changes; namely, fear concerning one's ability to support one's basic needs. Addressing this fear will also decouple labour from business, subsequently decreasing political pressure and creating some analytical space for policy alternatives for sustainable development. If corporations have both economic and social responsibilities, and institutions are embedded within civil societies rather than being separate from them, then corporations have an important role to play in the creation of meaningful work. Many people believe that this can be achieved through technology, which has the capacity to eliminate many routine tasks from the workplace. Technology, however, is a double-edged sword, it has often resulted in depopulating the workplace. In fact, some analysts contend that technological breakthroughs, so far from functioning as a panacea for carrying capacity deficits, actually contribute to increased environmental degradation and overshoot (Catton 1993).

Given the structural adjustments now occurring through globalization, free trade, computerization, robotization, and corporate concentrations, some kind of basic income is necessary to support human beings as they adapt to the transition to sustainable development. There are also important questions concerning power and distribution and its effects on civil society. Michael Wolzar (1983) puts the issue clearly:

> A radically laissez-faire economy would be like a totalitarian state, invading every other sphere, dominating every other distributive process. It would transform every social good into a commodity. This is market imperialism ... What is at issue now is the dominance of money outside its sphere, the ability of wealthy men and women to trade in indulgences, purchase of state offices, corrupt the courts, exercise political power ... the exercise of power belongs to the sphere of politics, while what goes on in the market should at least approximate an exchange between equals (a free exchange).

With respect to a basic income security, Dobell (1996: 198) refers to the notion of a minimum participation income, the foundation for which is a social contract that "assures a basic income paid as an economic return to all citizens for two reasons: first, as participants in productive social networks and active contributors to social wealth creation; and, second, as owners of the social capital, represented by social networks and community knowledge, and of the scarce natural capital, represented by the ecological commons, that together form the foundation for market activity." The importance of social networks, social wealth, and women's work is not counted in our current ways of recording income and expenditures. As well, the principle of citizen ownership of natural capital is completely ignored in the settling of national accounts.

We could finance a basic income scheme through green taxes rather than using them to offset taxation on income, as Hawken (1997) suggests. Further, the possibility exists that, in the long run, with the convergence of economic and social imperatives, such a scheme might be more cost effective than the current employment insurance scheme. The right to meaningful work would assume greater value than the right to employment insurance. Hirst (1994: 180) argues that it is "the one reform that would make extensive associational experiments possible, since it provides a basic plank of universal income support on the basis of which large-scale experiments that lead to diversity and heterogeneity in provision might be acceptable."

All of these changes must be accompanied by a corresponding change in the way we make decisions concerning what we value as a civil society. If we consider the nature of sustainable development problems such as global warming, ozone depletion, biodiversity loss, and overpopulation, then it is clear that they are becoming increasingly more complex and interactive. These problems are more and more frequently caused by local human impacts on air, land, and oceans – impacts that slowly accumulate and then trigger sudden abrupt changes that directly affect the health and innovative capacities of people, the productivity of renewable resources, and the well-being of societies everywhere. In a democratic society, there is no single right answer to these complex, interacting problems; rather, we must accept the fact that there are multiple realities that can only be resolved by the plurality of interests affected.

Key Economic Imperatives

1 use multiple measures to provide a more robust picture of human well-being rather than relying solely on one measure (GDP)

2 get the prices right

3 eliminate ecologically damaging and economically perverse incentives

4 improve performance indicators

5 move from pioneer to climax economics; the rapid growth and exploitation of new possibilities typical of the pioneer stage will give way to a state of stable maturity in which maximum amenity is obtained from minimum resources, and energy is devoted primarily to the maintenance of the current capital stock rather than new growth.

(Ophuls 1977)

Moving from this global context, whose impacts are mirrored in Canada (albeit on a different scale of impact and severity than in many countries), let's turn the page to look at the Canadian context, particularly as it relates to governance. In order to effectively address questions of governance, however, it is necessary to first look at barriers to affecting changes in the polity.

7
Solitudes, Silos, and Stovepipes

Suppose you own a pond on which a water lily is growing. The
lily plant doubles in size each day. If the lily were allowed to
grow unchecked, it would completely cover the pond in 30 days,
choking off the other forms of life in the water. For a long time
the lily plant seems small, and so you decide not to worry about
cutting it back until it covers half the pond. On what day will
that be? On the twenty-ninth day, of course. You have one day to
save your pond.

– Meadows, D.L., J. Richardson, and G. Bruckman,
Groping in the Dark

In spite of the overwhelming ecological evidence that we are destroying
the very natural resource life-support systems that form the basis for
human life, there appears to be a systemic failure on the part of human
activity systems to meaningfully and effectively implement sustainable
development policies and practices. A central question we have to ask is:
Why, in the face of this overwhelming evidence, has there been this systemic failure? Systems that appear to be based on rational-expert decision-
making models may, indeed, be supporting and perpetuating decision
making that is based on ill-founded conceptions of natural systems and
inherent psychopathological structures supported by outdated paradigms,
metaphors, and myths (see Chapter 2). For example, three distinct views
have dominated perceptions of ecological causation, behaviour, and management. The first is an equilibrium-centred, or "nature-constant" view, and
it emphasizes constancy of behaviour over time. The second is a multiple-
equilibria-states view, and it emphasizes the existence of a number of stability regions and the role of instability in the maintenance of the resilience
of ecological systems. The third is a "nature-evolving" view, and it highlights organizational change and the surprises it generates (Holling 1994).

In addition, human activity systems are continually maintained and reinforced by a variety of vested interests that are committed to perpetuating
the status quo, with its existing distribution of power and access to resources
and rewards. Moreover, the failure to address the underlying nature of unsustainable policy choices arises from deep assumptions about how the
world works. These assumptions, which actually comprise our worldviews,
or mental models (Bateson 1972; Capra 1991; Kuhn 1962), are rarely examined in the light of current realities. As I discussed in Chapter 2, they are
often detectable as implied beliefs about the nature of the world. I also

examined two inhibitors of effective action: (1) the pervasiveness and persistence of dualistic thought in Euro-American systems and (2) the dominance of prevailing paradigms, myths, and metaphors. In this chapter, I will examine how the behaviour of the Canadian federal government has contributed to the gridlock around the implementation of sustainable development imperatives.

Experiential Context

Over the course of my twenty-three years as a public servant at the federal level, I have had a number of interesting and challenging assignments. Upon joining the government in February 1976, I worked mainly on strategic policy development and the machinery of government issues (such as wage and price controls, program reviews of personnel management systems, regulatory reform, environmental programs, and strategies for macro-level changes in federal governance). As well, at the beginning of the 1970s, I worked on futurist research, at which time two seminal books came to influence my thinking and subsequent career choices: the Club of Rome's *Limits to Growth* (Meadows et al. 1972) and Schumacher's (1973) *Small Is Beautiful*. As my experience grew in starting up new organizations and managing change in federal systems, I participated in building two novel programs and their institutional structures: the diversification of regional economic development programs and the establishment of the Atlantic Canada Opportunities Agency and, more recently, the creation of the National Round Table on the Environment and the Economy. Since October 1988, I have been working exclusively in the area of sustainable development policy and planning. And since 1993 I have been working as a senior research associate with the Sustainable Development Research Institute at the University of British Columbia and with the Canadian Biodiversity Institute in Ottawa.

People in organizations, including educational organizations, find themselves hard pressed either to find actual instances of these rational practices or to find rationalized practices whose outcomes have been as beneficient [sic] as predicted, or to feel that these rational occasions explain much of what goes on within the organization.

(Weick 1976: 10)

Over the past two decades, I have directly experienced and observed the difficulties of effecting change in large bureaucracies, in spite of the political will to do so and of the rational information indicating the need for such change. Bureaucratic inertia and the tendency of bureaucracies to change incrementally has been written about extensively (Aucoin 1972;

Doern and Conway 1994). In my experience, the forces against change appear to be much more systemic, pervasive, and multifaceted than is normally appreciated, and they operate at both the group and individual levels. In many of the task forces, commissions, and senior management meetings in which I have participated, I have found that often the lowest common denominator prevails in decision making, in the face of information to the contrary. Early in my career, as I gained first-hand experience of irrational decision making, I started to question the expert-rational decision model. Increasingly I noticed that issues of power and control, as well as individual psychodynamics, were key features of decision making and that they operated at all levels within the system.

Although aware of the pervasive influences of early socialization on childhood development and learning, I was puzzled by the seeming inability of bureaucracies both (1) to appreciate the influence of their collective culture on their grasp of the reality of emerging phenomena and new information, and (2) to respond to these changing realities. There were clearly significant gaps between rhetoric and action. I began to perceive the influence of prevailing paradigms, myths, and metaphors as well as of the powerful vested interests committed to maintaining the status quo.

It is more appropriate to think of resources as managing humans than the converse: the large and more immediate are prospects for gain, the greater the political power that is used to facilitate unlimited exploitation. The classic illustrations are gold rushes. Where large and immediate gains are in prospect, politicians and governments tend to ally themselves with special interest groups in order to facilitate the exploitation.

(Ludwig et al. 1993: 35)

For example, the virulent opposition to and criticisms of the concept of limits introduced by the Club of Rome's 1972 document seemed out of proportion to the important ideas that were being raised. Growth and development were so firmly linked with the notion of human progress that to propose something else was viewed as sacrilege. Another example of the strength of dominant paradigms may be found in the lack of action resulting from the 1985 MacDonald Commission. The commission stated:

In many other places in this Report, we call for less government intervention; in the area of environmental regulation, however, we are obliged to call for more. Over the long term, the task of environmental regulation promises to be immense. We shall have to deal with growth in the number and size of projects that may adversely affect the environment, with an increasing number of pollutants and hazards, with the irreversible, and sometimes unquantifiable, effects of a growing range of industrial substances and processes, and with the emerging international aspects of our environmental responsibility. (MacDonald Commission 1985: 439-440)

In this case, the commission was one of the best organized task forces in the federal government; it had an extensive research budget and some of the best economic minds in the country were brought together. Yet most of its recommendations were not implemented. It is revealing that its recommendations on free trade, which it linked to the implementation of a guaranteed annual income scheme to ease the period of structural adjustment, were implemented without any mention of a guaranteed annual income. It seemed clear to me that government policies were being derived from fundamental and often unstated assumptions and values concerning the nature of the world and how it works.

Political Paralysis
The increasingly plural nature of Canadian society, combined with the increase in vested interests (Pal 1990; Pross 1992; Thompson and Stanbury 1984) around maintaining the status quo, results in a lack of political will at all government levels. And this is accentuated at the top of the pyramid; that is, at the federal level. In a world dominated by competing vested interests, the future is inevitably contentious (Atkinson 1991). The resources of these vested interests vary greatly. In 1985-86, for example, the Social Sciences Federation of Canada budgeted over $300,000 for representing its members' concerns; in 1980 the Consumers' Association had revenues of $1.7 million. In contrast, in 1988 the Canadian Nuclear Association budgeted $4,260,000 for its public information program (Pross 1992). Client capture works two ways at the official level. Departments capture groups (e.g., in 1986-87 seventeen federal departments paid $184,995,000 to over 500 groups [Finkle et al. 1994]), and groups capture departments (insofar as the same organizations, once funded, tend to get funded over and over again).

It is obvious that radical changes are urgently needed in the structure and processes of public service systems of administration, which were originally established to exploit and export natural resources as efficiently and effectively as possible, not to sustain them. The preceding chapters have argued that Canadian society – indeed, societies everywhere – is facing a concurrent decline in ecological, social and, economic capital: hence, the importance of creating incentives for people and economies to act more in harmony than in conflict with essential processes that control the dynamics and structure of ecosystems. And biodiversity is the key to the health and productivity of ecosystems (Folke et al. 1996; Kay and Schneider 1994). The three types of capital – ecological, social, and economic – are interdependent, and, because of scale and time effects, they lock us into a

Intellectual boundaries create the myriad specialisms that are then grouped into multitudes of human organizations. Arrangements for governance over provinces and districts or other spatially defined regions in Canada consist of a rich overlay of elected political bodies, special purpose administrative agencies, corporations, and other non-government organizations. Their collective abilities to analyze details and manage within artificial boundaries are not matched by comparable abilities to synthesize data into knowledge that extends across many of these same boundaries, as an understanding of systems requires.

(Francis and Lerner 1995: 149-150)

co-evolutionary spiral that can just as easily be negative and degenerative as positive and creative. Economic growth, total material consumption, and environmental degradation are now tightly bound up in complex and unsustainable systems at both local and global levels.

Ideas, however, are not isolated from the values and beliefs of the times from which they emerge, and most of these have not successfully engaged current political agendas. Nor have they been systematically addressed by many academics, researchers, and government policy makers. This poses a number of interesting questions. Why have dominant theories and models never been seriously challenged by alternative modes of thinking? Are these concepts incapable of critical defence? Why, in the light of growing evidence of increasing ecological collapse, have dominant paradigms not seriously been engaged in addressing alternative models and arguments? Why is there such great resistance to emergent concepts about society and the environment?

The reluctance to seriously address and re-examine dominant concepts and values is particularly perplexing given the wealth of evidence of increasing social and environmental degradation. Most of our basic indicators are consistently showing that the quality of our land, air, and water continues to degrade on an annual basis. Moreover, the accelerating and interactive nature of the impacts of modern industrial behaviour are becoming clear globally through such phenomena as global warming and the increasing size of the hole in the ozone layer. In the face of this evidence, the systemic failure of our socio-political institutions to address what some scholars have identified as shallow versus deep sustainable development is irrational at best, and extremely shortsighted in the long term.

Socio-political institutions are, of course, manifestations of the prevailing values and beliefs of the society of which they are part. Is it true that modern institutions are rarely capable of changing at other than incremental rates if, indeed, they are capable of changing at all? And what are the driving and restraining forces (Lewin 1951) working for and against emergent issues such as sustainable development?

Human societies, however, are capable of sweeping change, as is evidenced by the great revolutions of our past – the agricultural, the industrial, and the technological. In the nineteenth century, the Industrial Revolution swept across Europe without major resistance. At that time, society was far less structured, both politically and institutionally, than it is today; thus fewer forces were capable of resisting the sweeping tide of change. Now, in the twenty-first century, an entire complex system of institutions and organizations presents an often formidable gridlock, which is inimical to change. But why, in the face of overwhelming evidence that humanity may be fast approaching ecological limits or, as some scholars claim, that it may have even overshot those limits (Ehrlich and Ehrlich 1991; Meadows et al. 1992; Rees 1996), is there such institutional resistance to the sustainable development paradigm? Moreover, the probability of overshoot is increased with delays in feedback, which ensure that decision makers do not get, or believe, or act upon information that limits have been exceeded until long after this has occurred (Meadows et al. 1992). An example of this is the collapse of the Atlantic cod fishery, which I discuss in Chapter 9.

Driving and Restraining Forces

The sophistication of modern society and its organizational structures are supported by inherent and interlocking values and ideologies. These, in turn, are tightly coupled with structural barriers that systematically reduce the ability and, indeed, the capacity of new concepts and alternative models to challenge dominant paradigms. Often these interlocking values and ideologies are shared across institutions and between sectors. Over time, this gridlock produces an overwhelming inability to respond, even in the face of new information and facts that illustrate the importance of immediate action.

Existing technological alternatives also face relatively important barriers because of the positive externalities developed in the existing dominant technological path. Because of the existing routines, present tasks and qualifications, and existing user-producer relationships, the diffusion of a new (sustainable) technology is rather difficult and proceeds slowly. We face a situation of competing technologies, where the existing technologies benefit from dynamic scale and learning effects, particularly important for the diffusion stage.

(Lahaye and Llerena 1996: 207)

Moreover, for those working within institutions, the reinforcing nature of these driving and restraining forces for change are covert and deeply embedded in the historical web of interpersonal relations, conflict, and rationales. The result of this is that even newcomers are quickly influenced by the seemingly unquestionable rationale behind current actions. What may, indeed, be irrational behaviour is perceived as eminently rational because of the opacity of these driving and restraining forces. It is important, therefore, to examine these forces; to assess their validity in the light of current realities; and, ultimately, to address pathological gridlock by linking economics and ecology when engaged in decision making (Baskerville 1997). In fact, economics, ecology, and society must not only be linked, they must be linked both externally (to institutional structures and processes) and internally (to personal development) (Hill 1998). To effect meaningful change, it is necessary to identify the main social and economic forces that are currently driving ecological, social, and economic decline. We must identify both the proximate and underlying forces (Perrings et al. 1992) and create structures capable of providing the necessary incentives to redirect them. One of the main underlying forces is the overall structure of the federal government – a structure that results in inappropriate and ineffective government policies vis-à-vis sustainable development.

When one examines how hunting and gathering societies were organized and compares that with how modern societies are organized, a number of interesting trends become apparent. Hunting and gathering societies were more holistic in contrast to modern societies, with the latter's tendencies towards dualism and separations. Moreover, modern societies have placed an increasing emphasis on technology, centralization, and privatization (see Figure 7.1). As human scale has increased exponentially in recent times, there has been a corresponding increase in the concentration of production and industry in urban centers (Brennan 1997); this, in turn, has led to an increase in privatization. The more privatized human activity systems become, the more centralized they become. More concentration of ownership results in greater privatization, all of which results in increased reliance on technology to support the scale of human activities – a positive feedback loop. Centralization leads simultaneously to extended acquisition, which leads simultaneously to increasing scale, which leads simultaneously to increasing technology, which ultimately results in a hyperactive rhythm of global capitalism and homogenization.

When these four trends (centralization, technology, privatization, and scale) are transposed on two axes, the following pattern emerges:

It is our overall paradigms and values that determine the degree of separation of the three sustainable development imperatives. And this separation is further enhanced by centralization, our dependence on technological solutions, privatization, and scale, which are interactive and mutually reinforcing. Thus, there is a positive feedback loop between these four trends. The more that ecological, social, and economic imperatives diverge through disaggregate decision making, the more these four trends converge and support unsustainable activities that continue to lay the foundation for

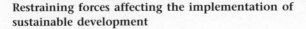

Figure 7.1

**Restraining forces affecting the implementation of
sustainable development**

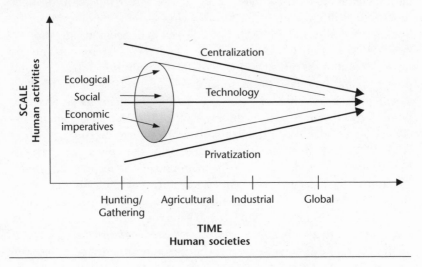

ecological and social collapse. Paradoxically, what appears to be increasing
options (through increasing technology and scale) is actually narrowing
future options through the growing divergence of the three imperatives.

Gridlock

In the absence of a guiding framework and clearly articulated principles
for operating across government, gridlock appears, from within the organization, to be eminently rational. This explains why, on the one hand,
you can have one department mandated to protect the environment and,
on the other, one that actively supports unlimited industrial expansion.
Current economic activities are encouraged through government programs
and incentives that result in continued exploitation of natural resources,
with increasing capital investment and expanding scales of activity. Paradoxically, the result is increasing dependency on the continued successes
of the first phase; that is, further exploitation of nature (see Figure 7.2),
which in the process results in a loss of resilience, thus increasing the
likelihood of unexpected crises and eventual system collapses. With this increasing dependency on the first phase comes denial of the results of decisions to maintain or expand economic subsidies. This, along with lobby
groups battling other lobby groups in their attempts to influence government decision makers, results in gridlocks that make effective decision
making impossible – whether it involves salmon, owls, fishing, and logging

in the Pacific Northwest; cod, poverty, and cultural survival in Newfoundland; or urbanization, wildlife, and water in the Everglades (Gunderson et
al. 1995a). Too often decisions represent the lowest common denominator
among the plurality of interests competing to influence governments (decisions made in order to minimize disruption over the short term).

Treasury Board President Marcel Masse has warned that governments are paying
too much attention to special interest groups and risk losing touch with ordinary
Canadians in shaping policies and services. He told the Association of Professional
Executives yesterday that politicians and public servants must find new ways to
"define" the public interest rather than letting powerful special interest groups
dominate the policy-making agenda. "Special interest groups have become
well-organized and their voices are heard like they're the voice of the majority ...
So what we have to do is find a way to consult all Canadians who are more directly
involved with all issues."

(Ottawa Citizen, 28 May 1998)

Holling and Meefe (1996), in their analysis of environmental resource
management systems, identify three additional underlying factors that contribute to this pathology. First, following upon the initial successful phase
(for example, insect pests are initially reduced through pesticide use), the
loss of ecosystem resilience is accompanied by management agencies shifting from their original social or economic purposes to increasing efficiencies
and reducing costs. Second, their personnel become increasingly isolated
from the systems being managed as their focus is politically directed from
research and monitoring to corporate agendas of cost efficiencies, technologies, quality management, and institutional survival. Third, one cannot
underestimate either the power of externalities or existing organizational
frameworks to maintain the prevailing paradigm. Leaving a particular
development path, therefore, depends upon the source of self-reinforcing
mechanisms. New relationships are called for, and these need to be com-
plemented by fundamental changes in government decision making along
with institutional reorganization.

   In addition to the restraining forces affecting the implementation of
sustainable development, as depicted in Figure 7.1, there is the lack of a
cohesive constituency, or what MacNeill (personal communication, 1998)
refers to as the "politics of sustainable development." As he further states:
"Perhaps the greatest weakness of sustainable development ... lies in the
fact that we have not yet begun to invent a politics to go with the concept." Although the National Round Table on the Environment and the
Economy may have stimulated some networks of collaboration around the
implementation of sustainable development (perhaps a necessary precursor

to developing a politics), sustainable development has yet to coalesce into a political force in Canada. The pervasiveness of "growth" in human societies as a positive and necessary social and economic good for human well-being, and its deeply embedded myths, is a main barrier to developing this new politic. Some of these myths are: "to grow is to progress," "to grow is to move forward," and "to do otherwise is to go backwards." Within such a dominant socio-economic paradigm (Figure 2.1) how does one sell the concept of sustainable development, which, if it is to be meaningfully implemented, means not just "doing more with less" but, ultimately, "doing less"? In fact, one of the reasons why the Conserver Society concept proposed by the Science Council in 1977 failed to reach the mainstream agenda was simply that many people associated the term "Conserver" with "less," and, for many who had survived the 1939 Depression, the conserver concept had negative psychological associations.

I believe that one of the main reasons a politics of sustainable development has not emerged is simply because of the fragmentation within key sectors involved in its promulgation – the development, environmental, health, peace, and women's movements. What would normally be a driving force for implementation – the interest of so many stakeholders – effectively prevents an overall coalition of interests. The problem is inherent in the nature of the beast. Sustainable development issues are broad and horizontal, cutting across all sectors of society. As well, problem solving and decision making in this domain are difficult precisely because solutions are not clear-cut and because the future consequences of alternative actions are uncertain (Brewer 1986; Brewer and de Leon 1983; La Porte 1975). In addition, the issues are often not rationally bounded because they are normative and involve complex bio-ethical issues such as recent debates around genetically modified organisms. Nor do they correspond to human political boundaries, demanding ecosystem approaches that respect ecological boundaries.

Hence, the stakeholders bring different perspectives and usually hold one issue to be primary. In addition, the stakes and values are high. Here, this very diversity may be dysfunctional in that it leads to intense fragmentation. Even within particular issues, there can be differing perspectives, often within a dualistic framework. For example, some see population as the driving force; others see consumption as the driving force; still others see both population and consumption as driving forces. And to complicate matters further, there is a major geographical division: the North/South split.

And with certain issues, questions of scale also arise. For example, with respect to biodiversity conservation, experts vary greatly as to whether they should work at the habitat, populations, or species level. The reconciliation of these competing perspectives, therefore, is central to the development of any coherent regime and a subsequent cohesive political force for sustainable development. The lack of a new politic (political constituencies) for sustainable development has also been affected by a lack of consensus on what the restraining forces for implementation are and the driving forces for unsustainability. In spite of a proliferation of innovative attempts, such as multistakeholder processes, seminal works such as Agenda 21 and others, the basic structure of governments and political decision making worldwide have changed very little, or, if they have changed at all, it has been incrementally. Indeed, there appears to be an inverse relationship between ecological literacy and seniority of decision making, making integrated decision making, which is so necessary for the implementation of sustainable development, an impossibility.

Moreover, "just as there is no single culture, there is no single meaning of sustainable development. You cannot homogenize development, unsustainable or otherwise, in the presence of what are multiple, distinctly heterogeneous cultures and actors. Pluralism must remain the criterion of efficacy ... The really big policy question [is] how to encourage the constructive interaction of these plural and ineradicable actors" (Thompson 1993: 55). It may well be that a sufficient politics for sustainable development will emerge only in those uncommon, complex moments when policies, problems, and politics converge so that the problems of the moment are tangential to the politics of the moment, which, in turn, are tangential to the policies of the moment (Roe 1998). Figures 7.3 and 9.2 provide a model for how governments could facilitate this convergence by deliberately avoiding debate over which perspective is morally superior or which issue more predominant. They could do this by creating semi-permanent coalitions that, with the attendant resources, would have the opportunity to develop more cohesive civil constituencies around sustainable development.

Although we lack a politics for sustainable development, there is no lack of politics in its decision making, once again, because it cuts across all sectors, thereby involving many interest groups, industry associations, and lobbyists, and because it is normative. And since government decision making is largely incremental, due mainly to its hierarchical and vertical structuring, analysis is sharply limited to alternatives that differ very little from the status quo. Policy is made iteratively, by trial and error, with minimal reliance on theoretical knowledge.

Institutional Incapacities

It is particularly disturbing that the inherent structures of two institutions that need to provide leadership in the promulgation of knowledge about sustainable development and its implementation – universities and governments – work against this. In the former, disciplinary organization and corresponding incentive structures work against interdisciplinary knowledge and research; in the latter the parallel sectoral, vertical solitudes, and the silo mentality (Bourgon 1996; Zussman and Jabes 1989) similarly work against the implementation of cross-cutting, horizontal policies and practices. Moreover, Mintzberg et al. (1996) argue that the real barriers to horizontal collaboration may well be vertical, in two ways. First, the very things that enable people to be promoted within a vertical hierarchy may impede them from encouraging horizontal collaboration. For example, in the public service executives are often promoted for their loyalty to their minister and the subsequent protection of departmental mandates. In academic institutions, the very characteristic of a good researcher – strong adherence to individual perspectives – militates against interdisciplinary research, which is highly collaborative. Second, people at the apex may see collaboration that is initiated informally as suspect.

Indeed, often new organizational initiatives that work horizontally, such as the National Round Table on the Environment and the Economy (NRTEE) and the more recent creation of the Policy Research Secretariat in the Privy Council Office, are seen as threats to existing departmental mandates and, in most cases, are actively or passively resisted or, when possible, ignored. Even within an organization, new entities have to earn their "space," as, for example, when the position of Commissioner for the Environment and the Economy was created in 1998, the NRTEE had originally recommended that it be separate from the Office of the Auditor General. Intense negotiations, however, ensured that it became a somewhat hybrid position within that office, with a responsibility to report both to the auditor general of Canada and to Parliament.

Expertise almost always means narrow, specialized, disciplinary expertise; few persons by training, experience, or predilection are prepared to engage in or promote comprehensive environmental decision-making. The idea of comprehensive environmental decision-making finds little institutional support in the ways universities, science, or the professions generally are structured, or in the ways persons in government or business are employed.

(Vig and Kraft 1990: 242)

In analyzing twelve key institutions of advanced Western industrial societies at the macro-, meso-, micro-, and socio-cultural levels, Perlmutter and Trist (1986) discovered that a fundamental mismatch existed, between many of their inherent structures/processes and the demands of the new environments that, paradoxically, they had configured. In other words, the original context within which these institutions had been created had changed so much that their current mandate was no longer relevant. For example, given the exponential growth in human populations, a family allowance scheme may no longer be appropriate. Furthermore, since the kind of dysfunctionality they found is not readily reversible under the prevailing dominant socio-economic paradigm, it is likely to persist as long as this fragmented paradigm remains the guiding framework for advanced industrial societies. Moreover, since this dysfunctionality emerges from the interplay of extremely powerful dynamic forces, it can be expected to increase (as is shown in Figure 7.1). Thus the dominant paradigms of both academe and the federal government collude in maintaining a gridlock that emphasizes small, incremental, maladaptive actions designed not to challenge the status quo.

Institutional failure at the macro level can be readily recognized by adding to the earlier Holling ecosystem model (Figure 4.1). For example, an analysis of the decisions of successive governments with respect to East Coast fisheries issues confirms the trends discussed below and illustrated in Figure 7.2, particularly with respect to research and monitoring issues (*Ottawa Citizen*, 4 July 1997; 16 November 1997; 10 December 1997).

Government institutions are "stuck" along the one axis, which keeps them endlessly cycling between the exploitative and conservation phases, and this prevents them from seriously considering alternatives. Consequently, there is never any analytical or policy space to investigate and develop these alternatives because doing so would be incompatible with

Figure 7.2

Federal government gridlock

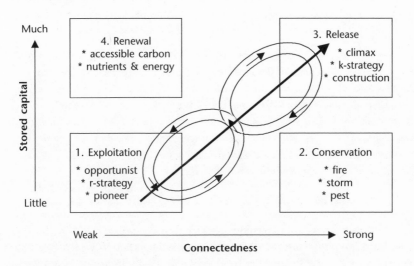

Source: Adapted from Holling 1986.

the short-term vested self-interests of business, governments, and even academe (which is increasingly driven by a colonizing granting system). When one is stuck in a spiralling pattern of exploitation and conservation, systemic learning cannot take place, and reactive rather than proactive policy choices become the norm. Because failure (which is necessary for learning) is anathema to bureaucratic organizations designed to project only positive images of their political leaders, responses to crises cause government systems to flip back to the exploitative stage. Unless this underlying structural conflict (Fritz 1996) is recognized and addressed, only incremental change and implementation at the margins will be tolerated. Over time, these flips between conservation and exploitation will occur faster and faster (Regier 1995b), and government policy development will become increasingly myopic and rigid (Gunderson et al. 1995a), further alienating our politicians from the publics they are supposed to serve and, paradoxically, further decreasing the very social capital upon which the integrity of governance depends.

When bureaucracies are faced with complex ecological systems characterized by complex interactions, masses of information that often seems contradictory, millions of species, and unknown phenomena and risks, they tend first to focus on those phenomena and cause-and-effect relations that conform to their decision-making structures and their dominant paradigms. This tendency to maintain apparent control by selecting only those variables that correspond to their "perceived rationality" serves to affirm the need for their continued institutional existence. Deep inquiry and cause-seeking behaviour, if it occurs at all, is restricted to the boundaries of their rational and physical domains, and each piece of new information and every selected task supports a monolithic authority network of centralized and decontextualized decision making (Edwards and Regier 1988).

The dangers arising from professionalism are great, particularly from democratic societies. The directive force of reason is weakened. The leading intellects lack balance. They see this set of circumstances, or that set; but not both sets together. The task of coordination is left to those who lack either the force or the character to succeed in some definite career. In short, the specialized functions of the community are performed better and more progressively, but the generalized direction lacks vision. The progressiveness in detail only adds to the danger produced by the feebleness of coordination.

(Whitehead 1925)

In addition to powerful external vested interests committed to maintaining the status quo, there are equally powerful internal vested interests. Together, these create a pervasive gridlock of resistance to all alternative paradigms and policy initiatives. In the case of the environment, these forces that restrain change have enormous repercussions at many levels, ultimately threatening the very survival of our species.

For example, the NRTEE was an innovative attempt in 1989 to open up the decision-making process of government by creating a multistakeholder body that, instead of advising ministers, had them sitting at the table as one stakeholder among others. In addition to government ministers, the other stakeholders at the table were industrialists, environmentalists, and public policy practitioners. Instead of following the more traditional institutional model of bringing together individuals and businesses that had common interests or goals, round tables were multipartite and reflected different backgrounds and experiences, different perspectives and insights, and different values and beliefs (Dale 1996). In one sense, they represented microcosms of society, with memberships that drew from the political level of governments, the corporate sector, academe, and a variety of public interest and professional groups. Multistakeholder bodies, such as the NRTEE, had the capacity to become a creative way to transform public institutions and to facilitate shared decision making. They were a unique vehicle for clearly articulating stakeholder values and for using them as a basis for creating an improved set of policy alternatives (Gregory and Keenery 1994). The federal body failed, however, to retain this uniqueness, and within three years of its creation it became a traditional advisory body, without the active involvement of ministers, as had been the case in the first two years of its existence.

Why? Because new organizational models threaten existing institutional arrangements, mandates, and power relations, by their very creation. Hence, the NRTEE was perceived to be a serious threat to Environment Canada as well as to some of the departments involved in managing natural resources. As well, in a marked departure from public administration in Canada, federal cabinet ministers sat at the table to which others, without any bureaucratic filter whatsoever, had direct access. Hence, as is the case with most of these newly created groups, their access to the highest level of decision makers slowly eroded. They moved from reporting to the prime minister to reporting to the deputy minister and so on down the line. This change in reporting level is usually accompanied by a corresponding change in the level and stature of appointments so that, over a period of time, they are effectively captured and silenced by those departments under threat and, eventually, are closed. This pattern, more or less, could be observed with the former Science and Economic Councils as well as with the Canadian Economic Advisory Council, all of which were disbanded in the 1980s. The current structure of the federal government has, consequently, remained unchanged, maintaining the very structures that so impede such horizontal initiatives as sustainable development. They are more comfortable with their known solitudes, stovepipes, and silos than they are with change.

Even recent innovations, such as the position of Commissioner for the Environment and Sustainable Development, created in 1997, appear to have had little effect on the basic underlying structural tensions within the federal government. In his third report to Parliament, Brian Emmett stated that, even with respect to toxic substances (one of the more easily bounded sustainable development issues): "I am particularly concerned that federal departments are deeply divided on many key issues. They do not share a common vision of how toxic substances should be managed. They disagree on such issues as the degree of risk posed by some industrial chemicals, the interpretation of federal policy and the need to take action on it, the relative merits of voluntary and regulatory controls, and their own respective roles and accountabilities" (Emmett 1999: 10). Moreover, of the twenty-eight sustainable development strategies tabled in 1998, there were key implementation gaps, particularly in the establishment of clear and measurable targets (which was again mentioned, this time in Emmett's 1999 report, as a serious deficiency).

Another matter of concern is the effectiveness of new processes such as national, provincial, and municipal roundtables with respect to changing government decision making and influencing policy decisions. This raises questions about whether or not shared decision making can exist within a Cabinet committee decision-making framework. This subject merits serious consideration if shared decision making is to be meaningfully realized. The question of the relationship between duly constituted multistakeholder bodies, especially when convened by governments, and constitutional decision making should be addressed, or else these bodies may ultimately contribute to paralysis of the decision process through excessive participation, reverting back to reliance on "experts" and traditional backdoor lobbying by vested interests.

Integrated Solutions

How, then, can the federal government transform itself to respond to our current trajectory of increasingly degraded brittle ecosystems, rigid management, and dependent societies leading to crises (Gunderson et al. 1995b)? How can the government become a relevant instrument for the magnitude of social change required to ensure that Canada becomes a sustainable society in the twenty-first century? How can the federal government reconcile competing vested interests in an increasingly plural society, not to mention competing paradigms and conceptual frameworks?

The integration of ecological, social, and economic imperatives requires changes in attitudes, structures, and behaviour at both societal and personal levels. These changes cannot be imposed, or even effectively fostered, through consultation; rather, they must be sought through the collaborative efforts of all involved (Gibson and Tomalty 1995). In addition, a comprehensive understanding of linked natural and human activity systems requires the synthesis of a number of mutually supportive conceptual frameworks. These include participatory action research and collaborative inquiry (Freire 1970; Reason and Rowan 1981b; Torbert 1991), strategic questioning (Peavey 1986), soft systems methodologies (Checkland and Scholes 1990; Meadows et al. 1972), self-organizing properties (Kay 1994; Odum 1983; von Bertalanffy 1968), ecosystem properties (Holling 1986; Kay and Francis 1995; Regier 1995b), co-evolutionary models (Bateson 1979; Norgaard 1994); values-based thinking (Keeley 1992; Keeney 1996; and Orr 1994), and multistakeholder processes (Dale forthcoming).

In addition, as discussed in Chapters 2 and 7, interdisciplinarity and transdisciplinarity, as well as integrated modes of inquiry, are required if we are to really understand sustainable development. This is because competence in this area can never be based on complete knowledge but must rely on the best available information and expertise, intuition, responsible experimentation, and common sense. Given the complex interactions between environmental and social systems (and, particularly, the current difficulty of reconciling social and ecological imperatives), this interdisciplinarity must integrate the various disciplines within both the natural and social sciences. It should be noted that, whereas many ecological imperatives relate to absolutes (such as each species' specific needs for food and space), social imperatives are relative and much more flexible. Although it may not be apparent in the short term, in the long term, ecology, not economics, determines the bottom line of human systems.

It is through the dynamic interactions between ... communities that new configurations of the knowledge net emerge by creating new meanings, new linguistic routines and new knowledge.

Their hermeneutic attitude means they avoid debate in favour of dialogue unless compelling reasons call for a dialectic communicative process. They realize that the debate is a win-lose polarizing strategy that rarely results in true synthesis or creative insights. Dialogue, in contrast, is mutually reinforcing, working together through languages. It is a realization that we can assume a perspective-taking orientation and benefit from opening ourselves to the horizon of another.

(Boland and Tenkasi 1995: 352 and 366)

A helpful technique for exposing dominant thought, methodologies, prevalent paradigms and alternative opportunities involves the use of strategic questioning (Peavey 1986). Strategic questions, as defined by Peavey, are questions that make a difference. They facilitate our ability to move from stuck positions, to create options and liberate creativity, to dig deep in order to expose roots, to avoid defensiveness, to avoid simple yes-no questions, to empower rather than to manipulate, to question assumptions, and to express our higher values. It is for these reasons that they can facilitate positive co-evolutionary change.

Strategic questioning, coupled with the use of holistic models, can be extremely helpful in supporting responsible (and co-evolutionary) government decision making at both the political and bureaucratic levels as well as within the population at large. The building of systems models, both hard and soft, can help to identify gaps in knowledge about complex systems and serve as effective planning tools for policy analysts, decision makers, and stakeholders for at least six reasons. First, they have the capability to bring research information and analysis directly to those making resource management decisions without having to go through a filter of bureaucratic interpretation. Second, they make explicit the uncertainties and difficult choices related to risks and time preferences. Third, they can expose innovative policies by making use of spatial replication, thus allowing decision makers to clearly see the effects of their trade-offs. Fourth, they can facilitate more flexible responses to both natural and human-made surprises. Fifth, they can expose gaps in information and knowledge, and this leads to the development of more precise research agendas. And sixth, by creating a visual image, they can evoke an emotional response, and this leads to more direct action (Westley, personal communication, 17 August 1998). Holistic models, therefore, may be an important visual tool for enhancing responsible sustainable development decision making, which entails a wide variety of actors being able to appreciate and understand the meaning of complex self-organizing and open systems. Furthermore, this complexity necessitates greater use of integrated modes of inquiry, such as the provision and facilitation of accessible and influential multistakeholder pluralistic fora.

If there is more than one "sustainable" outcome, is the governance system that is capable of identifying alternatives better than one that identifies only one that is preferred? Is there a difference? Does it matter? I think this is related to the point that we need systems that are "safe to fail", that have alternatives both in terms of small decisions and large outcomes. I think the governance system that fulfills these criteria is multicentric, decentralized, networked, more coordinating than managing. At the same time, I realize that because of the artificial spatial/jurisdictional boundaries that governance needs to grow outside of the bounds whose scale extends beyond the scope of localism. So maybe a "sustainable" governance system is able to detect the right scale of issues and match it with action – either through building external or global networks, or by allowing decentralization.

(Pinter, Electronic Dialogue, 30 September 1997)

It is clear that the linear "one problem, one solution" approach is no longer either adequate or appropriate and must be replaced by an integrated ecosystem and social system analysis that considers people as a part of, and not apart from, nature. Emphasis on open, self-organizing, and holarchic systems (SOHO) could provide an alternative approach for changing our sense of relatedness to one based on inclusion rather than exclusion. This approach to understanding respects the complexity of organizational forms, and considers function and change in open systems within the context of their dynamic interactions within and without their respective environments. As a result of such interactions, these systems manifest emergent properties, as in co-evolution. Uncertainty and surprise are fundamental features of such open systems (Holling 1993a), as are the related ideas of flexibility, and changing and fluid boundaries among system parts. SOHOs can be regarded as being arranged in nested holarchies, in which the parts are reciprocally interdependent with the whole, being alternately dependent and independent. SOHO and soft system methodologies serve an enlarged decision-making framework able to accommodate situations in which facts are uncertain, reality is evolving, values are in dispute, stakes are high, and decisions are urgent. Ecological systems are, indeed, dynamic, inherently uncertain, and have potential multiple futures (Holling 1996).

Governments are so fragmented and lacking in holistic systems-analysis capabilities that the task of responding to sustainable development imperatives seems overwhelming. Managers and scientists live and work in vastly different cultures and, as a result, often view the world from very different perspectives and act on the basis of different values, both of which are limited in different ways. The meaning of potentially useful information, therefore, can diverge widely between these two groups, resulting in inaccurate communication and paralysis on the part of political decision makers in the face of what appears to be conflicting or incomplete information. Many analysts are calling for a more enlarged kind of science. For example, Lee (1993) uses the phrase "civic science" to emphasize the point that managing complex systems should be more participatory, open to learning from errors, and able to profit from success. Funtowicz and Ravetz (1991, 1993) have argued for a post-normal science that addresses the management of uncertainty through an extended, inclusive peer community, a more democratized knowledge, and the recognition of a multiplicity of forms of success. Hill (1998) has emphasized the importance of focusing not on the "oligopolistic" initiatives but, rather, on relatively small overall meaningful acts that one can guarantee will be carried through to completion, and a public celebration of successes (so that we may be buoyed by them) as well as of failures (so that we may learn from them). Since sustainable development issues involve conditions of high variability, complex interactions, and possibly cumulative effects in ways not yet well understood, I argue that, in addition to an extended scientific peer community, they require considerably enlarged decision-making contexts. Accurate scientific information is essential, but not sufficient, because the normative nature of most sustainable development issues argues for enlarged contexts for decision making (Dale forthcoming).

Clearly, given their overall convening power, governments can play a key role in providing for and organizing atomistic sets of individual users into interactive, institutionalized, and culturally cohesive groups. In spite of industry insistence over most of the 1970s and 1980s that governments should drastically reduce their role in the private sector, they play an important third party role in bringing players to the table and in arbitrating, if they choose, between competing vested interests. These groups could then acquire the ability to manage and initiate concrete actions for addressing the complex sustainable development issues facing twenty-first century civil societies everywhere. As well, governments are the most logical leaders for this role because, due to the electoral process, they are more generally accountable than are either the business community or the nongovernmental community.

Untidy Interfaces
What is now required to achieve changes in governance of the magnitude needed are principle-centred dialogues that bring together many of the alternatives discussed in previous chapters, including ecology, holism, feminism, alternative models (such as steady-state economics), chaos theory, and other emergent sources of wisdom. Principle-centred discourses are fora similar to search conferences in that they re-examine fundamental assumptions, thus allowing for critical discourse on policy alternatives. The following model (Figure 7.3) depicts how these pluralistic decision-making fora might be structured to enhance decision making for sustainable development.

The above model represents only a first step in integrating the contributions of experts and stakeholders, who will necessarily vary depending upon the specific issue. Most important, it would shift public discourse towards a new centre in which the instrumental rationality of state and corporate managers would be balanced by the ethical judgments and aspirations of the wider polity (Karlberg 1997).

When values and stakes are high, both ecologically and socially, then the decision-making stakes must be recognized to be correspondingly high for both present and future generations. But, pluralistic fora cannot have all voices reflected at the table, and most problematic are those of other species and future generations; and yet their "interests" generally entail the highest stakes. The only way to balance this inadequacy is to provide the

Figure 7.3

Framework for responsible decision making

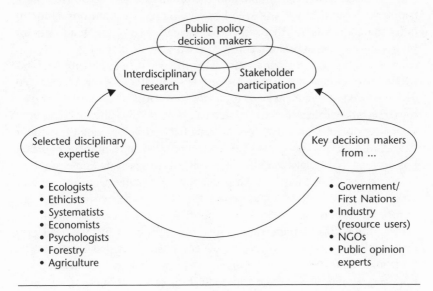

widest representation possible within these fora. For example, by paying attention to gender balance, and access to power and resources, much broader (and deeper) awareness of the difficult trade-offs to be made may be achieved.

The accuracy and relevance of the information selected for examination is key to the success of these pluralistic fora and for effective decision making that must make meaningful trade-offs. The integrity of this information is limited by the ability of our current socio-political institutions to generate active and responsive (and co-evolutionary) management systems that promote learning and innovation. It is also inhibited by policies that may or may not recognize that processes and products are mutually interrelated.

It is only through the interface of the three overlapping central circles in the above model that the most innovative and effective solutions for the problems associated with sustainable development will emerge (Kay 1994) and that the plurality of interests will be expressed. These untidy interfaces open up conceptual spaces for new policy directions both within and between organizations. These dynamic and untidy interfaces represent the paradox of decision making that must take into account both uncertainty and surprise. The ability to live within this paradox requires individuals who are able to transcend disciplinary perspectives and to work with paradoxes of stability and change, order and chaos, sustainability and development (Holling 1989/90), the short term and the long term, the near and the distant, and the simple and the complex (Hill 1998). It requires people with the ability to transcend gaps in knowledge and information in order to make decisions that sometimes have irreversible consequences for future generations, to simultaneously deal with the parts and the whole, and to balance the needs of our species with the needs of the many "others" with which we share this planet. Coupled with these kinds of enlarged decision-making fora is the need for a cross-government, co-evolving holistic framework within which to formulate policies that would rapidly promulgate the principles and practices of sustainable development throughout Canadian society, a need that has been identified by a number of stakeholders (e.g., Tyrchniewicz and Wilson 1994). If this holistic framework is to be operationalized, then we need principles for making decisions pertaining to sustainable development (see Chapter 8) as well as criteria for determining whether or not policies are supportive of sustainable development.

In addition to a common cross-government framework, we need new institutional structures that are better equipped to deal with the broad horizontal issues now facing Canadian society. These new institutions, however, require fundamental paradigm shifts or, at a minimum, a loosening of the resistance to entertain what is currently defined as alternative thinking. Rather than tight hierarchical structures, we need fora that are diverse and that can support the coupling of ideas for emergent innovation and creativity, especially locally. Of particular importance is redesigning our institutions so that their communities are better able to understand ecological system dynamics and respond to the early indicators of change affecting their resilience and positive functioning. If human activity systems are to be ecologically sustainable, then they need to ensure that ecosystem resilience is maintained, even though the limits on the nature and scale of their activities are inherently uncertain and may remain so, at least in the foreseeable future. In addition, we need to reform our information systems, especially the way scientific and technological information is provided to decision makers. In particular, we need to be able to respond to both negative and positive feedbacks from these systems rather than ignoring them due to short-term political trade-offs between ecological, social, and economic imperatives. As evidenced by the fisheries collapse (which I provide as a case study in Chapter 9), ignoring underlying ecological change and early indicators of ecosystem breakdown will always result in the collapse of the social and economic imperatives. As a start, we need to loosely couple our institutional structures and to introduce more organic ways of organizing, so that we can be in closer relationship to the ultimately more powerful ecological structures and functions. I discuss this in greater detail in Chapter 9.

8
Reconciliation

> The problem of grace is fundamentally a problem of integration
> and that what is to be integrated is the diverse parts of the mind –
> especially those multiple levels of which one extreme is called
> "consciousness" and the other the "unconscious." For the
> alignment of grace, the reasons of the heart must be integrated
> with the reasons of the reason.
>
> – Gregory Bateson, *Steps to an Ecology of Mind*

The focus of this chapter is on the need for a guiding, cross-government framework that is based on sustainable development and strategic imperatives, out of which emerge principles for decision making and strategic objectives. Chapter 9 will discuss a framework for governance based on changing the boundaries of government decision making through dialogue. This enlarged decision-making context, however, is dependent upon the implementation of what I term a reconciliation framework. As I have argued, the nature of sustainable development issues means that no one sector can address such sweeping social reconstructions without enlarging the scope of traditional decision making.

Changing the Aperture

In such interdependent systems as nature-human systems, resilience in any of the ecological, social, and economic imperatives is a property of the joint system. Thus, the system equilibria are a product of the dynamics of both natural and produced capital, and the stability of those equilibria are characteristic of the system (Common and Perrings 1992). The complexity of relationships within and between each of the three imperatives makes it unlikely that one can predict long-term consequences of actions – particularly out-of-balance actions that cause, for example, the extinction of other species. The ability of a system to absorb changes without breaking down is limited, but it is not proportional to the perceived magnitude of the change. This realization is the foundation for my insistence that none of us can totally "predict" or "manage" what will or will not happen when we perturb living systems. We must pay attention to the consequences of human actions and be ready to modify them when necessary. In order to be able to respond, however, it is vitally important that decision-making systems be able to receive key ecological information, to work in meaningful ways within appropriate time frames, and to modify scale where necessary. Governments now mainly respond to positive feedback loops because of the powerful vested interests that work to maintain the present system; negative feedback loops are either ignored or dampened. A negative feedback loop is a chain of cause-and-effect relationships that initiates a change in one element around a circle of causation until it comes back to change that element in a direction opposite to that of the initial change. Whereas positive loops may generate runaway growth, negative feedback loops tend to regulate growth, to hold a system within some acceptable range, or to return it to a stable state. A positive feedback loop can be a "virtuous circle" or a "vicious circle," depending upon whether the type of growth it produces is wanted or not (Meadows et al. 1992). It is my contention that a plurality of powerful vested interests works to block negative feedback information from reaching political decision makers and that, because of their profound ecological ignorance, these people interpret what is actually vicious positive feedback as a social good.

Living with and acknowledging high levels of uncertainty is an essential attribute of the competency required for governing and being governed in an information society.

Living constructively and productively with uncertainty, then, will be at least as much a matter of discovering and applying new myths, values and boundaries that define the norms and processes of government as it will be one of adding more information.

(Michael 1993: 84)

For example, returning to Figure 7.1, governments have been strongly influenced by the dominant belief that larger is better, as evidenced by the mega-project approvals following the oil crisis in 1972. Within the same department (Natural Resources Canada), large-scale energy projects began to be supported at the same time as energy conservation was becoming a major concern. Due to the dominant socio-economic paradigm, eventually there was less and less emphasis on energy conservation, especially as the oil crisis abated. Hence, the notion of large being better resulted in a positive feedback loop, as it also supported such government objectives as creating more employment and satisfying federal-provincial imperatives. What resulted was a vicious circle (see the example of the East Coast fisheries in Chapter 9).

What is now needed is an integrative approach based on a fundamental reconciliation between the three imperatives (ecological, social, and economic) in human activity systems. Reconciliation of these three imperatives is the first step towards integration and it is a necessary condition for the implementation of sustainable development. Without a guiding framework and clearly articulated principles for decision making, government departments will tend to work against one another (as is the case, for example,

when energy conservation programs operate alongside the ongoing development of large-scale mega-energy projects). In addition, given the plurality
of vested interests that are now influencing government decision making,
without a clearly articulated common direction to coordinate its various
policy responses, this kind of schizophrenic behaviour is exacerbated.

When human responsibility does not match the spatial, temporal, or functional scale of
natural phenomena, unsustainable use of resources is likely, and it will persist until the
mismatch of scales is cured.

(Lee 1993: 561)

Policy failures can often be traced to a lack of mutually compatible central
organizing principles, ideas, and methods (Byers 1991; Gunderson et al.
1995b; Kasperson et al. 1988; Merton 1936; Sahl and Bernstein 1995). The
vested interests for maintaining the status quo are very sophisticated when
it comes to influencing government decision making. Indeed, it is my
contention that the fragmented nature, overlap, and duplication within
government, and its current organization (e.g., agriculture, industry, and
natural resources), actively works against the effective implementation of
sustainable development. And this results in a policy gridlock, which is
anathema to meaningful action.

Just as ecological systems are non-linear, and instability and uncertainty
are critical elements in their change process, so, too, are human social systems. Non-linear systems are evidenced by relationships between variables
in which the relationship between cause and effect may not be propor-
tionate. Thus, in non-linear systems seemingly minor changes or disturbances may generate positive feedback, or amplifications, resulting in
wholesale structural and behavioural changes. These outcomes may range
from new states of equilibrium to novel states of increased complexity and
organization or even to "chaos," at which point predictability and organization break down (Kiel 1991). Moreover, open systems, which characterize
ecological, social, and economic systems and which are known as dissipative structures, consist of a variety of subsystems interacting in a non-
linear fashion. Dissipative structures are continually subjected to a variety
of disturbances, both from the external environment and from existing
subsystems. Dissipative structures remain relatively stable in the face of
some disturbances; however, it is possible for a relatively minor disturbance to amplify existing non-linear interactions and to drive the structure
to a state of extreme instability.

During this period of instability the structure may reach a critical point,
which is referred to as a bifurcation point (Prigogine and Stengers 1984).
Once the destruction of the pre-existing structure occurs, it is impossible to

determine in advance which direction change will take: whether the system will disintegrate into "chaos" or leap to a more differentiated, higher level of organization (ibid., xv). Of particular interest to government policy makers is the fact that it is impossible to predict the evolutionary pathway, or branch, that the system may follow at any particular bifurcation point. It is also impossible to predict the specific nature of the resulting new configuration.

Is there any way to short-circuit the process, to avoid or at least shorten the periods when the system is rigid and unresponsive, maximize the periods in which the system is tuned to its environment and responding creatively? As Holling has pointed out, the ideal may be the social equivalent of the endotherm: some exchange of loss of internal variability (as long as it is associated with specific kinds of regulation) for heightened ability to explore, sense, and respond to a variety of external environments. How would the principles translate into management of change?

(Westley 1995: 393)

When one considers the present interaction of natural and human activity systems, ecological, social, and economic systems must be considered as evolving, non-linear systems. The relationships between their variables are dynamic because of their increasing interdependence; their interlocutory effects; their time, place, and scale effects; and their co-evolutionary relationships. The continuing emphasis by human activity systems on traditional command and control management policies, prediction, and centralized hierarchical decision making is clearly antithetical to the implementation of sustainable development.

The nature of sustainable development requires integrated, comprehensive decision making in which problems and solutions are considered with regard to their interrelated, interconnected totality. Caldwell (1963) has argued that much of the inadequacy of environmental decision making is the fault of the predominant segmental character of policy – what I have referred to as solitudes, stovepipes, and silos.

So they set about, first of all, educating themselves about acid rain. They read all the scientific data. They became experts on acid rain. In the lobby business, there are no permanent friends and no permanent enemies. There are only permanent interests.

("Acid Rain Lobby Disbands," Morningside, *20 November 1990)*

Moreover, it is clear from past environmental successes (e.g., acid rain and the Intergovernmental Panel on Climate Change [1995]) that scientific consensus and coalitions with the environmental non-governmental community are key to advancing common agendas around sustainable development issues. Governments have a key role to play, therefore, in stimulating the creation of such coalitions and building key constituencies around prioritized issues.

A Reconciliation Framework

The reconciliation framework I am proposing builds on the scientific consensus reached around the *World Scientists' Warning to Humanity* (Union of Concerned Scientists 1993). This statement was signed by over 100 international members of the scientific community. Any workable framework must be holistic enough to transcend current sectoral and vested interests, since without addressing current power issues in the Canadian polity, any applied research would be naive (Westley, personal communication, 17 August 1998). Through an electronic collaborative inquiry process, my co-researchers and I developed the framework I present here.

What follows are the overall criteria that we believe to be applicable across all government bodies with regard to developing principles of sustainable development. All such principles must:

1 be easily understood,
2 be applicable in diverse contexts,
3 be transferable across space and time scales,
4 deal with individual concepts and ideas in concrete terms,
5 identify possibilities for both radical and transformative change and positive incremental change, and
6 be regularly revisited, critically evaluated, and updated whenever appropriate (Brown, Electronic Dialogue, 2 February 1998).

We also agreed that whatever we propose must be achievable in our lifetimes (Dale, Electronic Dialogue, 10 June 1997).

In a brief review of sustainable development principles I found that most were not generic enough to transcend dominant paradigms. They tended to be anthropocentric, and sometimes so vague that they were meaningless. I believe that normative principles have to be constructed at a metaphysical level, as a kind of metalogue (Bateson 1972) so that specific goals and objectives become emergent priorities. In other words, if the normative principles are sufficiently inclusive and not coercive, then they facilitate participation. In this way, various sectors are empowered to develop their goals and objectives without sacrificing their autonomy. Fundamental to this framework is the belief that the principles of sustainable development must, as much as possible, be derived from the structure, processes, and functioning of ecological systems. And they must be incorporated into human activity systems so that we can begin to work with nature, rather than against it. Most fundamentally, human activity systems are themselves embedded within natural systems; thus the biophysical carrying capacity provides an upper boundary on socio-economic carrying capacity (Daily and Ehrlich 1996b). The articulation of values was also crucial to the pre-analytic development of our guiding framework.

Accordingly, we developed the following reconciliation framework, starting with the definition of sustainable development presented in Chapter 3, and building upon the *World Scientists' Warning to Humanity* (Union of Concerned Scientists 1993). The framework entails a definition, five strategic imperatives, principles for decision making, and four strategic objectives. Within this overall framework, sectoral departments could then define their specific goals, targets, and timetables.

Definition
Sustainable development can be regarded as a process of reconciling three imperatives: (1) the ecological imperative to live within global biophysical carrying capacity and maintain biodiversity; (2) the social imperative to ensure the development of democratic systems of governance in order to effectively propagate and sustain the values by which people wish to live; and (3) the economic imperative to ensure that basic needs are met worldwide. And equitable access to resources – ecological, economic, and social – is fundamental to its implementation (adapted from Dale et al. 1995).

Strategic Imperatives
These strategic imperatives were developed by the Union of Concerned Scientists in 1993, based on their belief that human beings and the natural world were on a collision course and that fundamental changes were necessary in order to avoid it. This warning has been endorsed by over 1,670 scientists (including 104 Nobel laureates) representing 88 countries, including the 19 large economic powers, the 12 most populous nations, 12 countries in Africa, 14 in Asia, 19 in Europe, and 12 in Latin America.

1 We must bring environmentally damaging activities under control to restore and protect the integrity of the earth's systems on which we depend.
2 We must, for example, move away from fossil fuels to more benign, inexhaustible energy sources to cut greenhouse gas emissions and the pollution of our air and water. Priority must be given to the development of energy sources matched to Third World needs – small-scale and relatively easy to implement.
3 We must halt deforestation, injury to and loss of agricultural land, and the loss of terrestrial and marine plant and animal species.

4 We must manage resources crucial to human welfare more effectively, giving high priority to efficient use of energy, water, and other materials, including expansion of conservation and recycling.
5 We must stabilize population. This will be possible only if all nations recognize that it requires improved social and economic conditions, and the adoption of effective, voluntary family planning.
6 We must reduce and eventually eliminate poverty.
7 We must ensure gender equality and guarantee women control over their own reproductive decisions.

Principles for Decision Making
These principles were an emergent property of the electronic collaborative inquiry that involved twenty co-researchers and was conducted between September 1996 and December 1998. Wherever possible, they represent our best attempts to develop principles for human activity systems derived from ecological systems (although clearly some are human constructs such as equity).

Cyclical processes
Achieving sustainable levels of production and consumption requires the fundamental redesign of human activity systems from linear input-throughput of production processes to closed loop operations. Inspired by the models of organisms and natural ecosystems, industrial production systems must reduce energy use and recover waste heat; reduce, reuse, and recycle materials across the life cycle of a product; minimize entropy by designing products to limit downcycling and to facilitate repair, refur-bishment, remanufacturing, reuse, and recycling; and dematerialize some activities and products by using digital rather than material methods of consumption (Cairns, Electronic Dialogue, 29 April 1998).

Diversity
Diversity is the spice of life (Rothman, Electronic Dialogue, 20 March 1998). It is an essential feature of all self-organizing systems, whether socio-economic, political, or ecological. To homogenize diversity and foster

---

Diversity must also be the codeword for the way we manage ourselves. Not only shall we need to draw from a wide range of cultural and minority options to improve the quality of our lives, but also to draw upon a broad, participatory power base in our political systems to oppose and reverse present trends toward homogeneity-over-centralization, the abuse of power, and our uncaring society.

(Myers 1985: 254)

uniformity is to rob any complex system of future evolution, adaptive capacity, and, ultimately, of its essence (Lister, Electronic Dialogue, 22 April 1998). Consequently, functional diversity must be conserved as the basic source of system maintenance and regeneration.

Dynamic, self-organizing, open, holartic systems (SOHOs)
SOHOs are important analogues for human decision making; they are organic models of complex systems that occur in nature. They adapt to and accommodate change as a normal event. Such systems are diverse and flexible, and, therefore, resilient; that is, they actively respond to learned experience, which facilitates their adaptability and, ultimately, co-evolution. In this way, the system is able to accommodate and adapt to change and to regenerate (Lister, Electronic Dialogue, 24 April 1998). Any system, no matter how resilient, can be pushed to a "point of no return" or to a threshold beyond which limiting factors become so severe that recovery (at least within periods that would be meaningful on the human timescale) becomes impossible (Dasmann et al. 1973).

A lasting social advance will entail the identification of a set of nonbureaucratic principles at the domain level. These principles may be called socioecological, as contrasted with those of bureaucratic extensionism or self-sufficient, dissociative reductionism. Socioecological principles imply the centrality of interdependence. Entailed is some surrender of sovereignty along with considerable diffusion of power. There is no overall boss in a socioecological system, though there is order, which evolves from the mutual adjustment of the parts; who are the stakeholders.

(Trist 1983: 271)

Enlarged decision-making contexts
When it comes to sustainable development, decision making cannot take place in isolation by any one sector of civil society, including governments. Rather, it requires new levels of integration that bring natural and social scientists together with public policy practitioners and NGOs. What is needed are transdisciplinary fora and dialogues that enable the expression of a multiplicity of legitimate perspectives as well as the examination of public policy questions pertaining to sustainable development and its attendant moral, aesthetic, and valuation questions (Dale, Electronic Dialogue, 26 April 1998).

Equity
The notion of equity must accommodate multiple and complex realities. These emerge from a globalism that includes different realities of place

(i.e., different continents), of time (i.e., different generations), and of form (i.e., different life forms). It must encompass not only the visible outcome of process, but also the process itself, whether it is as formulated as (some) decision-making processes are or as unformulated as (some) aspirations can be. Ultimately, equity is about the sharing of power (Vainio-Matilla, Electronic Dialogue, 18 March 1998), and it may well be that it cannot be actively planned for but, rather, is an emergent property of functional diversity at all levels of decision making (Dale, Electronic Dialogue, 25 July 1998).

Information

Information meaningful to sustainable development decision making is dependent upon integrative modes of inquiry between the natural and social sciences as well as upon multiple sources and modes of evidence. Since information is constantly evolving, just as are living systems, its integrity is vitally dependent upon the ability of human activity systems to perceive and respond to both positive and negative feedback loops, particularly in the area of policy development for natural resource management (Dale, Electronic Dialogue, 26 April 1998). Ecological information must be given at least the same weighting as social and economic information in management practices and policy decisions (Wiens 1997).

The other problem with feedback is that there are often conflicting feedbacks provided. In the case of the North Atlantic cod fishery, for example, one feedback (only detected belatedly because of the problems in the models used to assess the fishery) was the declining size of the stock. A second feedback resulted from the overcapitalization of the fishing fleet. With fortunes invested in hardware, the fishers needed large catch allowances and pressured politicians for high catch quotas. Given a population estimate with a higher degree of uncertainty associated with it (a common occurrence in assessments of natural systems) and pressure for higher catch quotas from the voters, the politicians listened to the latter feedback.

(Pope, Electronic Dialogue, 28 November 1996)

Feedback loops

Since complex systems have both changing and largely unknown natural boundaries, it is conceivable that human activity systems could badly misjudge which components and parameters to consider in their decision-making processes. The ability of decision makers to be able to effectively respond to both negative and positive feedback from ecological, social, and economic systems is critical to effective decision making with regard to sustainable development (Brown, Electronic Dialogue, 10 August 1998).

Integrity
A thing is "right" when it tends to preserve the integrity, resilience, co-evolutionary potential, and beauty of natural and human systems. It is wrong when it tends otherwise (adapted from Leopold 1949) (Dale, Electronic Dialogue, 22 August 1998).

Humility
Human systems are not apart from but, rather, are a part of natural systems. Life and nature are bigger and more powerful than any force that humans could ever bring to bear, and it is foolish to think it could be otherwise. Humility means seeing ourselves, our knowledge, our institutions, and our systems of governance as vitally interdependent with the natural world. It means recognizing our place as one among many. Rather than believing that we can manage our "environment," we must recognize that the only thing we can manage is our behaviour and impacts upon the environment. Greater sentiency implies greater responsibility for, rather than dominion over, nature (Geuer, Electronic Dialogue, 10 August 1998).

Limits
Just as natural systems are subject to biophysical limits, so all human activity systems are subject to scale. In other words, the greater the human population, the greater the ecological space humans occupy; ultimately leading to collapse if we exceed biophysical limits. The ultimate limit on human activities is, therefore, the biosphere. Although these limits may be more plastic thanks to technology and human ingenuity, they are ultimately finite (Sims, Electronic Dialogue, 10 August 1998). Humans cannot escape the limitations imposed by the resources of the biosphere (Dasmann et al. 1973). It may well be that the more human activity systems co-evolve with natural systems, the more these biophysical limits will become absolute human limits (Dale, Electronic Dialogue, 21 July 1998).

Multiple contexts
Human beings are context dependent. In our attempts to make sense of our world, we are heavily influenced by individual perceptions and mind-scapes, dominant socio-economic paradigms, and prevailing myths and metaphors. Personal and collective awareness of these multiple contexts, and our distressed tendency to maintain the status quo, act as barriers to new thought, innovation, and creativity. Making those tendencies explicit is key to being open to understanding new information (Dale, Electronic Dialogue, 26 April 1998).

Multiple perspectives
Multiple perspectives expand our decision-making processes by bringing different kinds of knowledge to the table. This principle challenges our reliance on dominant scientific approaches to sustainable development that, while remaining important tools, can only provide us with a partial view of a problem and its solutions. Multiple perspectives involve enlarging our ideas about who are the "experts" and what kinds of information are important. They mean seeking multiple sources of observations about our natural world as well as its social and economic spheres. This process should bring to the fore the different assumptions, values, and goals embodied in different perspectives (Massey, Electronic Dialogue, 26 April 1998).

Mutuality
Health and a functional, meaningful existence depends upon the organism's faculty for mutual synthesis with others and the environment (Williamson and Pearse 1980). All human activity systems are subjectively interdependent and embedded within natural systems, and both are engaged in overall mutual and co-evolutionary processes. Each influences the other, often in complex and subtle ways (Dale, Electronic Dialogue, 26 April 1998).

Precautionary principle
Rather than awaiting certainty, governments (and others) should anticipate potential environmental harm in order to prevent it. Consequently, it is essential that we become better at recognizing and responding to early indicators of system damage. Given the uncertainty and difficulty of predicting the nature of the limits of the co-evolutionary human/nature system, it would be prudent for human activity systems to live below rather than at penultimate biophysical limits. Given the complexities involved, decisions concerning the appropriate scale and nature of human activity systems, and the subsequent space our systems occupy, can be made only within enlarged decision-making contexts (Dale, Electronic Dialogue, 22 August 1998).

Resilience
This is the ability of a system (for example, an ecosystem or a system of government) to adapt to change while maintaining critical aspects of its original condition and function. If we wish to use the concept of resilience, then we must be explicit about what aspects we value and think are important to maintain, even as conditions change (e.g., total biodiversity, democratic processes, etc.) (Middleton, Electronic Dialogue, 13 April 1998).

Democracy understood as communication (Dryzek 1990) together with democratic
citizenship as part of a social learning process provides some evidence that individuals
can decline environmental goods and avoid or limit environmental bads ... Democratic
citizenship in short permits the possibility of the voluntary creation and maintenance
of an ecologically rational social-nature interaction, informed by moral as well as
scientific considerations. This is because it is communicative (rather than instrumental
rationality) which characterizes ecological rationality and the possible realization of
sustainability.

(Doherty and de Deus 1996: 125)

Scale

Phenomena present themselves on multiple scales. Mismatches between
the scale of a problem and the scale of human responses to it can result in
inappropriate policy initiatives. We have to develop operationally acceptable ways of scanning across scales by expanding our perceptual, analytic,
and planning horizons; and we must organize our policies around the
multiple scales found in natural systems (Pinter, Electronic Dialogue, 2
April 1998). Efforts must be made to adjust the scales of management to
those of natural processes (Wiens 1997). The impacts of multiple scales can
be addressed only through the implementation of environmental measures
at a domestic jurisdictional level appropriate to the source and scope of the
problem, and appropriate to effectiveness in achieving objectives. Where
there are significant transborder impacts, there should be international
cooperative efforts (Pinter, Electronic Dialogue, 2 April 1998) as well as
nested levels of decision making (Pope, Electronic Dialogue, 15 April 1998).

Systems approach

A systems approach to a problem involves trying to understand and
actively learn from whole living systems and their interconnectedness. It
involves an integrated and inclusive set of approaches to and methods of
problem solving based on the knowledge that human and natural systems
are complex, dynamic, resilient, and adaptive. The acceptance that uncertainty is an inherent quality of living systems is central to a systems
approach (Lister, Electronic Dialogue, 24 April 1998).

Triangulation

Triangulation involves the use of multiple methods, procedures, and/or
theories to acquire deeper understanding of what might or should be done
to improve any given situation, given its inherent complexities. We insist
that both conventional and novel analytic methods triangulate from as

many directions as possible in order to help us determine what we could be doing better when facing issues whose empirical merits are either unknown, not agreed upon, or both (Dale, Electronic Dialogue, 22 August 1998, adapted from Roe 1998).

Values

As sustainable development is a normative and ethical concept (Robinson et al. 1990), values are central to any dialogue, policy development, planning, and actions. Our values are deeply embedded in our cultural symbolism, our institutions, and our religions, and they collectively influence decision making at all levels (Pinter, Electronic Dialogue, 8 February 1997). Making the plurality and diversity of values explicit through values-based thinking is critical to sustainable development (Dale, Electronic Dialogue, 26 April 1998).

Strategic Imperatives

These strategic imperatives are by no means exhaustive but are meant to illustrate the minimum effort necessary to begin the rapid implementation of sustainable development policies, programs, and practices. Moreover, I anticipate that each department would expand upon these imperatives, depending upon their particular contexts.

1 It is imperative that all government policies and planning integrate ecological information into the development of their programs. In order to be both more effective and to minimize the likelihood of subsequent negative surprises, government must take into account interrelationships within ecological systems (e.g., cyclical flows, diversity, limits, and maintenance) (see Figure 8.1).

Figure 8.1

Interrelationships within ecological systems

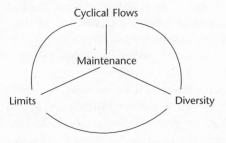

2 All government policies, planning, and programs must begin to replace short-term economic incentives with those that support the restoration and maintenance of ecosystem resilience; one by-product of this will be long-term economic sustainability (Holling and Meefe 1996). This imperative also requires policies for full-cost pricing; that is, for transferring environmental and social costs to prices paid by firms and consumers.

3 Governments must develop ways for individuals to innovate and to learn, and they must support them in doing so. An example is the application of actively adaptive environment management approaches, whereby policies become hypotheses and management actions become minimal-risk experiments to test those hypotheses (Holling 1978; Walters 1986).

Discursive democracy is ecologically rational, particularly from the point of view of sensitivity to feedback signals, complexity, generalizability and compliance; moreover, it promotes sensitivity to signs of disequilibrium in human-nature interactions because their sine qua non of extensive competent participation means that a wide variety of voices can be raised on behalf of a wide variety of concerns.

(Hayward 1995: 206)

Adaptive management demands that we consider a variety of plausible alternatives to the way we approach our world; consider a variety of possible strategies; favour actions that are robust with regard to uncertainties; hedge; favour actions that are informative; probe and experiment; monitor results; update assessments and modify policy accordingly; and favour actions that are reversible (Ludwig et al. 1993).

4 Governments must engage people as active partners in the process of developing public policy.

5 Governments must develop local partnerships among broad constituencies so that all stand to gain (or lose) from good (or poor) resource management (Holling and Meefe 1996), thereby enabling us to learn our way collaboratively into the future.

6 Governments must develop systems of governance that can accommodate the time, place, and space of natural systems through achieving greater synergy between ecological boundaries and socio-political boundaries. An example of this is the ecological framework developed by two federal government departments: Environment Canada and Agriculture and Agri-Foods Canada. Based on the direction to think, act, and plan in terms of ecosystems, and to move away from monitoring individual elements to a more comprehensive approach monitoring and reporting on the environment, these departments developed a nationwide ecological framework. The framework is composed of three main levels: ecozones, ecoregions, and ecodistricts.

de Groot (1992: 475) proposes establishing a partnership with nature in order to generate what he refers to as "partnership ethics": "Setting relations among people and between people and nature in a single ideal of communicative response, partnership ethics are different in many ways from the ethics of rights, obligations, stewardship and intrinsic value on the one hand, and from 'Deep Ecology' metaphysics on the other." In his partnership ethic framework, unlike within the reconciliation framework, being part of nature not only biologically but also spiritually becomes co-constitutive for being human.

The problem with a partnership ethic is that, first, in order for people to adopt such a framework they have to agree with its underlying values, and values have proven to be intractable with regard to many sustainable development issues. Second, a partnership, in my opinion, must be based on equity between partners, and, once again, this raises the ongoing philosophical debate regarding questions of sentiency of humans and other animals. This is why a reconciliation framework, which is based on the fundamental integration of ecological, social, and economic imperatives, may be more easily accepted. It is simple and is founded upon the basic reconciliation of formerly competing interests – interests that have brought humankind to its current level of environmental degradation. It also avoids the traditional polarization and trade-offs between the three imperatives. And it argues for ecological rationality (Dryzek 1990). This framework offers a non-regressive reconciliation with nature that is founded upon a basic ethic of communicative action – one that is egalitarian, uncoerced, competent, and free from delusion, deception, power, and strategy (ibid.).

Structural Antecedents
The adoption of a reconciliation framework across government departments, therefore, would not be imprisoned within the dominant socio-economic paradigms and vested interests that work to preserve them. Rather, it would transcend them and provide a new "rationale" for doing what it is we do. This rationale could be easily communicated to the wider publics, and it would avoid the paralysis of inaction that results when opposing sides use uncertainty and differing scientific perspectives to argue their respective cases. This is not to say that values are not central to a reconciliation framework; rather, it is to say that their articulation emerges from the reconciliation process itself. As well, equity may be an emergent property of reconciliation if diversity is accepted as a fundamental organizing principle of civil society. Such a framework, however, must be accompanied by new ways of government organizing (particularly with respect to policy development), to lead to appropriate actions for implementation in a timely fashion before we reach irreversible thresholds.

Governments adopting this framework would need to have different institutional characteristics than they do at present. At the end of this chapter I offer a description of those characteristics, adapted from Rueggeberg and Griggs (1993) (see Table 8.1). The two columns could be characterized as shallow and deep organizational change, respectively, with the left-hand column indicating an interim transition strategy, moving towards more fundamental changes on the right.

The difficulties are so great that maladaptive defenses are becoming massively in evidence ... : superficiality in which depth connection is lost; segmentation in which parts pursue their ends without reference to the whole; and dissociation in which people and groups cease to respond to each other.

Nevertheless, adaptation to complex environments is possible by appropriate value transformations. Critical are the design principles on which social institutions are built. The choice is between redundancy of parts (the machine principle) and the redundancy of functions (the organismic principle).

(Vickers 1972: xii)

A new sense of relatedness must permeate our institutions of governance, as redemocratization is critical when moving to the integrist model (Figure 2.3). Revitalizing democracy means restoring the moral basis of political life. We must come to realize that the personal is political and that there is no real separation between the public and the private spheres; to believe otherwise is to view the world through a distorted lens. We need a different view of what constitutes good governance. Informed and engaged publics, along with trustworthy, supportive, and inclusive institutions, facilitate democracy. Instead of being concerned with controlling and doing, governments should focus more on catalyzing community empowerment by developing (and leading) strategic partnerships. We must regain our capacity for release, innovation, and reorganization (Figure 7.2), and we must reintegrate these competencies into government policy development and program design (and redesign). Governments must concern themselves with creative renewal, and this will frequently involve devolving power and authority to the most effective level of government wherever possible. If this is not done, then the politics of separation will continue into the next decade.

Attempting to change definitions of what constitutes relatedness fundamentally challenges how we view nature and our relationship with it. One of our principal challenges, therefore, is to move from a single distorting-lens view of what constitutes integrity and culture to a multiple-apertures view with the flexibility to allow for co-evolving multiple perspectives. We must redesign human institutions to be in harmony with the functioning of natural systems, thus preserving the integrity of the self-organizing processes within ecosystems, human communities, and individuals alike. We need to encourage credible inquiry and discourse, often of the kind suppressed within organizational systems (Bella 1994).

Policy inquiry recognizes the uncertain and tentative nature of policy "knowledge" and accepts that there may be a variety of legitimate views on policy strategies. Policy development becomes an interactive process of inquiry among experts, interested parties and a broader public. Policy dialogue, then becomes an occasion for exploring and discussing options ... It does not deny or exclude the reality of political motivations and political pressures; rather, it allows policymakers to review different options and to consider those options. Policy dialogue and relevant policy inquiry are the essential underpinnings of the policy leadership that can only be provided by government.

(International Development Research and Policy Task Force 1996: 21)

We live in a world with multiple realities and pluralities, and we need to value both commonalities and differences. Emergent relations and processes can come only from the synergy of complementary differences, not from the preservation of traditional separations. Valuing one thing over another denies diversity and leads to separations that, on the surface, appear rational and natural but that, in reality, are based on the bankrupt politics of power and divisiveness. However, mere paradigm shifts are not likely to be sufficient. Political and social arrangements that implement these values will be essential for turning deeds into actualities (Ophuls 1977). The following table, adapted from Rueggeberg and Griggs (1993), examines some of the institutional characteristics that would facilitate the implementation of sustainable development in a world with multiple realities, pluralities, and diverse values.

Table 8.1

Institutional characteristics that support sustainable development

Integrated and coordinated

Integrative: each part of an institutional system interprets its mandate broadly to take into account all three dimensions of sustainability (social, economic, and ecological).

Comprehensive: each part of the institutional system recognizes all values associated with the resources it addresses and/or services it delivers. It employs the principle of "full cost accounting" in assessing the outcomes and impacts of decisions.

Coordinated and transactive: each part of the institutional system recognizes linkages with other parts of the system, seeks to harmonize its activities with those of others, and promotes a coordinated approach to achieving overlapping activities.

Efficient and effective

Efficient: the institutional system seeks to reduce overlaps and redundancies in the mandates and activities of its component parts; two or more parts of the system do not duplicate efforts. This criterion recognizes, however, that some degree of overlap is necessary to support integration and to ensure the "robustness" of the system in being able to respond to unexpected events.

Effective: each part of the institutional system has a sufficient mandate and the required level of staff and resources to run processes, make decisions, implement results, and monitor or review outcomes as necessary to achieve its objectives. The operation of the system produces meaningful results from the

Reconciliation

Integrative: all decision making for sustainable development fundamentally integrates ecological, social, and economic imperatives within a guiding framework.

Comprehensive: competing paradigms and conflicting worldviews are explicitly recognized and made transparent as part of the decision-making process. Multiplicity of perspectives and multiple contexts are venues for expression.

Transcendent: each part of the institutional system recognizes that it is a part of a larger whole whose goal is to further democracy through strengthening civil society.

Flexible and responsive

Flexible: unnecessary overlap and duplication are eliminated through integrated decision making and the development and continual refinement of a guiding framework for operating across government.

Effective: resources are efficiently and effectively deployed to respond to emerging issues, particularly at the domain level.

perspective of those operating in the system as well as from recipients of services provided by the system.

Long-term and adaptive

Strategic and anticipatory: the system is perceptive, looking for present and future opportunities and challenges. It establishes priorities to take action based on an assessment of the scope of impacts, irreversibility of decisions or actions, and urgency; in addition, it has the capacity to address short-term crises, undertake long-term planning, and also anticipate and respond to issues that occur at "in-between" speeds.

Precautionary: the institutional system recognizes that social, economic, and ecological limits exist, though they may not be definable. It takes a cautious approach to problem solving and decision making to ensure that outcomes are within those limits.

Reflexive and adaptive: the institutional system has the capacity to keep up with changing values and knowledge and to review and improve decision-making processes. It has the mandate and tools required for self-evaluation and self-modification. It shows leadership not only in questioning the way things are done, but whether in fact the "right" things are being done. This is not just a latent capability but an active role.

Long-term and responsive

Strategic and restorative: the system responds equally to ecological, social, and economic feedbacks; in particular, it has the ability to recognize and respond in a timely fashion to negative feedbacks from ecological systems, especially with respect to the loss of diversity at all scales.

Contextual: systems of governance recognize and respond to the differing time, place, and scale phenomena of natural systems and human activity systems, recognizing that there are absolute limits on human activities imposed by the biosphere. Accordingly, decision-making systems reconcile an ecological framework of spatial boundaries with socio-political boundaries, taking into account the finite limits on place and scale imposed by the biosphere. A cautious approach is to live below those limits, rather than near or at the limits, in order to maximize resilience of all systems.

Responsive: decision-making processes are enlarged policy-making contexts, transdisciplinary fora that bring together a multiplicity of stakeholders with relevant experiences to bear on the issue, particularly natural and social scientists, public policy practitioners, and the non-governmental community.

▶

Open, balanced, and fair	Open and inclusive
Representative: each part of the system provides opportunities for all affected interests to be represented in processes, decisions, and actions.	Equitable access: involvement in decision making by the plurality of interests concerned is key. Diversity of representation in processes, decisions, and actions, plus employment of a multiplicity of approaches is emphasized.
Equitable: the system ensures that the costs and benefits of decision-making processes and their outcomes are distributed fairly among those affected, providing appeal mechanisms for those who feel that their interests have been overlooked or undetermined.	Embeddedness: identification with our connectedness, and also recognition of our being a small part of a larger grouping, provides a foundation for concerns for history, inter-generational and global equity, and awareness of the needs of "others" (Josselson 1996).
Participatory and collaborative: the institutional system provides opportunities for individuals and groups representing different interests to cooperate in decision making and take actions which affect their future while sharing responsibility for outcomes.	Networks of collaboration: the institutional system recognizes the complexity, incomplete knowledge, and uncertainty inherent in living systems, and that no one sector can solve the complex societal issues involved. Their role is to stimulate networks of collaboration around "domains of interest," leading to solutions and concrete actions.
Responsive and accountable: each part of the system responds in a timely fashion to the constituency it serves and provides mechanisms by which individuals or groups can be held responsible directly by that constituency for a decision or action; these mechanisms are not so rigid as to inhibit creativity.	Integrity: integrity of information is critical to the responsiveness of the system, particularly negative feedbacks from ecological systems. In order to be able to respond to negative feedback information, subsidiarity is fundamental.
Conflict-resilient: the system provides mechanisms to deal constructively with conflicts within and between its component parts, and with other institutional systems.	Open: mutual learning occurs in open policy dialogues, which value discovering main areas of both agreement and disagreement.

Source: Left-hand column adapted from Rueggeberg and Griggs 1993 (reprinted with permission of the Canadian Council of Ministers of the Environment); right-hand column, Dale 1998.

9
Dialogue and Governance

The principle of rough equality suggests ... that diffuse feedback
processes in the natural world should be matched by diffuse
decision processes in human societies.

– J.S. Dryzek, "Green Reason:
Communicative Ethics for the Biosphere"

In spite of a significant increase in the number and kinds of laws, policies, and programs directed at managing natural systems (over 120 international treaties and conventions, and over 250 agreements at regional and local levels have been established since the 1970s [Holdgate 1996]), there remains a substantial gap between the formal intent of such laws and their actual effect on natural systems. These implementation gaps can be partly accounted for by the inadequacy of organizational structures and administrative processes pertaining to the management of natural systems.

A network is a set of elements related to one another through multiple inter-connections. The metaphor of the net suggests a special kind of interconnectedness, one dependent on nodes in which several connecting strands meet. There is the suggestion both of each element connecting through one another rather than to each other only through a center.

(Schön 1983: 190)

Given the nature of sustainable development imperatives (see Chapter 3), it is clear that the present organizational capacity of the federal government (see Chapter 7), with its predominant vertical structures, calls for a redesigned institutional order (Paquet 1997). Some of the main organizational issues are fragmentation; jurisdictional gaps; polarization of interests; jurisdictional conflicts; piecemeal and uncoordinated polices; conflict of resource uses; and lack of coordination, trust, communication, and collaboration (Lowry and Carpenter 1984). Indeed, as the Commissioner for the Environment and Sustainable Development noted in his 1999 report: "Some of the most pressing issues facing governments today cut across departmental mandates and political jurisdictions. Effective co-ordination is essential for meeting our sustainable development challenges – governments are not very good at it" (Emmett 1999: 7). Another major barrier is the Anglo-American view that, since we live in a market society, there is no need for any philosophy of governance (Paquet 1997). Yet another is the declining trust in government: 67 percent of Canadians say they have little or no confidence in their political leaders (Environics 1995).

Because, in most industrial cultures, competition is valued more than collaboration, the more agencies responsible for the management of natural systems, the greater the risk of interdepartmental conflict; thus, the greater the need for interagency coordination and communication. As well, significant gaps and time lags in the implementation of management efforts, and continual changes in environmental and social conditions, increase the turbulence of the fields in which these organizations exist (Emery and Trist 1972). There is thus a fundamental mismatch between the structures, processes, and functioning of natural systems and those of governmental organizations. This limits the latter's ability to both respond effectively to early warning signals from ecological systems concerning the cumulative human impacts on the environment and to act in collaboration with them.

In its 1997 report, the World Bank called for the reinvigoration of public institutions, maintaining that an effective state is the cornerstone of successful economies; without it, economic, social, and personal development is severely limited. Good government is not a luxury but a vital necessity for civil societies. A precondition for the rapid diffusion of sustainable development principles and practices is, therefore, the development of effective institutions. Thus, the current structures of our institutions must be recognized as key barriers and humanly devised facilitators of human interaction. They structure incentives in human exchange, whether political, social, or economic, and shape the way societies evolve (North 1990). Institutions are in a position to provide leadership for positive human actions, but if they are inflexible and isolated, then they can readily become maladaptive and inimical to positive change.

A Fisheries Case Study

Policy failure has been identified as a major barrier to the implementation of sustainable development, being responsible, for example, for much of the current environmental damage in the agricultural sector (FAO 1991; Hill 1998). Another example of policy failure is the fisheries. From the mid-1960s to the mid-1980s human population boomed from three billion to four billion. And in 1989 the catch of ocean wildlife climbed to a high of nearly 90 million tonnes. However, since then, despite increased effort, new materials, and even better means of finding fish, the annual catch has declined; and for some fisheries the populations have crashed. This has happened in spite of the best efforts to evaluate maximum sustainable yields (MSY).

Paradoxically, commercial fishing already costs much more than it contributes to the economies of the nations of the world. At present the annual catch worldwide brings in about US$70 billion and costs $124 billion to land. The difference – $54 billion – is made up in subsidies, in tax dollars paid by others, including those in Canada who are supporting out-of-work cod fishers (Earle 1995).

With respect to the limitations of our knowledge, Ludwig et al. (1993) argue that resource questions pertaining to potential yield cannot be answered reliably because learning about natural resource systems is limited by a lack of research replicates and controls, a lack of treament randomization in natural experiments, and changes in underlying systems. This highlights the two views on managing renewable resources. One view suggests that more intense detailed scientific research on biological systems will provide improved understanding and that this, in turn, will lead to better management. The other view argues that the space and time scales of many major systems are such that traditional scientific research will not provide additional useful understanding and that improved design of the monitoring and management systems will provide greater benefits. Holling (1993b) and Lee (1993) both argue that there is an important role for scientific research but not if it is merely disciplinary, reductionist, and detached from people, policies, and politics. Holling further argues that the needed research should be interdisciplinary, non-linear, focused on the interaction between slow processes and fast ones, and emphasize the study of cross-scale phenomena. On the other hand, Hilborn et al. (1995) state that one of the key lessons to be learned from the study of the sustainable exploitation of fish, wildlife, and forests is that successful management rests not so much on better science as on the implementation of better institutional arrangements for controlling exploiters and creating incentives for more sustainable behaviours.

Mistakes in scientific assessment have played a major role in the collapse of some potentially sustainable harvested systems. For example, when Canada took over the extended management jurisdiction (the 200-mile limit) of its East Coast fish stocks in the late 1970s, after a period of intense fishing by foreign fleets, scientists overestimated the remaining cod stocks off Newfoundland by over 200 percent. This led to a Canadian policy that virtually destroyed the cod stock by 1991 (Findlayson 1994; Hutchings and Myers 1994).

And we do not seem capable of learning from our past. The fisheries industry has always been characterized by boom and bust cycles.

There is growing evidence that, between 1845 and 1880, increased fishing was having a negative influence on marine resources. As early as the 1840s a significant public demand pressured government to regulate the use of new fishing gears to protect cod stocks ... With hindsight and late twentieth century awareness, we can now understand that frequent fishery failures and a necessary shift to more intensive technologies, when set beside rapid population increase and large fluctuations in Newfoundland salt cod and seal exports, combine to point to a likely ecological problem. (Cadigan 1996)

A more recent failure is the collapse of the West Coast herring fishery in the 1960s. At that time, herring was used mainly for fertilizer and pet food. Given the increase in demand for herring, decisions were taken to use bigger boats and more efficient technology; this, of course, resulted in the crash of the herring fishery. It was reopened in the 1980s on the basis of a 20 percent spawning biomass. In addition, markets had changed, the chief product now being herring roe for the Japanese market, with the remainder being used for pet food. This is one of the information failures: we do not seem to be able to learn from historical precedents, and, in moving to species substitution, we perpetuate the same mistakes.

With respect to the East Coast cod fishery, the Atlantic cod take reached its highest level before the end of the 1960s, with a slight blip at the beginning of the 1980s (Environment Canada 1992). In fact, the stock has been declining since then, and the catch rate, from the time that the 200-mile limit was introduced in 1977 (effectively placing the responsibility for managing eastern Canada's groundfish fisheries with the federal government), rarely made the total allowable catch. Moreover, the graph on the size of mature cod at seven years of age, from 1976 onwards, showed a persistent downward slope (Environment Canada 1992). Thus, in addition to Fisheries and Oceans scientists, Environment Canada scientists would also have been aware of this persistent decline and its ecological ramifications (as, indeed, would scientists in other government departments and fisheries experts in academic institutions).

In the past century, without much thought about the consequences, we have removed from the sea literally billions of tonnes of living creatures, of wildlife, and added to it billions of tonnes of toxic substances. Fish, whales, shrimps, clams and other living things are widely regarded as commodities not as vital components of the living system upon which we are utterly dependent.

We have a hard time thinking of fish as valuable unless they're dead. True, too, of whales, of trees, and much of the rest of nature in times past. Our accounting system regards these things as free. What is taken is regarded as direct income without affecting costs other than what it has cost to take them out of their natural setting.

(Sylvia Earle's address to the International Union for the Conservation of Nature Conference, Montreal, October 1997)

Another question with regard to information failure is, why did academic researchers and organizations (such as the Royal Society of Canada) fail to signal this persistent decline before it reached threshold limits? This introduces the question of the role of scientists in educating the public, and of making their research accessible and available to a far wider audience.

It would appear that there were many factors involved in the overestimates of the cod fishery. A discrepancy between the availability of cod to the inshore and offshore fisheries, respectively, was being reported as early as 1986, with the latter arguing that their catches were low because of overexploitation on the part of offshore trawlers. Ironically, Winters' (1986; cf. Hutchings et al. 1997) conclusions were that the size of the cod stock had been overestimated since 1977 and that this was caused by excessive reliance on abundance indices derived from commercial trawler catch rate data and by the violation of assumptions of the multiplicative model used in the assessment procedure. Contrary to the consensus expressed by Lear et al. (1986), which concluded that cold water temperatures were responsible for low inshore catches in 1985, Winters documented a statistically significant negative association between inshore catch and offshore exploitation rate, concluding that the decline in the inshore catches since 1982 had been due to the increase in the offshore exploitation rate (Winters 1986).

Thus, the links between technology, scale, employment, and concentration became firmly entrenched. The unintended effects of government policies aimed at reducing the fleets were, paradoxically, to reward those who could take a bigger catch within a shorter period of time (i.e., scale) because they had more efficient vessels (i.e., high technology). This resulted in low employment and the loss of community resilience.

The ambiguity and imprecision surrounding jurisdictional authority would seem to have undermined the scope of federal environmental policy historically and contributed to a weak enforcement regime. However, the effects of federalism on policy outcomes are difficult to isolate from the impact of other factors; among them the predominance in government and industry circles of a development/production-oriented technology, and the existence of closed policy networks in which industry and government officials have collaborated in the formulation of policies and environmental implications.

(Skogstad and Kopas 1992: 49)

Politically, the Progressive Conservatives were elected in 1982, and John Crosbie held the portfolio of minister for fisheries from 1984 to 1988;

between 1988 and 1992, he was both minister for fisheries and minister for the Atlantic Canada Opportunities Agency (ACOA). Needless to say, Crosbie, along with such Atlantic Canada players as Stuart McGinnes, Dalton Camp, and Senator Lowell Murray, was a powerful force in the Mulroney Cabinet. Jobs in Atlantic Canada have always been precious, and it would be safe to say that, during this period, they took precedence over any ecological concerns, over the long-term social implications of overfishing, and, apparently, over the scientific information that was then being presented to Cabinet. Unemployment in Newfoundland was increasingly exacerbated, and the age-old dichotomy of jobs versus the environment became increasingly volatile. It is no surprise, therefore, that the Conservatives decided to maintain the status quo, increasing the size of fishing vessels and inshore fish plants (recall the herring collapse of the 1960s), and reducing the take by the inland fishers. I have often asked my policy colleagues whether, at that time, any consideration was given to the idea of sustainable employment. Would it not have been more sustainable to continue to employ more small-scale inland fishers than to make the decision to allow factory-freezer trawlers, technology that allowed the catch to increase and that masked the fact that the catch was getting smaller and smaller? The barriers model (Figure 7.1) illustrates the gridlock that occurs when an increase in scale leads to centralization (moving from small-scale fishers to trawlers to fish plants), which, in turn, leads to increased technology and privatization, thus resulting in greater scale and increased divergence of the social, economic, and ecological imperatives.

In 1982, in Newfoundland, Fisheries Minister Crosbie announced the decision to increase the size of the ships, and this was met by cheers from the audience. The audience, however, was comprised mainly of the captains of the bigger ships and the employees of the new big plants; it did not include many inshore fishers. Many analysts believe that the East Coast cod fishery was doomed with the big ships.

One has to ask the question, would the uncertainties regarding the status of northern cod in 1986 have been summarily dismissed by a scientific establishment with no political or governmental affiliation?

If the above scenario is accurate, then it reflects an information failure at the individual level and points to one of the weaknesses of a rigid, hierarchical decision-making system within which one individual, either because of political or bureaucratic leverage, can attain so much power that he or she can influence an entire group, in spite of ecological information to the contrary. It may also reflect an information failure between government departments, in that the lead department channels information to

Cabinet and, if that information is "shaped" by policy advice that seems to question the accuracy of the data rather than concentrating on the long-term indicators, then effective decision making is curtailed. The number of bureaucratic and political points that have been so shaped may never be known, as confidentiality provisions pertain to any information that is given for the advice and consideration of Cabinet.

Further complicating estimates of the health of the cod fisheries were a number of environmental factors. Temperatures had been decreasing on the East Coast for some time, and it appears as though one of the effects of this is that fish are moving south, with Arctic cod moving down the coast (Hutchings and Myers 1994). Another complex variable is the role of other predators, notably seals (although there is evidence that seals will not go after cod when they are hard to find [ibid.]). This debate is still ongoing, and it is complicated by the fact that seals eat capelin – a fish species whose numbers are also declining. Thus it is easy to ignore human exploitation as the primary cause of the fisheries collapse and to point to environmental determinants and other species. This denial of the underlying causes of the current collapse, coupled with an inability to learn from previous collapses, ensures the inevitability of multiple future collapses.

Another overall trend was the reduction, in the 1960s, of taxonomy and systematics work (discovering and describing biological diversity, including naming species), when the emphasis on new technologies swept right through Canadian universities. This new science and technology push resulted in the emergence of many young academics who embraced the new socio-technological paradigm rather than the fundamentals of biology and their associated emphasis on the importance of monitoring and evaluating systems.

This highlights another information failure, the lack of a long-term strategic direction or a scientific research framework, lending a balance between basic and applied work, thereby avoiding major gaps for the future.

One has also to question the nature of the scientific information itself. As an article in the *New Scientist* (10 February 1996: 90) states: "Mealy-mouthed advice from scientists is providing politicians with excuses for their failure to save the world's fisheries, according to a report released to the House of Lords. It urges researchers to 'give much firmer advice in a form which the political managers could not ignore.'" Although some analysts have stated that the scientific community failed to adequately convey the aspects of uncertainty surrounding the fisheries, it may well be that the political decision makers simply cannot deal with uncertainty. They want definite answers, whereas scientists are used to couching their information in probabilities. Thus, there may have been a fundamental mismatch with regard to information needs for decision making between government scientists, government policy makers, and politicians.

Because the social imperative took precedence, more fishers were artificially maintained through the non-fishing season through unemployment insurance, thereby employing more workers than the resource would have naturally supported. The trade-off of jobs versus fish could have been avoided by the creation of an integrative framework in which the three imperatives were reconciled.

As well, there were simply too many fishers chasing too few fish (Walters and Maguire 1996). In fact, the government's unemployment insurance scheme may have actually created an incentive for overfishing, as it provided for fishers and their families during the non-fishing seasons, thus supporting more fishers than the ecological base could maintain. And, further compounding the overcapacity problem, was the fact that, as the catch became less, the government lowered the number of weeks necessary to qualify for unemployment insurance, thus further supporting the fundamental instabilities that led to the ultimate crash. Technology was also an important variable. According to Walters and Maguire (1996), trawlers exerted by far the largest share of fishing mortality during the 1980s and 1990s.

The collapse of the cod fisheries became what I have earlier referred to as a "vicious" cycle, where overcapitalization and increasing technology became a positive feedback loop to political decision makers and their advisors. And, despite the lessons that have been learned from the fisheries collapse, there is little evidence that Fisheries and Oceans has engaged in any organizational learning or modified its bureaucratic structure and mode of decision making. For example, a 1998 letter from the Coalition of Gulf Fishermen (whose members include the Federation of Gulf Nova Scotia Groundfishermen, the Prince Edward Island Fishermen's Association, the New Brunswick-based Maritime Fishermen's Union, and the Alliance des pêcheurs du Québec) to then fisheries minister David Anderson stated: "Nothing will effectively capture the fury we have at the blatant disregard you are demonstrating towards the vast majority of 'professional' fishermen in the Southern Gulf of St. Lawrence." Their specific complaints included allowing draggers and trawlers into the cod fishery; possibly allowing a winter cod fishery in the gulf; requiring fishing boats to carry very expensive observers in order to ensure that regulations are respected; and making trawler nets meet mesh size requirements that invite the capture of small, commercially useless fish. The letter states that the use of trawlers became popular when governments decided to treat the fishery as an industry. "But all over the world, we see it is folly to industrialize the catching of fish. The trawlers and draggers are too efficient" (*Ottawa Citizen*, 13 July 1998). The stovepipes and silos appear to be cast in concrete.

When the sub-systems of society were less interdependent, policies could be more discrete and separate agencies could administer their own programs with minimum interference to each other. The greater degree of interdependence has changed this situation. Diffuse problems now arise affecting several sectors or indeed the whole of a society and these problems tend themselves to be interconnected. Examples would be poverty, obsolescence, urban decay, pollution, overpopulation, regional disparities, water and other natural resource management issues and intergenerational conflicts.

(Emery and Trist 1972: 89)

It would appear that, paradoxically, in spite of occurring in a sophisticated information age, natural resource collapses are the result of fundamental and multi-level information failures. We have quite considerable proof of the validity of Figure 7.1: the more ecological, social, and economic imperatives diverge (entailing increasing scale, increasing technology, increasing centralization, and increasing privatization), the more inevitable is total collapse. As well, compartmentalization is a common feature of human activity systems, but it is antithetical to the understanding of ecological systems and processes. Disciplinary and institutional barriers constitute a formidable obstacle to the synthesis of ecological understanding and the free flow of intellectual process (Kerr and Ryder 1997). Unless this decision-making gridlock is exposed and new policies developed, our policies will either continue to maintain the status quo or change only at the margins.

Paquet (1997) also identifies rationalities, non-rational reasons, and unconscious psychodynamic processes as barriers to sustainable development. Alternative rationalities are regarded negatively because they threaten current power relationships; non-rational reasons are often invoked to prevent a full debate on dominant paradigms; and psychodynamic processes, such as anger, denial, and face-saving behaviours, operate partly unconsciously when leaders are forced to consider alternative agendas. Clearly, we must have public debates about the limitations of the old paradigms, in order to create analytical and reflective space for the development of policy alternatives within government.

Necessary Structural Changes

What ways, then, are appropriate for spanning the multiple and contending outside stakeholders that government must engage if it is to participate in enlarged decision-making contexts? Such contexts are unlikely to be established unless a new socio-governmental context emerges through the spread of trans-bureaucratic organizations and the creation of a common ground insofar as necessary changes are concerned (Emery and Trist 1972).

Our belief that we are independent agents deters us from recognizing how very much our beliefs and behaviour, our ways of evaluating persons and events, are shaped by our myths and our habits. Our prevailing beliefs about what is "naturally" worthy of aspiring to and doing – our myths – and reflexive dependence on what has worked well before – habit – are attractive ways to leave our minds uncluttered, our behaviour reliable, and our anxiety levels low. Institutions and organizations depend on just those attractions to appeal to stakeholders and membership. Thus learning, which mostly upsets beliefs and habits in individuals and organizations, is hardly likely to be embraced easily and enthusiastically, even though there is a growing, and sometimes powerful, recognition of the need for change.

(Michael 1995: 469-470)

Numerous case studies (e.g., the New Brunswick forestry policy, the Everglades, Chesapeake Bay and its watershed, the Columbia River Basin, the Great Lakes Basin Ecosystem, and the Baltic) have underlined the importance of building consensus and collaboration in solving natural resource problems (Berkes et al. 1998; Westley 1995). We need to move from closed to open policy-making processes; from issues that are single-sector and domestic to issues that are transdisciplinary and global; from government as controller and monitor to government as catalyst and leader; from citizen participation based on exclusive invitation and exclusion to citizenship based on rights, competency, and inclusion; from policy analysts as technical specialists to policy analysts as individual members of transdisciplinary teams; from management that is primarily vertical to management that is both horizontal and vertical; from homogenization to diversity; from a horizon that is short-term and reactive to one that is long-term, proactive and multiple in time, place, and scale; and from adaptive, reactive management to proactive, co-evolutionary management.

Gunderson et al. (1995b) argue that being adaptive means, among other things, being able to respond to environmental feedbacks. Although I earlier cautioned against the dangers of adaptation, I would argue that even with adaptation, human activity systems must, wherever feasible, mimic ecological systems. Our modern context no longer provides any space – ecological, social, economic, and perhaps even psychological – for continued quantitative growth. It is no longer a case of having the room to manage our environment, if indeed it was ever possible; rather, we are in a situation where we have to design systems of governance that allow us to collectively manage and change the fundamental nature of our impacts. We are now beyond adaptation, for, in many ways, adaptation means accepting the dominant socio-economic paradigms and simply adapting our behaviour to the inevitable negative outcomes. Rather than adaptive management, our long-term solutions require proactive, responsible, co-evolutionary management (see Table 8.1). We now have to develop ways of organizing that work in synergy with ecosystem functions and processes, recognizing natural limits and maintaining rather than exploiting resilience and diversity. We need to encourage decision-making contexts that facilitate the integration of multiple knowledges and experiences. The need for integration and synthesis is particularly evident in problem-oriented, human-centred, change-sensitive, future-oriented, and holistic endeavours that deal with new knowledge of human nature, the interdependence of social issues and problems, globalization, and the interdependence of all human knowledge systems (Hill 1979). One immediate and relatively easy way of meeting these realities is through opening up government policy-making processes and increasing dialogue.

Open Policy Processes

By employing more open-ended policy processes that engage the users of resources and key decision makers from civil society, feedback loops come closer to the locus of decision making, with the result that officials can no longer ignore or deny the long-term outcomes of their actions. The dialogue framework that I am proposing integrates some features of matrix management by prioritizing policy domains across government and shortening feedback loops through multistakeholder processes. It also bridges science and policy through enlarging transdisciplinary policy-making and decision-making contexts, supported by expanded external networks of collaboration. Given the co-evolutionary nature of our contemporary environmental contexts, traditional bureaucratic models are clearly dysfunctional; therefore, we need advances in institution building at the level of interorganizational domains (Trist 1983).

Government is an organizational construct that is often stalled in bureaucratic or political gridlock. Governance on the other hand, implies a far broader social act that calls on a variety of agents and values to deal with the fierce demands of global interdependence.

(Young and von Moltke 1993: 4)

Governments can then become the nexus of both generalized and specialized resources, which can be applied to the joint creation of social policy and action. The most important role of government is transformed to being a catalyst for action (Westley and Vredenburg 1996b). Governments and their institutions would become the mediating factor that determines the collective relationships between social groups and the ecosystems upon which they depend (Berkes'et al. 1998). They could assume this role because, ideally, the electoral process renders them accountable to the public and, thus, capable of being an "honest" broker for civil society. Furthermore, they have access to the requisite resources.

These collaborations, however, must transcend dualism (Dillon 1988) and avoid the temptation to assert the superiority of the opposite in order to prove the worth of the alternative. They must recognize that our concepts of biology and nature are already distorted by gender and power relations (Jiggins 1994); they do not merely reflect the given structure of reality.

It may be that by accepting the notion of biophysical limits, coupled with the idea of carrying capacity, at different scales – locally, regionally, nationally, and globally – we may achieve some policy changes. It is imperative, however, that we not wait until we approach critical boundaries. This is because threshold effects are leading to collapse, foreclosing future options. As well, given the increasing interlocutory effects, and our inability to respond to negative feedback loops until we reach or near critical thresholds, there must be a better way, given human ingenuity and innovation. I believe that Vitousek's work could become a powerful metaphor, coupled with the concept of limits to the biosphere, for getting people to look at their position within the world they inhabit and the room they are leaving for "others."

(Dale, Electronic Dialogue, 17 November 1996)

Any framework for governance, therefore, must tie policy development to illuminating deeply rooted values and beliefs about how the world works. This is because, as argued in previous chapters, human activities can no longer be sustained according to current biases and imbalances. Respect for diversity and nurturance, and a potential for oneness mediated by reciprocity, should be regarded as integral to our human condition (ibid.). Indeed, the strength of civil society in the twenty-first century can be expected to become increasingly dependent upon interconnected webs of relationships and reciprocal influences.

Sahl and Bernstein (1995) have created a framework for developing policy in an uncertain world. Given that there are multiple concepts, frameworks, approaches, and tools that are available as inputs for policy development, these authors stress the importance of explicitly organizing and choosing among divergent alternatives. There are a range of policy options, including containment, accommodation, adaptation, management, mitigation, and suppression. In their model, making our paradigms explicit and examining their appropriateness is an important part of achieving appropriate sustainable development policies. This then feeds back into the considera-tion of policy approaches, strategies, and tactics.

Working from Habermas' (1990) study on discourse ethics, which argues: (1) that the pluralism and complexity of modern life make it impossible to formulate universal, abstract, and strictly objective solutions to problems and (2) that public agreement can be arrived at and tested only through a public process, I have modified Sahl and Bernstein's model.

Thus the policy development process is opened up to an enlarged decision-making context that is able to incorporate the diversity of public values and paradigms of which governments need to be cognizant (see Fig-ure 9.1). Debates about competing perspectives, and about preferred states, are replaced by discussions about policy alternatives. Values then emerge through the course of dialogues about preferred policy alternatives rather than at the macro-level of preferred states. Most important, however, this modified model opens up the process to feedback and evaluation from outside government. In this way, governments will become sensitive to negative as well as positive feedback loops. The detection of feedback and the evaluation of processes and outcomes should be conducted by those directly affected by the policies; that is, by stakeholders closest to the prob-lem (i.e., multiple scales).

My model also differs from Sahl and Bernstein's in that it assumes that, because paradigms exist at a deeper level of consciousness than do values, paradigmatic thought influences values. As Tomkins (1962: 13) observes, "the world we perceive is a dream we learn to have from a script we have not written ... Instead of putting a mirror to nature we are ... putting the mirror to a mirror."

Figure 9.1

Responsible policy dialogue

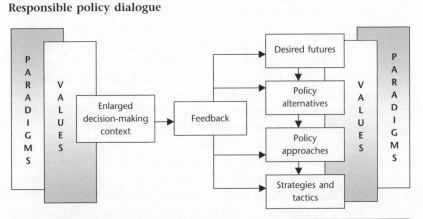

Source: Adapted from Sahl and Bernstein 1995.

In addition to opening up the policy process, there is an equally pressing need to build new domain-based linkages and competencies to deal with meta-problems such as sustainable development (Trist 1983). Sustainable development spreads horizontally across the conventional divisions of knowledge in the natural sciences, the life sciences, the social sciences, and the humanities. It also spreads horizontally across departmental structural arrangements. Assuming that our present modern context is a turbulent and "hostile" environment, it can be made less threatening by explaining problem solving at the level of the domain; that is, at the political level.

Domains are based on what Vickers (1965) called "acts of appreciation." Appreciation is a complex perceptual and conceptual process which melds together judgments of reality and judgments of value. A new appreciation is made as a new meta-problem (Chevalier 1966), a problematique, or "mess" (Ackoff 1975) is recognized.

The importance of the regulation by stakeholders can scarcely be over-emphasized, for there is considerable danger that the organizational fashioning, the institution building, the social architecture required at the domain level in complex modern societies will either take the wrong path or not be attempted at all.

(Trist 1983: 270-271, 273)

As discussed in earlier chapters, however, the domain of sustainable development is fundamentally about values. When these values are so absolute as to render immoral any compromise by the stakeholders at the table, then parties cannot bargain in good faith. Effective dialogue is dependent upon how extreme and non-negotiable individuals hold to their particular views. These values are also, of course, strongly influenced by the worldviews that participants bring to the dialogue. Stakeholders have to accept that, by entering into a multistakeholder process, they are, by definition, agreeing to search for mutually advantageous, although not always easily reconcilable, solutions that are common to society as a whole. They are engaging in what Trist (1983) refers to as joint appreciation. They are also agreeing to develop a new negotiated order that transcends their own personal agendas, a mechanism that Gray (1989) sees emerging from the interaction.

Figure 9.1 also assumes greater uncertainty, more orientation towards the future, and greater interdependence; and this necessitates more comprehensiveness (Emery and Trist 1972). Moreover, it assumes that the constraints of bureaucratic structure and norms are more limiting than are human cognitive processes, which can be stimulated to greater creativity by moving outside of the bureaucratic constraints of single organizations and by considering issues at a meta-level (Gregory and Keenery 1994). It also assumes, through the creation of networks of collaboration rather than more permanent referent organizations, that power differences can be minimized and that new hierarchies and other bureaucratic rigidities will not develop. Thus it allows for creative renewal.

Deconstructing Silos and Stovepipes

Whereas Trist (1983) argues for the establishment of more permanent, less fluid, and more central organizations (such as, for example, referent organizations), I argue for more organic, responsive policy domains around emerging and emergent issues across government. These domains need to be supported, however, by networks of collaboration for policy development that lead to an enlarged advisory context for political decision making. In some cases, depending upon the particular issues and whether or not decision making can be devolved, it may lead to new, enlarged decision-making contexts. In this way, the sectoral departments' client constituencies will be exposed and enlarged through the transdisciplinary fora, becoming more inclusive and national rather than just federal. As well, with government serving as a supportive resource, these fora can become semi-permanent and more stable than most of the loose ad hoc coalitions that currently exist, thereby creating a counter-balance to existing vested interests.

Domain appreciation is likely to be guided by the recognition of two principles: (i) that the quality of life is affected by the quality of the social reality at all system levels (not merely the individual), and in all dimensions of value (not merely the economic); and (ii) that welfare and development have become inter-dependent in the transition to post-industrialism – welfare in its widest connotation of growth (change) that is progressive and order-producing rather than regressive and disorder-producing.

(Emery and Trist 1972: 97)

It is crucial, however, that the deliberations of these collaborative networks be open and transparent so that the political level becomes more accountable. So, for example, if the government chooses to ignore the policy advice given by these networks, it would be forced to make transparent the political trade-offs involved. For example, in the United States, once the scientific advisory panels have given their advice to the government, they can publish their findings and recommendations. In addition to making scientific advice available to the wider Canadian public, these transdisciplinary fora bring together the science, academic, and policy communities. They transcend the vertical solitudes between these communities, by removing the opportunity for the policy development process, diluting or, in some cases, ignoring the internal advice of its specialists.

In this non-hierarchical model, no one community is regarded as above or below the other. In the event that consensus is not achieved around selected issues, then the disagreement is forwarded to the political level for its decision, and, at the same time, it is made public. Bringing both the external scientific and other academic advisors to the same table with public policy practitioners and specialists leads to the creation of mutual learning and direct feedback processes. This is not to say that everything can be solved by consensus. Indeed, as mentioned above, the exposure of major areas of disagreement is just as important in these enlarged, open, decision-making contexts. Churchman (1979) advocates seeking disagreements rather than agreements in order to identify problems, rather than seeking adaptive solutions to persistent conflicts, provided there are competent decision makers available to make the final decisions.

Network roles such as systems negotiation, underground manager, broker, and facilitator vary in character and yet make common demands on their practitioners, each of whom attempt to make of themselves a node connecting strands of a network which would otherwise exist as disconnected elements. The risks of the roles are many, since the broker may often be squeezed between the elements they are trying to connect. The need for personal credibility is high, since each role demands that the person be acceptable and believable to different organizations and persons, each of whom tends to hold different criteria for acceptance.

(Schön 1971: 200)

This kind of civil society participation in open policy dialogues works "horizontally" across government and society rather than from the bottom up from citizens to government. In the Netherlands, and especially in Canada, horizontal participation is especially important at the provincial level, where sectoral provincial regulations and plans (e.g., within the environmental, agricultural, housing, and traffic sectors etc.) have to be integrated into national strategies. Participation is not only an end in itself, but also a means for policies to be effectively implemented. Almost all literature on participation says that it "is necessary for [the development and implementation of] effective policies" (Roe 1998: 380). In the Third World, for instance, the truly successful environmental projects are invariably those founded on voluntary effort (Chambers 1988; Scoones and Thompson 1994). This opening up of the federal government policy development process may well lead to new alliances between the natural and social sciences, and between science and the state (Norgaard 1989).

Living, dynamic, and complex systems can be adequately understood only through a multiplicity of tools, techniques, methodologies, and perspectives. The policy development process can no longer be an exclusive, closed process involving only internal experts; rather, it must be open to plural methodologies, to broader communities with transdisciplinary knowledge, to shortened feedback loops that facilitate responses to both negative and positive information, and to multistakeholder creativity and evaluation. Multiple insights, methods, worldviews, and disciplinary perspectives would allow us to become more aware of the complexity of social and ecological systems as well as of the difficulties of taking appropriate actions. The enlarged policy process model described above, however, has to be accompanied by complementary structural changes within government – changes that actively facilitate an enlarged policy process. Vested interests include industry associations, corporate lobbyists, individual firms, and NGOs. Many of these interests centre exclusively on one department, such as Agriculture Canada, Industry Canada, and Natural Resources. And, at times, they may coalesce in interesting new alliances, depending upon the particular issue being addressed, making, at times, for strange bedfellows, in all innocence on the part of the less sophisticated interests. For example, there are some very interesting new and wider coalitions building in civil society, as is evidenced in the recent Seattle demonstrations against the World Trade Organization and in powerful industrial interests in biotechnology.

When faced with a dizzying array of interests, especially broad horizontal interests such as sustainable development, there often occurs a decision-making gridlock that results in the perpetuation of the status quo. In order to counter this, I offer a framework for governance based on dialogue (see Figure 9.2).

In this model, the main domain(s) of appreciation, and their associated policy themes, would be publicly identified by the incoming administration in the Speech from the Throne. Domain(s) of appreciation operate at a meta-level of organization, cutting horizontally across existing structures. In this way, the domain level(s) are established in conformity with the democratic values of the political party in power. (Given my arguments in the preceding chapters, and the guiding principles for decision making, I would suggest that, in our current context, there is only one umbrella domain of appreciation – sustainable development). In this model, domain collaboration becomes an inter-organizational means to achieving a desired end that no single department can achieve by acting unilaterally (Wood and Gray 1991). As well, some policy domains may cut across some, but not necessarily all, sectoral departments, and participation will have to be negotiated on a domain by domain basis rather than in the free-for-all that now predictably degenerates into inter-departmental territorial battles. Shifting the focus from departments to domains opens up an inter-organizational policy space within which collaboration and greater effectiveness and efficiency are possible.

The current federal roles of doing, controlling, and monitoring are thus replaced by leadership and catalyzing dialogues through networks of

Figure 9.2

Transdisciplinary networks of collaboration

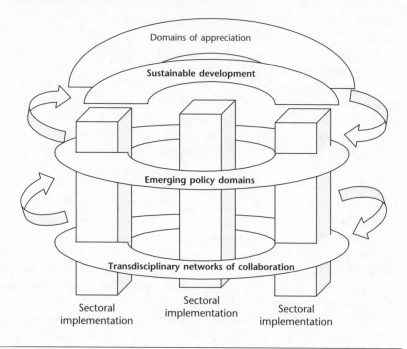

collaboration around clearly communicated policy domains. Collaboration is defined as "an interactive process having a shared transmutational purpose and characterized by explicit voluntary membership, joint decision-making, agreed-upon rules, and a temporary structure" (Roberts and Bradley, cited by Wood and Gray 1991: 143). In this way, these new networks challenge the power of traditional vested interests by making advice and information more transparent, diverse, and open to the enlarged, post-normal scientific and academic context outside government. Expertise is no longer limited to internal and external corridors of power and now reflects the plurality of knowledges and expertises throughout the country and beyond. This diversity of expertise creates enlarged and expanded space for enabling the exposure of dominant paradigms and meta-barriers, allowing for the creation of policy alternatives. It also exposes fundamental conflicts and leads to periods of sustained reflexivity around key strategic themes. Schutz and Weber (1967) defines reflexivity as the ability to periodically suspend our natural attitude and notice the taken-for-granted ways in which our communities of knowledge are constructed and interpreted. This can open novel possibilities for changing them. For only sustained

reflection can identify hidden paradoxes and dominant contextual para- ✳
digms and, thus, facilitate innovative and creative solutions that emerge
from the synergy generated by these transdiciplinary networks of collaboration. In this way, Ottawa policy making, often perceived by the provinces as
incestuous, insular, and isolated – a view which has contributed to the public's inability to identify with its government – is democratized and opened
up for improvement. Through collaborative negotiations, stakeholders can
be identified and can develop a common language; norms and values governing ongoing interaction can be established; authority, responsibility, and
resources can be allocated (Westley and Vredenburg 1996a); and exposure
to wider values and paradigms held by diverse stakeholders can be facilitated. This kind of lateral-flexible organizational form relies on peer-to-peer
relationships (as opposed to vertical hierarchies) in developing policy
advice from multiple communities of knowing, based on the concept of a
community of knowing as an open system (Boland and Tenkasi 1995).

The question of standing is also paramount to these new collaborations,
as are the criteria that determine who is and is not a stakeholder. Selection
of stakeholders must be rigorously defined for each process, and it must
be eminently defensible. And there are accountability issues. Because accountability is so diffused in the NGO community, and because industry
accountability pertains only to private shareholders, we must acknowledge
that elected governments have the greatest accountability to the public.
Without government participation, there is the possibility that collaborative groups will simply become a glorified, if somewhat more elevated,
form of consultation for governments or entrenched interests to use to add
weight to their own agendas.

A basic procedure for the conduct of any collaborative group is that, if
participants cannot agree upon who should be at the table, then the
process should be immediately stopped. Similarly, the parties should define
the sectors or areas to be represented at the beginning of the process, as
bargaining after the fact renders the entire process subject to lobbying
by vested interests. Participants may attempt to increase their stakes at the
table by artificially creating sectors in order to increase the number of seats
they have at the table. If the selection criteria for stakeholders are not
defensible, then the body is not duly constituted and, thus, is illegitimate.
Moreover, if these bodies do not reflect the voices not normally heard, then
they will not be responsive to current public demand. Canadians are not
demanding more of the same but, rather, greater representation in, and
legitimacy of, decision making.

These domains have to be loosely coupled, overlaying the vertical departments, thus allowing for the ongoing creative destruction and renewal
discussed in Chapters 4 and 7. Loose coupling suggests the idea of building blocks that can be grafted onto, or severed from, an organization with

relatively little disturbance to either the blocks or the organization itself (Weick 1976). The domain and the departments would thus be responsive to one another, yet each would preserve its own identity and some level of physical separateness. In this way, policy deliberations and expanded public dialogue would be separated from implementation, and departments would be responsible for implementing programs and regulations that are consistent with overall policy agendas determined by the political level through the advisory mechanisms of policy domains. What is available for coupling and decoupling within an organization, however, is an eminently political question, and this allows politicians to have greater leverage on the system. Under conditions of loose coupling, it is anticipated that considerable effort would be devoted to examining constructions of social reality, examining alternative paradigms and linguistic work, and exposing dominant myths and metaphors.

Applying the Model

Returning to the fisheries case study, let us now integrate the various components of the models, combining Figures 3.2, 7.3, 9.1, 9.2, and the guiding framework developed in Chapter 9, and examine whether enlarged decision-making and policy contexts would have made a difference. This case study illustrates a number of policy failures and structural impediments. First, there was strongly conflicting scientific advice concerning the size of the stocks and the reasons for their decline. Second, there were vertical stovepipes between the internal scientific advisors and the policy development process. Third, there were vertical silos and apparent differences between external fisheries scientists and department scientists. Fourth, scientific advice was, in some cases, presented in a language not easily understood by non-scientists. Fifth, the Cabinet decision-making process was opaque in two ways: (1) any advice that is given to Cabinet, both from its scientific and policy advisors, is regarded as confidential and thus is not subject to the Access to Information Act; (2) as the Cabinet decision-making process is not open, the trade-offs and issues involved in decision making are not available for more critical examination. Last, it would appear that regional disparities played a large role in these trade-offs, giving one Cabinet minister disproportionate influence over both the delivery of information to Cabinet and its final deliberations. If my proposed models were to be used, then the policy development process would be opened up to many more of the stakeholders in the Atlantic Canada cod fishery. Stakeholders are defined as agencies and citizens having a stake in the outcome of decisions – as people who are able to influence the key constituencies affected by the outcomes of the deliberations (Dale forthcoming). This clarification is necessary, I believe, because everyone can claim to have a "stake" in the environment; and since multistakeholder bodies are assumed to be convened in order to influence government decision making and/or policy deliberations, it follows that participants are at the table in order to bring various constituencies to bear on the issue(s) involved in the discussions. Another assumption is that, because multistakeholder processes involve dialogue, some conflict will be inevitable. This necessitates expert facilitation and the realization that consensus will not necessarily be reached in all cases; lack of consensus may be as informative as consensus.

In the case of fisheries policy development, key stakeholders would include the users of the resource, takers and managers of the resource, provincial and federal senior policy practitioners, individual fishers, the owners of fish-processing plants, fishing associations, well-known academic fisheries specialists (e.g., Ludwig, Hillbourne, and Walters, whose views differed strongly from those of the DFO), internal government scientific advisors, community activists, and environmental NGOs.

If the federal government had used the guiding framework developed in Chapter 8 (e.g., the limits, precautionary, resilience, and scale principles), it is highly unlikely it would have made the decisions it did. Adopting a systems approach, for example, may have eliminated some of the polarized scientific advice concerning whether the size of the stock was being primarily affected by a change in ocean temperatures or overfishing. Most likely, stock size would have been shown to be the result of both effects dynamically interacting in novel and unknown ways. In addition, the effects of scale would have been highlighted through the participation of single-hook-and-line fishers and owners of the factory freezer trawlers. This framework would certainly have prompted a discussion of values as well as the exposure of the dominant paradigmatic thinking underlying various positions. And it would have led to asking an extremely important question: is it more sustainable to employ individual hook-and-line fishers or to employ large-scale factory freezer trawlers? Could a sustainable fisheries accommodate both? Ironically, in light of the collapse of so many fishing communities, it now seems one of the most critical civil society questions we should have asked.

Of course, the composition of expertise at the table is of primary importance in exposing differences and allowing for consensus. The selection of experts who have both interdisciplinary and disciplinary expertise is critical for integrative modes of inquiry between the natural and social sciences. Exposing scientific differences may have led to more meaningful information being shared with political decision makers, either in terms of illuminating differences or reaching a consensus. Concentration on the size of the stock masked the underlying human over-exploitation, and this would have been exposed through my proposed dialogue.

One of the main barriers facing sustainable development is the fundamental lack of ecological literacy within the public service and, even more so, within the political community and the general public (Orr 1994). How information is presented and communicated to these groups is crucial. If participants cannot agree on a common information base, then the process must be stopped until this issue is reconciled, for power dynamics during the direction-setting phase largely involve efforts to control the negotiations and the flow of information (Gray 1989). It is crucial to recognize that there is no such thing as perfect or value-free information and that more information does not necessarily mean better information. These requirements must be identified at the beginning of the process, as must the best means of securing information. With this preliminary direction, specialists can be instructed to begin compiling common databases and alerting one another to information gaps, in order to allow stakeholders to decide how crucial these gaps are to their deliberations. Gaps are inevitable, however, because of the existing inadequacies in sustainable development information, and these collaborative networks must collectively decide whether or not they can proceed on the basis of the best available information. An additional benefit of these duly constituted networks is that, by including community stakeholders (particularly activists and environmental NGOs), scientific information can be directly communicated to non-scientific colleagues.

Multistakeholder bodies have the capacity to become a creative way to transform public institutions and facilitate shared decision-making. They can be a unique vehicle for clearly articulating stakeholder values and using them as the basis for creating an improved set of policy alternatives (Gregory and Keenery 1993). They will fail, however, if they serve only to legitimize existing hierarchical structures; if they become hostages to expertise, and if they are constrained to dispute resolution models. Their strength lies in building upon the stakeholders' current knowledge base and by bringing their different experiences, values and judgments together to identify in some cases, the trade-offs; in others, the policy solutions; in others, resolution of specific issues; and hopefully, in others, entirely new solutions that leap over existing paradigms.

(Dale forthcoming)

Consensus also plays an important part in these new processes. If a duly constituted transdisciplinary body reaches a consensus, then there is a stronger moral imperative for the government to consider its decisions, especially if government has been an active participant. Of equal importance, however, is what occurs when a transdisciplinary dialogue exposes areas where value conflicts are intractable. At times such as these, stakeholders have to recognize the legitimate right of the government to resort to more traditional decision making. Consensus is not always possible and, indeed, not all conflicts can or should be resolved through these bodies. Consensus may prove to be elusive in the near term, especially when existing information does not allow participants to meaningfully assess the ramifications of their decisions or to move beyond win-lose scenarios. The availability of information, and whether or not it is integrative, is crucial to these processes. Consensus can be built only if there is agreement on a shared information base that facilitates a common understanding.

One of the tragedies of the collapse of the Atlantic cod fishery is that the controversy was, in fact, being debated in academic fisheries journals. Unfortunately, these journals have very limited circulation. The fisheries debate would have reached the wider publics by making the debate transparent through transdisciplinary fora. Perhaps this would have exerted different pressures on the political decision makers, rather than leaving it subtly in the hands of the vested interests operating at that time. In addition, had my model been employed, it would have bridged the internal solitudes between policy development experts and their scientific advisors. In many departments, scientific advice is fed into the policy development process, and since this is also based on an internal advisory process, one never knows to what extent the advice is accepted or ignored; nor does one know the trade-offs made at the bureaucratic level, even before it reaches the Cabinet decision-making level. A key feature of these collaborative fora would be that, once their advice is given to Cabinet, it could then be made public. Thus Cabinet becomes more accountable for the trade-offs it makes and whether or not it chooses to ignore expert advice. As well, my model would limit the power of any one individual as a result of this greater transparency and accountability.

Networks of Civic Engagement
Dialogue – at the same time, in the same place, and with a continuity of stakeholders – leads to a deeper understanding of sustainable development issues than do traditional forms of expertise. The creation of an external transdisciplinary network of collaboration around sustainable fisheries would have acted as a counter-balance to the vested interests (i.e., the fish processing industry and its promotion of factory freezer trawlers) influencing Cabinet during the East Coast fisheries dispute.

In fact, in the long run, these networks of collaboration have the capacity to become networks of civic engagement, as they mirror the horizontal organization of social and political networks rather than current power-based hierarchies. A more appropriate role for governments in the twenty-first century may well be to support processes that increase social capital, as this will ultimately lead to a strengthening of both ecological and economic capital. In reality, the social capital embodied in norms and networks of civic engagement seems to be a precondition for economic development as well as for effective government (Cox 1995; Putnam 1993b). Furthermore, it may be hypothesized that the establishment of common ground will reduce disassociation and alienation. Current experience (outside the usual narrow range of social encounters) with regard to lack of common ground inhibits needed exploration and increases isolation (Emery and Trist 1972: 189). Wise policy can encourage social capital formation, and social capital itself enhances the effectiveness of government action. I propose going a step further and having governments actively lead the creation of networks of collaboration that stimulate greater civic engagement. For I believe that the effectiveness of government and, ultimately, the vibrancy of democratic systems of governance, are dependent upon the strength of civil society, which, in turn, is dependent upon creating communities of learning and knowledge through the establishment of transdisciplinary networks of collaboration.

How does social capital undergird good government and economic progress? First, networks of civic engagement foster sturdy norms of generalized reciprocity. Trust lubricates social life. Networks of civic engagement also facilitate coordination and communication and amplify information. When economic and political dealing is embedded in dense networks of social interaction, incentives for opportunism and malfeasance are reduced. Dense social ties facilitate gossip and other valuable ways of cultivating reputation – an essential foundation for trust in a complex society. And finally, they embody past success at collaboration, which can serve as a cultural template for future collaboration.

(Putnam 1996: 2-3)

10
Conclusions

If I stand back and look as objectively as I can at the earth, what
I see are populations made up predominantly of stressed,
malfunctioning humans against a backdrop of predominantly
stressed, malfunctioning ecosystems.

– S.B. Hill, in *Absolute Values and the*
Search for the Peace of Mankind

I have described how ecological, social, and economic capital is declining
globally, albeit at differing times, places, and space scales. The more the
three imperatives for sustainable development continue to diverge, the
more there appears to be an increasing convergence towards worldwide
human and natural systems collapse. Moreover, given the increasing co-
evolutionary nature of human and natural systems, this collapse will be
inevitable. The greater the divergence between these three imperatives,
therefore, the more rapid the decline.

The implementation of sustainable development is, consequently, one of
the most important human imperatives of the twenty-first century, requiring strong leadership by local, regional, and national governments. The
adoption of a reconciliation framework across governments is critical to
the ability to provide consistent and effective leadership to other sectors
of civil society, in order to diffuse sustainable development concepts and
practices, before we reach irreversible critical thresholds. Guiding frameworks based on the reconciliation of the three imperatives – ecological,
social, and economic – are critical if governments are to take a leading role
in implementing sustainable development. And governments are the most
logical convenors of the stakeholders who need to be at the table. As discussed throughout this book, the complexity of the issues demands deep
structural changes in the way we do business, the way we conduct our
day-to-day lives, and the way we make decisions. The only way that such
changes will occur, however, is through exposing the dominant paradigms,
values, and restraints that work together to support the existing powerful
movement for resistance on so many levels.

There are many alternative, as opposed to traditional, ideas circulating
within society (e.g., postmodernism, feminism, postnormal science, deep
ecology, participatory action research, bioregionalism, and systems theory)
that have yet to be included in mainstream agendas. These emergent
approaches and sustainable development paradigms provide important
new information about the ways in which our human activity systems

work; they also inform us about our understanding of the natural world and our interrelationships with it, with one another, and with other species. Although the current dominant socio-economic paradigms, metaphors, and myths act as powerful barriers to change, we must be aware that emergent schools of thought can become just as linear and reductionist as the former if they are not seen as transcendent. That is, they have the potential to become reductionist if they are regarded as the only truth, and if people believe their reality derives from the natural world. Emergent schools of thought are simply a new way of thinking about the real world and human relationships; essentially, they offer a paradigm shift with regard to how we deal with information and its circulation. The potential of these new ways of relating with the world will not be realized, however, if they do not challenge our fundamental beliefs and values and cause us to change our behaviour towards our world; our relationships with each other; and, most important, our relationships with other species.

What metaphors? Ones that map a fluid, amorphous, problematic, information-rich world of multiple myths such as: reciprocity, resilience, circularity, emergence, birthing, dying, development, balance, mirroring, ebb and flow, cultivation, seeding, harvesting, potential, fittingness, both/and, multiple causality, and multiple consequences ...

There are metaphoric potentials from the realm of ecology with its concepts of interdependence – you can't do just one thing – diversity, resilience, competition and collaboration, carrying capacity, vulnerability, cyclicity, continuity, and, again, time for development.

And embracing all these, are the learning-related metaphors: discovery, exploration, adventure, questing, knowledge, insight, new experience, risk, vulnerability, error, success.

(Michael 1993: 87-88)

These emergent paradigms are resisted for a wide variety of reasons at all levels: individual psychodynamics, socialization, disciplinary educational systems, and institutional gridlock. I have chosen to focus on the latter because the many stovepipes and silos within our institutions, along with the deep solitudes in our country, are major restraining forces against the implementation of sustainable development. These forces work together to produce an increasing decision-making gridlock, where, quite often, the lowest common denominator prevails because of the extensive trade-offs that are made in the hierarchical, dualistic, rational-expert decision-making model that currently operates in the federal bureaucracy.

Another powerful barrier to sustainable development is the fundamental lack of ecological literacy in governments, most particularly at the political level. Politicians work in an environmental context of urgency, denial of alternatives, and unreasonable deadlines; this, of course, militates against sustained reflexivity and opportunities for new learning are virtually non-existent. Thus the political decision-making level of government becomes even more dependent upon the quality of information it receives from its public service advisors as well as the many external sources hoping to exert their influence. Bureaucratic stovepipes, coupled with vested interests, have created a positive feedback loop for change that, at best, only marginally, if ever, disrupts the status quo (or extrapolations of it).

Future Research Agenda

Given the co-evolutionary relationship between human and natural systems, I have assumed that many of the same structures and processes necessary for sustaining natural systems are important analogues for sustaining human activity systems. Consequently, in order to begin writing about ecological imperatives, I had to learn (as would most Canadians) about ecological systems and how they function, albeit at a certain level of generality. Although I originally intended to look at characteristics of ecological systems that could link both human and natural systems, time constraints and the scope of the research kept this endeavour at a preliminary level. This is an important critical area for future research, however, as is learning how to communicate key ecological information to both the public service and political decision-making levels.

In evaluating local carrying capacity, we must consider large-scale impacts on other ecosystems as well as temporal effects (Dale et al. 1995). Many social systems have developed patterns that deviate significantly from the way ecological systems function. Such patterns have been able to persist, however, because we have compensated for these deviations by transferring costs to the future, to other locations, or to the buffer/sink capacity of the surrounding ecosphere. This can work only in a world in which the impacts of cultural/social subsystems are smaller than is the rate of ecosystem carrying capacity regeneration (or where the uncertain capacity of the future is forced to absorb added burdens from the past). My co-researchers and I assumed that human activity systems were most like the third circle in Figure 3.1. In other words, we are already approaching the critical threshold limits of the biosphere, and we have already borrowed extensively from the capital of future generations. Furthermore, there was unanimous agreement that there are critical limits to both biosphere functioning and to human carrying capacity. The capacity of human systems to apparently transcend time, place, and scale through globalization and the unlimited use of resources and technologies, although seeming to allow human systems to supersede ecosystem principles in the short term, results in the discounting of ecological services that are critical for all life.

Hopefully, human activity systems will be able to respond to sustainable development imperatives before too many more future options are foreclosed, particularly with respect to biological and cultural diversity. There are complex societal decisions to be taken concerning the relative scale and size of human activity systems in relation to natural systems – particularly since, in general, human carrying capacity can be increased only at the expense of other species (Dale et al. 1995). The degree of biodiversity in the natural world will be highly dependent upon our ability to nurture diversity within human activity systems. When diversity within human systems is valued and actively planned for, then, it is more likely that biodiversity will be maintained, and greater equity may well be an emergent property.

Diversity means variety. Diversity comes in many different forms, each of which is a relationship that fits precisely into every other relationship in the Universe and is constantly changing.

(Maser 1992: 11)

How to promote and maintain diversity (of space – mental, physical, cultural, and spiritual; of place – built and non-built; of organization – self and process, structure and function; and of scale – at the micro, meso, and macro levels) are crucial human questions. In addition, we have to ask the fundamental question: how much human carrying capacity are we prepared to support at the expense of other species? And what repercussions will this have for our own species over the long term? How much is enough (Durning 1992)?

Human carrying capacity, coupled with an awareness of the "limits" of the planet's carrying capacity, argues for a co-evolutionary system of managing human impacts on natural systems, based on respecting the critical linkages between their respective structures and processes, both positively and negatively. At a minimum, such a co-evolutionary framework must include the reconciliation of economic, ecological, and social imperatives within the context of sustainable development. It must also emphasize the importance of closed loop feedback systems, especially with regard to systems that are becoming increasingly open. And it implies a notion of "limits" that applies equally to both physical and human spheres. Perhaps rather than just being concerned with carrying capacity, we should also be concerned with "caring capacity," a relational understanding rather than an understanding derived only through reason and intellect.

This raises such complex social and ethical questions as: What are the characteristics of the co-evolutionary relationships between natural and human systems? What values are prerequisites for this co-evolution? What conditions facilitate its development? Are there ways to respond more proactively to negative feedback loops in our co-evolutionary relationships?

How do human systems determine their appropriate carrying capacity – locally, nationally, and globally? Is carrying capacity plastic, as some experts claim, as a result of human ingenuity and potential new technologies, or is it fixed? Other metalogue questions involve the nature and scale of the limits to the biosphere. Rather than relying upon adaptive management, which I see as a reactive response, we should proactively bring the best knowledges, experiences, and expertise to bear on these questions. And we should ask deeper questions, such as: What does it mean to be human? What do we really need as human beings? What kinds of civil societies do we really want to create? How can we manage our growing impacts on the biosphere, given our current projected population rates? Are there ways to introduce more congruence between the needs of human activity systems and the regeneration and maintenance of key ecological services?

These questions will not be asked, never mind addressed, unless governments change the nature of their relationship with and to the polity. Such change must take place through enlarged policy development processes and decision-making contexts based upon transdisciplinary and pluralistic networks of collaboration. Sustainable development issues are, by their very nature, expansive and unconstrainable within traditional boundaries; they push at the frontiers of our current knowledge and experience, and continually test society's values. The importance of regarding the rich diversity of knowledge (and not just scientific knowledge) as a public good is highlighted by these processes, which involve complex organizational, informational, power, and conflict issues. Deep down, they are based on psychological processes that underlie our ability to deal with complex issues, the resolution or non-resolution of which have ramifications not just in the present, but also for future generations as well. The means necessary to achieve the ends in many of these issues is simply not clear in our present context.

Transdisciplinary networks of collaboration have the capacity, I believe, to transform our public institutions and to facilitate more effective shared decision making, based on civil society dialogues. Such collaborative networks can be a unique vehicle for clearly articulating stakeholder values and using them as the basis for creating an improved set of policy alternatives. They will fail, however, if they serve only to legitimize existing hierarchical structures. They will also fail if they become hostages to expertise and are limited to dispute resolution techniques. Their strength lies in building upon the stakeholders' current knowledge base by enabling them to bring their different experiences, values, and judgments together to identify, in some cases, the areas of disagreement and trade-offs; in others, the agreed policy solutions; and in others, the resolution of specific issues. Perhaps these fora can even lead to the creation of entirely new approaches to sustainable development that leap over existing paradigms. And by making them semi-permanent, a new "politics" of sustainable development may emerge.

Ultimately, however, these transdisciplinary collaborative networks will fail if stakeholders cannot put aside their disciplinary perspectives, dominant paradigms, and current operational contexts. This means that, in the long run, in order to achieve a fundamental reconciliation of the ecological, social, and economic imperatives, the personal imperative also has to be recognized as an integral part of public life – for the personal is, indeed, political. In the long term, the health of civil societies everywhere depends upon the reconciliation of the ecological, social, and personal imperatives and increased dialogue.

We know enough to act now (Dale and Hill 1995), and yet it is not enough simply to change the structure of organizations and institutions; we must involve Canadian civil society. It is clear that, virtually without exception, the more civic the context, the better the government (Putnam 1993a). And strong civic societies may be more dependent upon the rationality of human processes through communicative and discursive dialogues than on the rationality of thought. Change, however, does not simply begin with the individual and spread to institutions in a linear fashion; rather, change results from complex feedbacks and iterations between individuals and institutions (Dale et al. 1997).

Although this story has been framed in terms of the ecological, social, and economic imperatives, in the long run it is the personal rather than the economic imperative that most demands our attention. The personal imperative involves personal reconciliation on many levels – individual, professional, and relational. I assumed it would be naive, however, to deny the dominance of the current socio-economic paradigm; I recognize that we need a transition strategy before moving to a framework based on this more fundamental integration.

It may be deterministic to predict what, ultimately, redesigned governance will look like, given that sustainable development is constantly evolving. Consequently, Figure 9.2 represents a transition phase. In the long run, a totally new structure would emerge within government that transcends its current vertical and sectoral departments. We may, in the future, be looking at a population of collaborations within a problem domain – some grassroots, some vision-led, and some government-mandated – and a consequent dismantling of our current adversarial federal-provincial system. Given the complexity of the particular problem domain being discussed, it may well be that government-mandated collaborations are the first step towards identifying common solutions, followed by vision-led and grassroots initiatives for implementation and subsequent follow-up. In other contexts, it may well be that a government-mandated collaboration may be the last in a cascade of deliberations. The current departmental form of government organization may well become completely deconstructed and reconfigured in new ways as a result of these collaborative networks.

Don't forget that effective movements for change are built by ordinary people who perceive themselves to be in "do-or-die" situations. Sustainable development may be one of the paths to survival – certainly the concepts are a crucial part of what we are all working towards – but to make it really come alive as an active force in the world we need to marry the academic frameworks to a plan of action, and the actions need to include every one of us.

(Geuer, Electronic Dialogue, 17 January 1998)

Another crucial question will concern the meaning of the personal imperative for civil society. How can the personal imperative be realized individually and collectively, both locally and globally? Perhaps the root of dualism is the apparent separation of the emotional sphere from the professional sphere, and the separation of our autonomous self from our adapted self (i.e., the self that emerges through continuous compromises, both professionally and socially) (Gruen 1986; Hill 1998). In our adapted states, we cannot recognize alternative responses other than through further adaptation to an increasingly unsustainable world. And emphasis on continual adaptation denies any responsibility on our part for changing the unsustainable forces in our current decision-making system. Just as the frog slowly boils to death when we slowly increase the temperature of the pot, so, too, we slowly adapt to the positive feedback loops between human and natural systems. Just as we unwisely introduce unsustainable feedback loops, so we can design for negative feedback loops that will demand a much higher awareness of the structures, processes, and functioning of ecological systems and the co-evolutionary nature of human and natural systems. How we communicate this knowledge to key decision makers whose ecological understanding is, at best, minimal, is a crucial question.

As well, the incorporation of different perspectives on "relationality," on love and compassion (particularly in professional milieus), may be a necessary precondition of sustainable development. Greater human progress may well follow from the integration of the intellect and the heart, leading to expanded notions of the value of life. If we had included all living beings within our value system, then a nine-month-old golden retriever puppy would not have died while twenty people watched, because property rights take primacy in human activity systems that are based on dominance and power and valuing human sentiency over that of other living beings.

11
Reflections

In the Introduction, I wrote about the loss of one of my most loved animal companions, Odessa Mamut, when I began to write this book. This was my first experience, as an adult, with prematurely losing someone I loved, and his death was particularly traumatic because of his suffering. Many people did not understand the nature and depth of my grieving for "just an animal," and I realized how ironic it was that my values about other beings, in fact, actually deepened and made the process of grieving far more painful.

Bereavement is one of the most humbling of experiences, something over which there is very little control. For grief has a rhythm and pathway that is different for every individual. If one does try to control emotions associated with loss and pain, they simply manifest themselves in numerous other ways: through physical illness and, eventually, if persistently blocked, emotional breakdowns and the destruction of relationships. For example, 90 percent of marriages break up over the loss of a child (Sanders 1992). Consequently, the very things that made me a good manager – the ability to control and predict, to lead when others were stressed – made me poorly prepared for accepting the free-flowing processes of grief. Even while writing about and accepting the chaos and randomness of ecological systems,

---

We went through the entire emotional sequence – grief, loneliness, reluctant responsibility – when we worked on the Club of Rome project twenty years ago. Many other people, through many other kinds of formative events, have gone through a similar sequence. It can be survived. It can even open up new horizons and suggest exciting futures. Those futures will never come to be, however, until the world as a whole turns to face them. The idea of limits, sustainability, sufficiency, equity, and efficiency are not barriers, not obstacles, not threats. They are guides to a new world.

(Meadows et al. 1972: xvii)

---

for example, I still believed that most parts of my life could be "controlled" and "managed." Previously, there had been a logical progression in both my personal and professional lives, and this lulled me into believing that "being" had a very logical continuity, that it contained no surprises, and that one could manage unexpected events by turning challenges into opportunities. The only people close to me who had died had all been in their eighties. Sudden and premature loss changed all that. It is horrifying how quickly life can change with one phone call. I became keenly aware of how good my former life had been, only now that it was irrevocably gone, almost in an instant.

Since beginning to write this story I have lost three other animal companions, and I thought that I had turned a new page. Many told me that there was a purpose to all this – something I strongly rejected, as why would I deserve any more "purpose" in my life than anyone else? This kind of statement seemed to speak of fire and brimstone, of punishment. I did not believe there was any particular reason why I should be singled out for more purpose than those around me. Unfortunately, the worst of times was yet to come.

On 10 May 1998 my beloved only child, Danny James Frazer, died. He was one of the most gentle, kind, and decent men I have known, and I am very privileged to be his mother. He had such wonderful integrity, to which I can now add a remarkable courage in trying to maintain it. Some people, when they are on earth, occupy only the space of a tree; but when they leave they leave the space of a forest. My beloved Danny was such a person. All of us who loved him are now trying to learn how to live at the edge of a forest. Just as your values determine the depth of your grief, the quality of the person you lose determines the depth of your loss. Paradoxically, I sometimes wish my son had not been so special, so gentle and kind. However, just as in nature, where some of the richest changes occur at the edges of ecosystems, so too, at the edge of the forest, I have an opportunity for the kind of creative reconstruction that can occur only if destruction is faced head on.

To lose a child is, I believe, one of life's greatest tragedies because it is so unnatural, and to lose an only child is to enter an abyss. In addition to the profound loss of the person, I feel I have lost my future, my grandchildren that will never be, my continuity, and parts of my identity. A terrible, singular void opens up. It is quite simply a primordial loss. I have been able to finish this book only because I know it is what Danny would have expected, and, in so doing, I try my best to honour him in death, as well as life.

Paradoxically, I now know more about the meaning and value of relationships through my experience with dying than through my experience with living – now that I no longer have those special beings I loved so much with me to share that wisdom. I don't regret the meals I didn't cook, the house I didn't clean; but I do regret the times I wasn't there for hugs and simply for taking long walks in the bush. For is not life simply relationships, love, compassion, and dynamic connectedness (Jantsch 1980)? And the meaning of "purpose" has emerged. Terrible events do not happen for a purpose, the purpose comes from how you take those events and live with them. For me, the purpose of Odessa Mamut's death was to teach me how to hold a dead body for the first time, without being afraid, and how to say goodbye. Without this prior learning, I would never have had the ability to say the graceful goodbyes to my beloved son, which I did on the morning of 10 May 1998, nor would I be here today writing these reflections.

In these last years, I have learned so much, for death holds a mirror up to everyone's soul, if only for a brief moment. For me, it feels as though the moment will last forever and ever. Many, quite naturally, are afraid of being in the space I now occupy. We live in a culture in which there is a massive denial of death and our own mortality. Most do not know what to say, and many say nothing. Many, because of fear, have tried to deny me the space to talk about my beloved son, and this becomes a double loss – first his death and then a denial of his entire existence. Many others have embraced me and wept with me. Many people have rushed, in great love, to try and fill the abyss. But just as Daly (1990) claims, there are no substitutes between natural or human capital, so there are no substitutes for the person you have lost. The missing future cannot be replaced; it is all so irreplaceable. Attempting to fill the abyss is another form of denial; and the failure to face the reality of a terrible loss has a great price. Just as many rush to fill the void in the paradox between sustainable and development, and by doing so merely tinker at the edges and maintain the status quo.

So people are at a loss as to what to do, how to help, how to comfort. If we valued becoming, rather than always focusing on being (Williamson and Pearse 1980)(or, better still, on both), then knowing what to do in the moment would not be so difficult. My sister remarked that all the wrong people are reading the books on grief, that it is the people who are not grieving who should be reading them. Perhaps the same thing is true for sustainable development: the wrong people are reading the information, and we are writing for and reaching the already converted.

Part of the grieving process is mourning the part of you that was lost along with the person you lost. I have entered a process of fundamental deconstruction, for my former life is gone forever. This deconstruction, however, will not take place unless there are "safe places" in which to express my grief, places that allow the process to unfold and a new self to emerge. The process is neither linear nor short-term, often awakens other losses, and often involves other interrelationships as well as being linked to the relationship and depth of attachment with the deceased. It appears that only by facing the wasteland of grief can creative reconstruction occur. Unfortunately, North American society allows very little space for living in this wasteland.

My lens has been changed forever, and only I can determine its new shape, if I can accept the risks of the free-fall of the abyss. I now live so keenly in the present that, for the moment, the past and the future have dropped away. Small things and details assume great importance: the ability to "manage" life's day-to-day trivia is reframed in the moment.

Presence is a moment when all ranges are present, or when we are experiencing the wholeness of the spectrum rather than the characteristics of just one of the ranges. It is a moment – a condition – when the totality of our existence synergizes and blends with our world, expanding the ranges of the reality we inhabit as well. And it does so through attunement, through weaving itself gracefully into our world.

(Spangler 1996: 77)

In spite of this "rawness," in most organizations one is allowed only four days of bereavement leave. For me, this reveals the massive denial of death and the ignorance and denial of grief that is so much a part of our culture. It reflects a deeply rooted structural psychopathology in support of the rational, expert model. It assumes that if you take a little time, then your normal self will return. How does one accommodate the loss of a loved one – a mother, a father, or a child – in just four days?

There are deep gender differences as well. I have been allowed much more "emotional space" than has Danny's stepfather; however, overall, we have both been expected to get over it in about two months. How does one answer the routine question, "How are you?" There is no way to answer that question, for I can no longer say, "Fine, thank you," as I used to (even when I felt unwell). No one, unless they have experienced loss of this magnitude, has any idea of the depths of despair, nor are we encouraged to communicate that despair, except nominally at the beginning of our mourning. Unless someone has experienced loss, they do not know the costs of simply existing every day. No one talks about the shock, the terrible separation anxiety, or the deep hopelessness. In spite of all our education, we know so very little about the meaning of life and death or its essential processes. And we fear them.

People's reactions to fear differ widely. Some respond with infinite compassion, some are quick to blame, to judge. Blaming and judging are often learned ways of coping, of distancing ourselves from pain. If one accepts that psychic pain is as painful, and perhaps even more painful, than physical pain, then what right do we have to judge those who choose to end their pain? Because we cannot directly see psychic pain, just as we cannot see many environmental problems, we tend to base our decisions on incomplete knowledge, inaccurate information, and fear of the unknown.

The one thing that's true of all exceptional patients is that they are people who have become authentic. They do not reach the point of death only to find that they've never really lived. Sometimes they only "really live" for a few moments before they die. But they have lived and they are ready to go, as their choice. They know who they are, where they've been and why. This makes it easier for them to let go, and for their loved ones to let them go when they are tired and sore.

(Siegel 1990: 246)

Death can help us face our own mortality and the meaning of life and death – if one seizes the moment. For a moment, one's values become so clear and immediately focused. Many people have told me that Danny's death helped them to re-examine their priorities. In some ways I am glad that he continues to live in some way by playing a role in other people's lives. But some days it is little comfort, for I will never hear him say "Mum" again. For those who have deeply loved and lost, it is such a solitary journey. People rush to try to make others feel better, to fill the void, but there is nothing to be done but to face it. There is no running away, just as there will be no running away when we reach the limits of the biosphere.

The language around death manifests our denial of one of life's essential processes. A particularly painful comment is, "You'll get over it." One quickly learns that there is no getting over it; rather, one learns how to live with it by accepting and developing a new pair of spectacles. What would my framework be like now if I had been taught, from a young age, different realities about death – its inevitability, its naturalness. What if, in particular, I had been taught that the death of the parts is necessary for the life of the whole, that perhaps there is an extended space-time continuum (Jantsch 1980). More important, if I had learned, as a young child, that I have control only over myself, how different would my relationships have been? How different would our relationship with the world be if ecological literacy were valued as deeply as written literacy?

As previously discussed, human activity systems cling stubbornly to continuous cycles of exploitation and conservation, allowing only a little release when external pressures become too great and seldom, if ever, engaging in deep renewal. If we saw death as a natural release, as creative destruction, and if we saw grief as an integral part of that destruction, then we would open up new spaces for renewal. By denying death and grief, we deny renewal (Westley, personal communication, 17 August 1998). Similarly, if we provide analytical space for policy alternatives, differing paradigms, and a plurality of values, then greater possibilities for institutional renewal would be opened, corresponding to current realities rather than remaining alienated and contributing to greater social fragmentation and divisiveness.

One of the main barriers to meaningful change in our current ways of being involves the fact that we are living in massive denial of the ecological information that surrounds us. I believe this involves complex issues of unresolved grief, for what we do to the earth, we do to ourselves.

We must, indeed, recognize 3 types of potential limits: the "outer limits," essentially of a material character, such as are considered in the Meadows' report, the "inner limits," which are those of the social system, and the "innermost limits," which reside within the human individual.

(Postel 1987: 9)

If we accept that there are limits to the biosphere, then we also have to accept that there are limits to ourselves, for we are, indeed, mortal. We live in massive denial of this: the health profession, for example, regards death as a mortal enemy – as something to be avoided, or at least postponed, at all costs. Perhaps if death were not closeted away and seen as an integral part of life, then it would allow for more creative destruction and renewal at all levels of the individual, psychic, emotional, mental, and spiritual collective.

Evolutionary leaps in self-organization, new forms of relationality and knowledges, seem often to occur during periods of extreme physical or emotional pain, grief, trauma, and death. The paradox is that acute clarity (Baeker 1997), vision, and vitality appear to occur during moments around life and death, joy and pain. Sustained reflection upon these moments of extreme clarity at the core of the paradox (Lister 1997), and at the heart of the void, may allow for the emergence of meaningful change. Change, however, involves giving up something; therefore, there is a process of mourning involved in accepting change (Day 1997). It is not easy to live in a void, but to deny the void is to deny personal development and, possibly, long-term survival – both individually and collectively.

When my son Danny was a little boy, and again especially over the last two years, when he was ill, I remember that, when coming home at night, I used to wish upon the brightest star: "Starlight, star bright, may I have the wish I wish tonight. May my lad be safe tonight." When I said my final goodbyes, I kissed his eyes, his nose, and his mouth, as I did when he was a little boy, and I asked him, if he could, to shine more brightly once in a while from the sky. I have, on occasion, seen a single star shining with great clarity and brilliance, just as Danny lived his life on this earth.

May he be running on the other side of the Rainbow Bridge
with our faithful companions, Odessa Mamut and Odessa Kara.
See you at the bridge, my beloved Danny.

Glossary

Allogenic succession: Succession resulting from changes in the external environment (usually geophysico-chemical) (www.biology.ualberta.ca/bio208.hp/).

Autogenic succession: Succession resulting from biological processes, including modification of the environment (www.biology.ualberta.ca/bio208.hp/).

Biodiversity: This refers to the totality of genes, species, and ecosystems within a region. The wealth of life on earth today is the product of hundreds of millions of years of evolutionary history. Over the course of time, human cultures have emerged and adapted to local environments, discovering, using, and altering their biotic resources. Many areas that now seem "natural" bear the marks of millennia of human habitation, crop cultivation, resource harvesting, and waste production. The domestication and breeding of local varieties of crops and livestock have further shaped biodiversity. For convenience, biodiversity can be divided into three hierarchical categories: genes, species, and ecosystems. These describe quite different aspects of living systems, and scientists measure them in different ways.

Genetic diversity refers to the variation of genes within species. There may be distinct populations of the same species (e.g., in India there are thousands of varieties of rice), and there may be genetic variation within a single population (e.g., it is very high among Indian rhinos and very low among cheetahs). Until recently, measurements of genetic diversity were applied mainly to domesticated species and populations held in zoos and botanical gardens; however, increasingly, these techniques are also being applied to wild species.

Species diversity refers to the variety of species within a region. Such diversity can be measured in many ways, and scientists have not yet settled on the best methods for doing so. The number of species in a region – its species "richness" – is one often used measure, but a more precise measurement, "taxonomic diversity," also considers the relationship of species to one another. An island with two species of birds and one species of lizard, for example, has greater taxonomic diversity than does an island with three species of birds and no lizards.

Ecosystem diversity is harder to measure than either species or genetic diversity because the "boundaries" of communities and of ecosystems are elusive. Nevertheless, as long as a consistent set of criteria is used to define communities and ecosystems, then their number and distribution can be measured. Until now, such schemes have been applied mainly at national and subnational levels, although some coarse global classifications have been proposed.

Many other expressions of biodiversity are also important. These include the relative abundance of species; the age structure of populations; the pattern of communities within a region; changes in community composition and structure over time; and ecological processes such as predation, parasitism, and mutualism. To meet specific management and policy goals, it is crucial to examine not only compositional diversity – genes, species, and ecosystems – but also diversity in ecosystem structure and function.

Human cultural diversity may be considered part of biodiversity. Like genetic and species diversity, some attributes of human cultures, such as nomadism and shifting cultivation, represent "solutions" to the problems of survival within particular environments. Like other aspects of biodiversity, cultural diversity helps people adapt to changing conditions. It is evident within language, religious beliefs, land management practices, art, music, social structure, crop selection, diet, human relationships, and numerous other aspects of human society (modified from the Global Biodiversity Strategy [World Resources Institute et al. 1992]).

Composition and levels of biodiversity (UNEP 1995)

Ecological diversity		Organismal diversity
biomes		kingdoms
bioregions		phyla
landscapes		families
ecosystems		genera
habitats		species
niches	**Genetic diversity**	subspecies
populations	populations	populations
	individuals	individuals
	chromosomes	
	genes	
	nucleotides	

Cultural diversity: This refers to human interactions at all levels (see **Biodiversity**).

Biomass: The weight of organisms (producers, consumers, decomposers) present at any one time is conveniently termed biomass (i.e., living weight), or standing crop. The size of a standing crop is not necessarily indicative of the level of activity; some ecosystems, such as a forest of large trees, have a large amount of relatively inert biomass (Odum 1975).

Biophysical carrying capacity: This refers to the maximum population size that an area can sustain under given technological capabilities (Daily and Ehrlich 1996a).

Biosphere: This refers to all of the earth's ecosystems as they function together on a global scale. We can also think of the biosphere as being that portion of the earth in which ecosystems can operate; that is, the biologically inhabited soil, air, and water. The biosphere merges imperceptibly into the lithosphere (the rocks, sediments, mantle, and core of the earth), the hydrosphere, and the atmosphere – the other major subdivisions of our earth spaceship.

Finally, it should be emphasized that, as with any spectrum, the levels-of-organization hierarchy is a continuous one; divisions are arbitrary and set for convenience and ease of communications (Odum 1975).

Carrying capacity: This is the population level for long-range survival (Odum 1971). Two levels are typically recognized: (1) the maximum, or subsistence, level (i.e., the maximum level for human existence) and (2) the optimum, or "safe," level (i.e., the level at which individuals are secure in terms of food, resistance to predators, and periodic fluctuations in the resource base) (Odum 1989). Since humans can vary widely in their impact on life-supporting resources, social scientists add a second dimension – intensity of use – to their concept of carrying capacity. Catton (1993) defines carrying capacity as the volume and intensity of use that can be sustained without degrading the environment's future suitability for that use.

Ecologists define carrying capacity as the population of a given species that can be supported indefinitely in a defined habitat without permanently damaging the ecosystem upon which it is dependent. However, because of our culturally variable technology, different consumption patterns, and trade, a simple territorially bounded head count cannot apply to human beings. Human carrying capacity must be interpreted as the maximum rate of resource consumption and waste discharge that can be sustained indefinitely without progressively impairing the functional integrity and productivity of relevant ecosystems (wherever the latter may be). The corresponding human population is a function of per capita rates of material consumption and waste output, or net productivity divided by per capita demand (Rees 1991). This formulation is a simple restatement of Hardin's Third Law of Human Ecology: total human impact on the ecosphere = population x per capita impact (Wackernagel and Rees 1996). Early versions of this law date from Ehrlich and Holdren, who also recognized that human impact is a product of population, affluence (consumption), and technology I = PAT (Holdren and Ehrlich 1974).

Civil society: This refers to the associations within which we conduct our lives. These associations owe their existence to our needs and initiatives rather than to the state (Dahrendorf 1995: 23).

Co-evolution: This involves reciprocal natural selection between two or more groups of organisms that have close ecological relationships but that do not interbreed. Ehrlich and Raven (1965), who first proposed the term, used their studies of butterfly caterpillars and plants as a basis for proposing the following hypothesis. Plants, through occasional mutations and gene recombination, produce chemical compounds, perhaps as waste products, which are not harmful to the plant but that turn out to be poisonous to insect herbivores such as caterpillars. Such a plant, now protected from the herbivore, would thrive and would pass on the favourable mutation to successive generations. Insects, however, are quite capable of evolving strains tolerant to poisons, as is dramatically shown by the increasing number of insects that have become immune to insecticides. If a mutant or recombinant appeared in the insect population and allowed individuals to feed on the previously protected plant, then selection would favour that genetic line. In other words, the plant and the herbivore evolve together because the evolution of the one depends on the evolution of the other. Pimentel (1968) has used the expression "genetic feedback" to refer to this kind of evolution (which he demonstrated with flies and wasps). Norgaard (1994) believes that genetic feedback should be taken into account when discussing issues related to sustainable development.

Ecology: This is the study of the earth's "households," including the plants, animals, micro-organisms, and people that live together as interdependent components. Because ecology is concerned not only with organisms, but also with energy flows and material cycles on the lands, in the oceans, in the air, and in fresh water, ecology can be viewed as the study of the structure and function of nature: it is understood that humankind is a part of nature (Odum 1975).

In ecology, the term "population," originally coined to denote a group of people, is broadened to include groups of individuals belonging to any kind of organism. Likewise, in the ecological sense, "community" (or "biotic community") includes all of the populations of a given area. The community and the non-living environment function together as an ecological system, or **ecosystem** (ibid.).

Ecosystem: This is a collection of interacting biological entities combined with the physical environment in which they live. This system is perceived to act as a whole (Woodley et al. 1993). The ecosystem is considered to be a unit of biological organization made up of all of the organisms in a given area (i.e., the "community") interacting with the physical environment so that a flow of energy results in a characteristic trophic structure and material cycles within the system (Odum 1975).

An important consequence of hierarchical organization is that, as components, or subsets, are combined to produce larger functional wholes, new properties emerge that were not present, or not evident, at the level below. Accordingly, an **emergent property** is one that results from the functional interaction of the components and, therefore, cannot be predicted from the study of the components apart from the whole unit.

It is convenient to recognize the ecosystem as being comprised of four constituents: (1) abiotic substances and conditions of existence – basic elements, compounds, and climatic regimes; (2) producers – autotrophic organisms, largely green plants; (3) macroconsumers – heterotrophic organisms, chiefly animals, that ingest other organisms or particulate organic matter; and (4) decomposers, or microconsumers – heterotrophic organisms, chiefly the bacteria and fungi that break down the complex compounds of dead protoplasm, absorb some of the decomposed products, and release simple mineral nutrients (usable by producers) as well as organic components that may provide food or that may be either stimulatory (e.g., vitamins) or inhibitory (e.g., antibiotics) (Odum 1975).

It is also convenient to subdivide the non-living, or abiotic, portion of an ecosystem into three components: (1) inorganic substances – the carbon, nitrogen, water, and so on that are involved in the material cycles of the ecosystem; (2) organic substances – the carbohydrates, proteins, lipids, humic substances, and so on that link the abiotic and the biotic; and (3) the climate regime – temperature and other physical factors that delimit the conditions of existence.

When considered from the ecosystem point of view, a lake, a forest, or other recognizable unit of the landscape has two biotic components: (1) an autotrophic component (autotrophic = "self-nourishing") that is able to fix light energy and manufacture food from simple inorganic substances, and (2) a heterotrophic component (heterotrophic = "other-nourishing") that utilizes, rearranges, and decomposes the complex materials synthesized by the autotrophs. These functional components are arranged in overlapping layers, with the greatest autotrophic metabolism occurring in the upper "green belt" (where light energy is available) and the most intense heterotrophic activity taking place in the lower "brown belt" (where organic matter accumulates in the soils and sediments) (Odum 1975).

The diversity of species tends to increase with succession. Maximum diversity of autotrophs in many ecosystems seems to be reached earlier in succession. A decrease in net community production and a corresponding increase in community respiration are two of the most striking and important trends in succession (ibid.).

Ecosystem integrity: This encompasses three major organizational facets: (1) the ability to maintain normal operations under normal environmental conditions, (2) resilience to changes (which can be catastrophic) in environmental conditions, and (3) the ability to engage in an ongoing process of self-organization.

Ecosystem services: These are the conditions and processes through which natural ecosystems, and the species of which they are comprised, sustain and help to fulfill human life. They maintain biodiversity and the production of such ecosystems goods as seafood, forage, timber, biomass fuels, and natural fiber as well as many pharmaceuticals, industrial products, and their precursors. The harvest and trade of these goods represent an important and familiar part of the human economy. In addition to the production of goods, ecosystem services are the actual life-support functions, such as cleansing, recycling, and renewal, and they confer many intangible aesthetic and cultural benefits (Daily 1997).

Emergent properties: These are properties of higher levels in the system that are not obvious from the properties of the parts. In fact, a clear view of the parts may preclude observation of the emergent property (Allen and Starr 1982).

Governance: This is a social function crucial to the viability of all human societies. It centres on the management of complex interdependencies among many different actors – individuals, corporations, interest groups, nation states – all of whom are involved in interactive decision making regarding issues that affect everyone's welfare (Young and von Moltke 1993).

Government: This refers to the acts, rules, procedures, instruments of power, and institutions by which the citizens of a country (or, more generally, the parts of any given system) communicate with and exert control upon each other so that the country as a whole maintains its unity and is directed towards specified ends.

Population: This refers to the organizing group of a particular species within a defined area. In practice, a population is simply all of the organisms of a particular species found occupying a given space. A population, as with any level of organization, has a number of important group properties not shared by adjacent levels (e.g., on the one hand is the organism, on the one other is the community). The most important of these population characteristics, or group attributes, are as follows:

Age distribution – the proportion of individuals of different ages in the group.

Birth rate, or, more broadly, natality (the latter includes organisms that arise from seeds, spores, eggs, and so on) – the rate at which new individuals are added to the population by reproduction.

Death rate, or mortality – the rate at which individuals are lost by death.

Density – population size in relation to a unit of space.

Dispersal – the rate at which individuals immigrate into the population and emigrate out of the population.

Dispersion – the way in which individuals are distributed in space, generally in one or more of the following three broad patterns: (1) random distribution, in which the probability of an individual occurring in any one spot is the same as the probability of it occurring at any other spot; (2) uniform distribution, in which components are more regular than random (e.g., corn in a cornfield); or (3) clumped distribution, in which individuals or other components are more irregular than random (e.g., a clump of plants arising from vegetative reproduction, a flock of birds, or people in a city).

Genetic characteristics – especially applicable to population ecology (e.g., adaptiveness, reproductive [Darwinian] fitness, and persistence [i.e., probability of leaving descendants over long periods of time]) (Odum 1975).

Population growth rate, or growth form – the net result of natality, mortality, and dispersal.

Primary production, or primary productivity: These are terms for the amount of organic matter fixed (i.e., converted from solar energy) by autotrophs in a given area over a given period of time, generally expressed as a rate (e.g., so much per day or year). Gross primary production is the amount stored in a plant for its own needs, while net primary production is the amount stored in a plant that is in excess of its respiratory needs and, therefore, is potentially available to heterotrophs. Net community production refers to the amount left after the biotic community, the autotrophs and heterotrophs, have taken all the food they need (Odum 1989).

Resilience: This refers to the ability of a system to maintain its structure and patterns of behaviour in the face of disturbance. Size of the stability domain of residence, strength of the repulsive forces at the boundary, and resistance of the domain to contraction are all distinct measures of resilience (Holling 1984).

Robust: This refers to a state in which the keystone structuring set of processes contain so much functional diversity and spatial heterogeneity that their regulatory role is able to maintain its integrity in the face of great changes in populations and/or in physical variables (Holling 1993).

Social capital: This refers to the shared knowledge, understandings, and patterns of interaction that people bring to any productive activity (Coleman 1988; Putnam 1993b). It also refers to the organizations, structures, and social relations that people build up independently of the state or large corporations (Roseland 1999). It contributes to a stronger community fabric and, often as a by-product of other activities, builds bonds of information, trust, and interpersonal solidarity (Coleman 1990). It also encompasses such features of social organization as networks, norms, and trust – features that increase a society's productive potential (Putnam 1993b).

Social carrying capacity: This refers to the maximum human population size that an area can sustain under a given social system, with particular reference to associated patterns of resource consumption (Daily and Ehrlich 1996b). The word "system" is used in its primary dictionary sense: a regularly interacting or interdependent group of items forming a unified whole (Odum 1975). Systems are groups of interacting, interdependent parts linked together by exchanges of energy, matter, and information. Complex systems are characterized by strong (usually non-linear) interactions between the parts; complex feedback loops that make it difficult to distinguish cause from effect; and significant time and space lags, discontinuities, thresholds, and limits (Costanza et al. 1973).

Stability: This concerns the propensity of a system to attain or retain equilibrium (i.e., a condition of steady state or stable oscillation). Highly stable systems resist departing from this condition and, if forced away from it, rapidly return to it with the least fluctuation. This is a classic equilibrium-centred definition (Holling 1984).

Succession: This refers to the way in which, after a disturbance, complexes of plants develop sequentially over time. Clements (1916) emphasized that succession led to a climax community consisting of a self-replicating assemblage of plants. The species of which that assembly is comprised are determined by basic climatic conditions – precipitation and temperature. Plant colonization and growth were seen as proceeding in a sequence leading to a stable climax. Initial colonization was carried out by pioneer species that could grow rapidly and withstand extremes of physical conditions. They so ameliorated those conditions as to allow the entry of less robust but more competitive species. Those species, in turn, inhibited the pioneers but set the stage for their own replacement by still more effective competitors. Throughout this process, biomass accumulates; regulation of biological, physical, and chemical processes becomes tighter; and variability is reduced until the stable climax condition is reached and maintained.

Succession (or ecosystem development) may be defined in terms of the following three parameters: (1) it is the orderly process of community changes that are directional and, therefore, predictable; (2) it is the result of community modifications of the physical environment and population structure; (3) and it culminates in the establishment of as stable an ecosystem as is biologically possible on the site in question. It is important to emphasize that this kind of ecological change is community controlled; each set of organisms changes the physical substrate and the microclimate (local conditions of temperature, light, and so on), and species composition and diversity is altered as a result of competitive (and other) population interactions (Odum 1975).

Systems perspectives (definitions taken from Principia Cybernetica Web http://www. pespmc1.vub.ac.be/SYSTHEOR.html):

System: 1) A set of variables selected by an observer (Ashby 1960). Usually three distinctions are made: 1. An observed object. 2. A perception of an observed object. This will be different for different observers. 3. A model or representation of a perceived object. A single observer can construct more than one model or representation of a single object. Some people assume that 1. and 2. are the same. This assumption can lead to difficulties in communication. Usually the term "system" is used to refer to either 1. or 2. "Model" usually refers to 3. Ashby used the terms machine, system, and model in that order for the three distinctions. 2) A set or arrangement of entities so related or connected so as to form a unity or organic whole. 3) Any definable set of components (Maturana and Varela 1987).

Systems theory: The transdisciplinary study of the abstract organization of phenomena, independent of their substance, type, or spatial or temporal scale of existence. It investigates both the principles common to all complex entities, and the models which can be used to describe them.

Systems theory was proposed in the 1940s by Ludwig von Bertalanffy, and furthered by Ross Ashby (1960). Von Bertalanffy was both reacting against reductionism and attempting to revive the unity of science. He emphasized that real systems are open to, and interact with, their environments, and they can acquire qualitatively new properties through emergence, resulting in continual evolution. Rather than reducing an entity (e.g., the human body) to the properties of its parts or elements (e.g., organs or cells), systems theory focuses on the arrangement of and relations between the parts which connect them into a whole (cf. **holism** below). This particular organization determines a system, which is independent of the concrete substance of the elements (e.g., particles, cells, transistors, people, etc.). Thus, the same concepts and principles of organization underlie the different disciplines, providing a basis for their unification. Systems concepts include: a system-environment boundary, input, output, process, state, hierarchy, goal-directedness, and information.

Systems theory is closely connected to cybernetics and also to system dynamics, which models changes in a network of coupled variable (e.g., the "world dynamics" models of Jay Forrester of MIT and the Club of Rome). Related ideas are found in the emerging sciences of complexity, studying self-organization and heterogeneous networks of interacting actors, and associated domains such as far-from-equilibrium thermodynamics, chaotic dynamics, artificial life, artificial intelligence, neural networks, and computer modeling and simulation.

- **Construct:** A hypothetical variable or system which does not purport to accurately represent or model given observations but has a heuristic or interpretative value concerning them. Constructs may be (1) ideal types as the economist's concept of rational behavior. Rationality can be formalized, leads to elaborate constructions for the motivation of economic behaviour, and stimulates empirical inquiries into why actual behaviour does not conform to it. Constructs may be (2) hypothetical entities, processes, or mechanisms which would explain the connections between observed causes and consequences if those entities, processes, or mechanisms existed. Human memory is such a construct. It bridges the gap between past experiences and current behaviour. Psychological examples are the Freudian id, ego, and super ego for which physiological evidence is principally unavailable. Finally, constructs may be (3) the algorithms capable of generating a certain process or product without evidence for whether this rather than another computational procedure is followed in practice.
- **Context:** The material that surrounds an item which helps define its meaning. The environment of something that establishes or classifies its meaning. In linguistics, the environment of a particular word may disambiguate the meaning of that word, e.g., the word "play" in "I saw a play" versus "I play the guitar." In communication, the context of a situation, which is comprised of all non-linguistic constraints including the social roles ascribed to the communicators, specifies the information of what is said relative to what could be said. In biology, the environment of an organism is similarly crucial in understanding what the organism does. In cybernetics, text and context are two complementary components (the subsystems) of one system, each of which could be considered to constitute or define the other's meaning.
- **Cybernetics:** (1) The science of communication and control in animal and machine. (2) Perhaps because the field is still young, there are many definitions of cybernetics. Norbert Wiener, a mathematician, engineer, and social philosopher, coined the word "cybernetics" from the Greek word meaning steersman. He defined it as the science of communication and control in the animal and the machine. Ampère, before him, wanted cybernetics to be the science of government. For philosopher Warren McCulloch, cybernetics was an experimental epistemology concerned with the communication within an observer and between observer and environment. Stafford Beer, a

management consultant, defined cybernetics as the science of effective organization. Anthropologist Gregory Bateson noted that whereas previous sciences dealt with matter and energy, the new science of cybernetics focuses on form and pattern. (3) A way of looking at things and a language for expressing what one sees.

Whereas general systems theory is committed to holism on the one side and to an effort to generalize structural, behavioural, and developmental features of living organisms on the other side, cybernetics is committed to an epistemological perspective that views material wholes as analyzable without loss, in terms of a set of components plus their organization. Organization accounts for how the components of such a system interact with one another, and how this interaction determines and changes its structure. It explains the difference between parts and wholes and is described without reference to their material forms. The disinterest of cybernetics in material applications separates it from all sciences that designate their empirical domain by subject matters.

In cybernetics, theories tend to rest on 4 basic pillars: variety, circularity, process, and observation. Variety is fundamental to information, communication, and control theories and emphasizes multiplicity, alternatives, differences, choices, networks, and intelligence rather than force and singular necessity. Circularity occurs in its earliest theories of circular causation or feedback, later in theories of recursion and of iteration in computing, and now involving self-reference in cognitive organization and in autonomous systems of production. Traditional sciences have shied away from if not exorcised the use of circular explanations. It is this circular form that enables cybernetics to explain systems from within, making no recourse to higher principles or a priori purposes, expressing no preferences for hierarchy. Nearly all cybernetic theories involve process and change, from its notion of information, as the difference between two states of uncertainty, to theories of adaptation, evolution, and growth processes. A special feature of cybernetics is that it explains such processes in terms of the organization of the system manifesting it, e.g., the circular causality of feedback loops is taken to account for processes of regulation and a system's effort to maintain an equilibrium or to reach a goal.

Cybernetics and systems science tend to focus on complex systems such as organisms, ecologies, minds, societies, and machines. Cybernetics and systems science regard these systems as complex, multi-dimensional networks of information systems. Some of the characteristics of cybernetic systems are:

- **Complementarity:** These many simultaneous modes of interaction lead to subsystems which participate in multiple processes and structures, yielding any single dimension of description incomplete, and requiring multiple complementary, irreducible levels of analysis.
- **Complexity:** Cybernetic systems are complex structures, with many heterogeneous interacting components.
- **Constructivity:** Cybernetic systems are constructive, in that as they tend to increase in size and complexity, they become historically bound to previous states while simultaneously developing new traits.
- **Development:** The process of a systematic unfolding of a system's structure. In biology, all molecular processes that underlie the growth to maturity of an organism. In psychology, the correlation between age and the capacity to engage in certain behaviours, particularly in children. In the economics of underdeveloped countries, the concept is politically controversial because it implies progressive structural changes from primitive to advanced forms and because this current use of the term by Western economists may serve technological imperialism. Nevertheless, the unfolding and growth of structures to their natural limits and their eventual replacement by new forms is observable, particularly in society, and without the need to refer to life-cycles or to assume progress, making development an important adjunct of the cybernetic concern with organization.
- **Evolvability:** Cybernetic systems tend to evolve and grow in an opportunistic manner, rather than be designed and planned in an optimal manner.

- **Feedback:** Information about the results of a process which is used to change the process itself. Negative feedback reduces the error or deviation from a goal state. Positive feedback increases the deviation from an initial state (Umpleby 1990). A circular causal process in which a system's output is returned to its input, possibly involving other systems in the loop. Negative feedback or deviation reducing feedback decreases the input and is inherently stabilizing, e.g., the governor of a steam engine. Positive feedback or deviation amplifying feedback increases the input and is inherently destabilizing, explosive, or vicious, e.g., the growth of a city when more people create new opportunities which in turn attract more people to live there.
- **Hierarchy:** (1) A form of organization resembling a pyramid. Each level is subordinate to the one above it. (2) An organization whose components are arranged in levels from a top level down to a bottom level. (3) A partially ordered structure of entities in which every entity but one is successor to at least one other entity; and every entity except the basic entities is a predecessor to at least one other entity. (4) Narrowly, a group arranged in order of rank or class; we interpret it to denote a rank arrangement in which the nature of function at each higher level becomes more broadly embracing than at the lower level.
- **Lag:** Metaphorically, trailing behind. In development, some variables may change faster than others and if they are dependent on each other these temporal differences, called lag, can cause structural stress within a system, e.g., in modern society, institutional developments tend to lag behind changes in technology causing many social problems from alienations to social inequalities and conflicts. In cybernetics, lag refers to the time for information to pass through one complete feedback loop. Lag makes regulation difficult.
- **Mutuality:** These many components interact in parallel, cooperatively, and in real time, creating multiple simultaneous interactions among subsystems.
- **Reflexivity:** Cybernetic systems are rich in internal and external feedback, both positive and negative. Ultimately, they can enter into the ultimate feedback of reflexive self-application, in which their components are operated on simultaneously from complementary perspectives, for example as entities and processes. Such situations may result in the reflexive phenomena of self-reference, self-modeling, self-production, and self-reproduction.
- **Synergy:** This derives from the holist conviction that the whole is more than the sum of its parts and, because the energy in a whole cannot exceed the sum of the energies invested in each of its parts, that there must therefore be some quantity with respect to which the whole differs from the mere aggregate. This quantity is called synergy.
- **Holism:** The process of focusing attention directly on the whole and its characteristics as a whole, without any recourse to consideration of its parts. A philosophical position claiming (1) that wholes cannot be taken apart and (2) that every apparent whole can be understood only in the context of the larger whole containing it. This belief is epitomized in the statement that "a whole is more than the sum of its parts."
- **Whole:** Without recognition of its parts, a whole is an essentially structureless and unanalyzable unity. If its parts are independent or randomly sampled by an observer, a whole has no outstanding quality other than that of being an observer's aggregate. If a whole is qualitatively different from a mere aggregate of its parts, the difference lies in its structure or organization. Thus any whole may be understood as, described in terms of, and considered equal to a structure or an organization of component parts. In some cases the properties of its parts may be ignored without appreciable loss of understanding a whole, particularly when parts are numerous, simple, and the same as in the objects of computer sciences, macro-economics, and quantum physics, all of which heavily rely on mathematics and their constructions. When parts are few, complex, different, and tenuously related, as in a marriage, the properties or the parts figure more prominently in the understanding of a whole and can not be ignored in favour of such wholes' organization.

Thermodynamics: The first law of thermodynamics was formally stated by Thomson in 1851: Energy can be transformed from one type to another, but it can never be created or destroyed. The second law of thermodynamics was first stated by Carnot (1824): No transformation of energy can occur unless energy is downgraded from a concentrated to a more dispersed form, and no transformation is 100 percent efficient.

References

Aaby, P., J. Bukh, I.M. Lisse, and A.J. Smitz. 1983. "Spacing, Crowding and Child Mortality in Guinea-Bissau." *Lancet* 161 (2-8342): 15-27.

Abramovitz, J. 1996. *Imperiled Waters, Impoverished Future: The Decline of Freshwater Ecosystems*. Worldwatch Paper 128, March 1996.

"Acid Rain Lobby Disbands." 1990. *Morningside*, 20 November. Ottawa: CBC Radio.

Ackoff, R.L. 1974. *Redesigning the Future: A Systems Approach to Societal Problems*. New York: John Wiley and Sons.

Agyris, C., and D. Schön. 1974. *Theory in Practice: Increasing Professional Effectiveness*. San Francisco: Jossey Bass.

–. 1978. *Organizational Learning: A Theory of Action Perspective*. Reading, MA: Addison Wesley.

Agyris, C., R. Putnam, and M.C. Smith. 1985. *Action Science: Concepts, Methods, and Skills for Research and Intervention*. San Francisco: Jossey Bass.

Allen, T., and T. Starr. 1982. *Hierarchy: Perspectives for Ecological Complexity*. Chicago: University of Chicago Press.

Altavatar, E. 1989. "Ecological and Economic Modalities of Time and Space." *Capitalism, Nature and Socialization* 3: 59-70.

Anielski, M. 2000. "Fertile Obfuscation: Making Money Whilst Eroding Living Capital." Paper presented at the Thirty-fourth Annual Conference of the Canadian Economics Association, University of British Columbia, Vancouver, British Columbia, 2-4 June.

Arrow, K., B. Bolin, R. Costanza, P. Dasgupta, C. Folke, C.S. Holling, B.-O. Jansson, S. Levin, K.-G. Maler, C. Perrings, and D. Pimentel. 1995. "Economic Growth, Carrying Capacity and the Environment." *Science* 268: 520-521.

Ashby, R. 1960. *Design for a Brain*. 2nd ed. New York: Riley.

Atkinson, A. 1991. *Principles of Political Ecology*. London: Belhaven Press.

Aucoin, P., ed. 1972. *The Politics of Management and Restraint in Government*. Proceedings of a conference sponsored by the Institute for Research on Public Policy, Toronto, Ontario, 19-20 September.

Baeker, G. 1997. Workshop at Lac Maskinonge, Quebec.

Bandura, A., D. Ross, and S. Ross. 1965. "A Comparative Test of the Status Envy, Social Power and Secondary Reinforcement Theories of Identificatory Learning." In *Readings in Developmental Psychology*, ed. J. Murray, 527-534. New York: St. John's University Press.

Barbier, E.B. 1987. "The Concept of Sustainable Development." *Environmental Conservation* 14 (2): 101-110.

Barbier, E.B., J. Burgess, and C. Folke. 1994. *Paradise Lost? The Ecological Economics of Biodiversity*. London: Earthscan.

Baskerville, G.L. 1997. "Advocacy, Science, Policy, and Life in the Real World." *Conservation Ecology*. http://www.consecol.org/Journal/vol1/iss1/art9/.

Bateson, G. 1972. *Steps to an Ecology of Mind*. San Francisco: Chandler.

–. 1979. *Mind and Nature: A Necessary Unity.* New York: Dutton.

Bella, D. 1994. Organizational Systems and the Burden of Proof. Presented at the Symposium on Pacific Salmon and their Ecosystems: Status and Future Options, University of Washington, Seattle, Oregon.

Berkes, F., and C. Folke. 1994. "Investing in Cultural Capital for a Sustainable Use of Natural Capital." In *Investing in Natural Capital: The Economics Approach to Sustainability,* ed. A.M. Jansson, M. Hammer, C. Folke, and R. Costanza, 128-149. Washington, DC: Island Press.

Berkes, F., C. Folke, and J. Colding. 1998. *Linking Social and Ecological Systems: Management Practices and Social Mechanisms for Building Resilience.* Cambridge: Cambridge University Press.

Bernstein, B. 1992. "A Framework for Trend Detection: Coupling Ecological and Managerial Perspectives." *Ecological Indicators* 2: 1101-1114.

Berry, T. 1988. *The Dream of the Earth.* San Francisco: Sierra Club Books.

Binswanger, H., M. Faber, and R. Manstetten. 1990. "The Dilemma of Modern Man and Nature: An Exploration of the Faustian Imperative." *Ecological Economics* 2: 197-223.

Bohm, D. 1996. *On Dialogue.* Ed. L. Nichol. London: Routledge Press.

Boland, R., and R.V. Tenkasi. 1995. "Perspective Making and Perspective Taking in Communities of Knowing." *Organization Science* 6 (4): 350-372.

Bolding, K. 1981. *Ecodynamics: A New Theory of Societal Evolution.* 2nd ed. Beverly Hills, CA: Sage Publications.

Bond, W. 1993. "Keystone Species." In *Biodiversity and Ecosystem Function,* ed. E. Schulze and H. Money, 237-253. Berlin: Springer-Verlag.

Borman, H., and S. Kellert, eds. 1991. *Ecology, Economics, Ethics. The Broken Circle.* New Haven and London: Yale University Press.

Boucher, M., ed. 1985. *Biology of Mutualism: Ecology and Evolution.* New York: Oxford University Press.

Bourgon, J. 1996. *Fourth Annual Report to the Prime Minister on the Public Service of Canada.* Ottawa: Privy Council Office.

Bowers, C. 1997. *The Culture of Denial: Why the Environmental Movement Needs a Strategy for Reframing Universities and Public Schools.* Albany, NY: State University of New York Press.

Bregha, F., T. Conway, J. Moffet, and P. Morrison. 1995. *Ecological Fiscal Reform: A Review of the Issues.* Ottawa: Resource Futures International.

Brennan, T. 1997. "Economy for the Earth: The Labour Theory of Value without the Subject/Object Distortion." *Ecological Economics* 20: 175-185.

Brewer, G.D. 1986. "Methods for Synthesis: Policy Exercises." In *Sustainable Development of the Biosphere,* ed. W.C. Clark and R.E. Munn, 455-475. New York: Cambridge University Press.

Brewer, G.D., and P. de Leon. 1983. *The Foundations of Policy Analysis.* Homewood, IL: Dorsey Press.

Bromely, H. 1989. "Identity Politics and Critical Pedagogy." *Journal of Applied Psychology* 63 (2): 197-205.

Brown, D. 1998. In *Sustainable Development: A Framework for Governance.* Ed. A. Dale. http://www.sdri.ubc.ca/addialogue.

Brown, L.R. 1995. *Who Will Feed China? Wake-Up Call for a Small Planet.* New York: W.W. Norton and Company.

Brown, L.R., C. Flavin, H. French, J. Abramovitz, C. Bright, S. Dunn, G. Gardiner, A. McGinn, J. Mitchell, M. Renner, D. Roodman, L. Starke, and J. Tuxill. 1998. *State of the World: A Worldwatch Institute Report on Progress Toward a Sustainable Society.* New York: W.W. Norton and Company.

Brown, L.R., C. Flavin, H. French, J. Abramovitz, C. Bright, G. Gardiner, A. McGinn, M. Renner, D. Roodman, and L. Starke. 1997. *State of the World: A Worldwatch Institute Report on Progress Toward a Sustainable Society.* New York: W.W. Norton and Company.

Brown, L.R., C. Flavin, H. French, J. Abramovitz, C. Bright, S. Dunn, G. Gardiner, A. Mattoon, A. McGinn, M. O'Meara, S. Postel, M. Renner, and L. Starke. 2000. *State of the*

World: A Worldwatch Institute Report on Progress Toward a Sustainable Society. New York: W. W. Norton and Company.

Brown, L.R., C. Flavin, and L. Starke. 1996. *State of the World: A Worldwatch Institute Report on Progress Toward a Sustainable Society.* New York: W.W. Norton and Company.

Brown, L.R., C. Flavin, S. Postel, and L. Starke. 1988. *State of the World: A Worldwatch Institute Report on Progress Toward a Sustainable Society.* New York: W.W. Norton and Company.

Brown, L.R., G. Gardner, and B. Halweil. 1998. *Beyond Malthus: Sixteen Dimensions of the Population Problem.* Worldwatch Paper 143. Washington, DC: Worldwatch Institute.

Brown, L.R., M. Renner, and C. Flavin. 1997. *Vital Signs: The Environmental Trends that Are Shaping Our Future.* New York: W.W. Norton and Company.

Brundtland Commission. 1987. *Our Common Future.* Oxford: World Commission on Environment and Development.

Bryant, D., D. Nielson, and L. Tangley, eds. 1997. *The Last Frontier Forests: Ecosystems and Economies on the Edge.* New York: WRI.

Burrell, G., and G. Morgan. 1979. *Sociological Paradigms and Organizational Analysis: Elements of the Sociology of Corporate Life.* London: Heinemann.

Byers, R.L. 1991. "Regulatory Barriers to Pollution Prevention." *Journal of the Air and Waste Management Association* 41: 418-422.

Cadigan, S.T. 1996. "The Sea Was Common and Every Man Had a Right to Fish It: Failed Proposals for Fisheries Management and Conservation in Newfoundland, 1855-1880." Occasional paper, History, Eco-Research, Memorial University of Newfoundland.

Cairns, S. 1998. In *Sustainable Development: A Framework for Governance,* ed. A. Dale. 29 April, http://www.sdri.ubc.ca/addialogue.

Caldwell, L.K. 1963. "Environment: A New Focus for Public Policy." *Public Administration Review* 23 (September): 138-139.

–. 1969. "Health and Homeostasis as Social Concepts: An Exploratory Essay." In *Diversity and Stability in Ecological Systems.* U.S. Brookhaven National Laboratory, Report of the symposium held 26-28 May, Upton, New York.

–. 1970. "The Ecosystem as a Criterion for Public Land Policy." *Natural Resources Journal* 10 (2): 203-221.

–. 1990. *International Environmental Policy: Emergence and Dimensions.* Durham: Duke University Press.

Canada. 1997. *Building Momentum: Sustainable Development in Canada.* Canada's submission to the Fifth Session of the United Nations Commission on Sustainable Development, 7-25 April. Ottawa: Minister of Public Works and Government Services Canada.

Canada's National Climate Change Process. 1999. *Canada's Emissions Outlook: An Update.* Analysis and Modeling Group.

Capra, F. 1991. *The Tao of Physics.* Boston: Shambhala Press.

–. 1996. *The Web of Life.* New York: Doubleday.

Caputo, J. 1987. *Radical Hermeneutics: Repetition, Deconstruction, and the Hermeneutic Project.* Bloomington: University of Indiana Press.

Carpenter, S.R., S.W. Chisholm, C.J. Krebs, O.W. Schindler, and R.E. Wright. 1995. "Ecosystem Experiments." *Science* 269: 324-327.

Casa Alianza. 2000. In United Nations Special Report, 31 March. Report of the Special Rapporteur on the Sale of Children, Child Prostitution and Child Pornography in Guatemala. Commission on Human Rights, 56th session.

Cassel, J. 1971. "Health Consequences of Population Density and Crowding." In *Rapid Population Growth: Consequences and Policy Implications,* ed. R. Revelle. Baltimore: Johns Hopkins University Press.

Catton, W.R. 1980. *Overshoot: The Ecological Roots of Revolutionary Change.* Urbana: University of Illinois Press.

–. 1993. "Carrying Capacity and the Death of a Culture: A Tale of Two Autopsies." *Sociological Inquiry* 63 (2): 202-223.

Cernea, M.M. 1994. "The Sociologist's Approach to Sustainable Development." In *Making Development Sustainable: From Concepts to Action,* ed. I. Serageldin and A. Steer, 6-10.

Washington, DC: World Bank, Environmentally Sustainable Development Occasional Paper Series No. 2.

Chambers, I. 1990. *Border Dialogues: Journeys in Postmodernity*. London and New York: Routledge.

Chambers, R. 1988. Farmer First: A Practical Paradigm for the Third Agriculture. England, University of Sussex: Institute of Development Studies.

Checkland, P. 1981. *Systems Thinking, Systems Practice*. New York: John Wiley and Sons.

Checkland, P., and J. Scholes. 1990. *Soft Systems Methodology in Action*. New York: John Wiley and Sons.

Cherfas, J. 1990. "FAO proposes a new plan for feeding Africa." *Science* 250: 748

Churchman, G.W. 1979. *The Systems Approach and Its Enemies*. New York: Basic Books.

Clements, F.E. 1916. "Plant Succession: An Analysis of Vegetation." Carnegie Institution, Monograph No. 242.

Cobb, C., G.S. Goodman, and M. Wackernagel. 1999. *Why Bigger Isn't Better: The Genuine Progress Indicator – 1999 Update*. http://www.rprogress.org/pubs/gpi1999/gpi1999.html.

Coleman, J.S. 1988. "Social Capital in the Creation of Human Capital." *American Journal of Sociology* 94 Supplement: S95-120.

–. 1990. *Foundations of Social Theory*. Cambridge, MA: Harvard University Press.

Collier, J. 1945. "United States Indian Administration as a Laboratory of Ethnic Relations." *Social Research* 12: 275-286.

Common, M., and C. Perrings. 1992. "Towards an Ecological Economics of Sustainability." *Ecological Economics* 6: 7-34.

Commoner, B. 1975. *Making Peace with the Planet*. New York: New Press.

Costanza, R. 1987. "Social Traps and Environmental Policy." *BioScience* 37: 407-412.

–. 1992. "Three General Policies to Achieve Sustainability." Paper presented to the Second Conference of the International Society for Ecological Economics, Investing in Natural Capital, Stockholm, Sweden, 3 August.

Costanza, R., ed. 1991. *Ecological Economics: The Science and Management of Sustainability*. New York: Columbia University Press.

Costanza, R., and C. Folke. 1996. "The Structure and Function of Ecological Systems in Relation to Property-Rights Regimes." In *Rights to Nature: Ecological, Economic, Cultural, and Political Principles of Institutions for the Environment*, ed. S. Hanna, C. Folke, and K.-G. Maler, 13-34. Washington, DC: Island Press.

–. 1997. "Valuing Ecosystem Services with Efficiency, Fairness and Sustainability as Goals." In *Nature's Services: Societal Dependence on Natural Ecosystems*, ed. G. Daily, 49-68. Washington, DC: Island Press.

Costanza, R., J. Audley, R. Borden, P. Elkins, C. Folke, S.O. Funtowicz, and J. Harris. 1995. "A New Paradigm for World Welfare." *Environment* 37 (5): 17-43.

Costanza, R., K. Wainger, C. Folke, and K.G. Maler. "Modeling Complex Ecological Economic Systems." *BioScience* 43 (80): 545-555.

Cox, E. 1995. *A Truly Civil Society*. Boyer Lectures. Sydney, Australia.

Dahrendorf, R. 1995. "A Precarious Balance: Economic Opportunity, Civil Society and Political Liberty." *Responsive Community* 5 (3): 13-39.

Daily, G.C., ed. 1997. *Nature's Services: Social Dependence on Natural Ecosystems*. Washington, DC: Island Press.

Daily, G.C., and P.R. Ehrlich. 1996a. "Global Change and Human Susceptibility to Disease." *Annual Review of Energy Environment* 21: 125-144.

–. 1996b. "Socioeconomic Equity, Sustainability, and Earth's Carrying Capacity." *Ecological Applications* 6 (4): 991-1001.

Dale, A. 1992. *Obstacles to Sustainable Development*. Ottawa: National Round Table on the Environment and the Economy.

–. 1996. "Multistakeholder Processes: Panacea or Window Dressing." Paper presented at University of Victoria, BC.

–. 1998. In *Sustainable Development: A Framework for Governance*, ed. Dale. http://www.sdri.ubc.ca/addialogue.

–. Forthcoming. *The Politics of Sustainable Development*. In the Life Sciences and Support Series of the United Nations. New York: United Nations.

Dale, A., and H. Regier. 1995. *Ecological Integrity and Protected Spaces: The Politics of Separation*. In the Proceedings of the Canadian Council on Ecological Areas Conference on Protected Areas in Resource Based Economies, Calgary, Alberta, 8-9 November.

Dale, A., J. Robinson, and C. Massey. 1995. *Reconciling Human Welfare and Ecological Carrying Capacity*. Vancouver: Sustainable Development Research Institute.

Dale, A., N.-M. Lister, and G. Baeker. 1997. Workshop at Lac Maskinonge, May.

Dale, A., and S.B. Hill. 1995. "Biodiversity Conservation: A Decision-Making Context." In *Achieving Sustainable Development*, ed. A. Dale and J.B. Robinson, 97-118. Vancouver, BC: UBC Press.

Daly, H.E. 1991a. *Steady-State Economics*. Washington, DC: Island Press.

–. 1991b. Elements of Environmental Macroeconomics. In *Ecological Economics*, ed. R. Costanza, 32-46. New York: Columbia University Press.

Daly, H.E., J.B. Cobb, and C.W. Cobb. 1989. *For the Common Good: Redirecting the Economy Toward Community, the Environment, and a Sustainable Future*. Boston: Beacon Press.

Daly, H.T. 1990. "Sustainable Development: From Concept and Theory Towards Operational Principles." Washington, DC: The World Bank.

–. 1994. "Fostering Environmentally Sustainable Development: Four Parting Suggestions for the World Bank." *Ecological Economics* 10: 183-187.

–. 1995. "Reconciling Human Welfare and Ecological Carrying Capacity." In *Reconciling Human Welfare and Ecological Carrying Capacity*, ed. A. Dale, J. Robinson, and C. Massey. Vancouver: Sustainable Development Research Institute.

Dasgupta, P. 1995. "Optimal Development and the Idea of Net National Product." In *The Economics of Sustainable Development*, ed. I. Goldin and L.A. Winters. Cambridge: Cambridge University Press.

Dasmann, R., J. Milton, and P. Freeman. 1973. *Ecological Principles for Economic Development*. London: John Wiley and Sons.

Day, T. 1997. E-mail Correspondence. 17 March.

Dayton, P. 1998. "Reversal of the Burden of Proof in Fisheries Management." *Science* 279 (5352): 821-822.

de Groot, W.T. 1992. *Environmental Science Theory: Concepts and Methods in a One-World, Problem-Oriented Paradigm*. Amsterdam: Elsevier.

de Moor, A., and P. Calamai. 1997. *Subsidizing Unsustainable Development: Undermining the Earth with Public Funds*. Toronto: Earth Council.

Demar, C. 1976. *Textes sur l'affranchissement des femmes (1832-1833)*. Paris: Payot.

DeMello, S., P. Boothroyd, N. Matthew, and K. Sparrow. 1994. "Discovering Common Meaning: Planning Community Development Education with First Nations." *Plan Canada* 34: 14-21.

Denzin, N.K., and Y.S. Lincoln, eds. 1994. *Handbook of Qualitative Research*. London: Sage Publications.

Derrida, J. 1984. "Deconstruction and the Other." In *Dialogues with Contemporary Continental Thinkers*, ed. R. Kearney, 107-126. Manchester: Manchester University Press.

Diamond, J. 1993. "Speaking with a Single Voice." *Discover* 14: 78-88.

Dillon, M.C. 1988. *Merleau-Ponty's Ontology*. Bloomington and Indianapolis: Indiana University Press.

Dixon, N. 1996. *Perspectives on Dialogue: Making Talk Developmental for Individuals and Organizations*. Greensboro, NC: Centre for Creative Leadership.

Dobell, R. 1996. "The Dance of the Deficit and the Real World of Wealth: Rethinking Economic Management for Social Purpose." In *Family Secure in Insecure Times*, Vol. 2: Perspectives, 197-226. Ottawa: Canadian Council on Social Development.

Dobson, A. 1990. *Green Political Thought: An Introduction*. London: Unwin Hyman.

–. 1995. "Biodiversity and Human Health." *Trends in Ecological Evolution* 10: 390-391.

Doern, B.G., and T. Conway. 1994. *The Greening of Canada: Federal Institutions and Decisions*. Toronto: University of Toronto Press.

Doherty, B., and M. de Deus. 1996. *Democracy and Green Political Thought*. London: Routledge.

Drescher, J., and M. Kepkay. 1997. "Ecoforestry at Windhorse Farm: Profile of a Working Operation." *Global Biodiversity* 7 (2): 13-16.

Dryzek, J.S. 1990. "Green Reason: Communicative Ethics for the Biosphere." *Environmental Ethics* 12 (3): 195-210.

Durning, A.T. 1992. *How Much Is Enough? The Consumer Society and the Future of the Earth*. New York: W.W. Norton and Company.

–. 1994. "Redesigning the Forest Economy." In *State of the World*, ed. L.R. Brown et al., 22-40. New York: W.W. Norton and Company.

Dyckman, T.R. 1981. "The Intelligence of Ambiguity." *Accounting, Organizations and Society* 6 (4): 291-300.

Earle, S. 1995. *Sea Change: A Message of the Oceans*. New York: Fawcett Columbine.

–. 1997. "Sustaining the Earth." Panel address, International Union for the Conservation of Nature Conference, Montreal, Canada.

Ebenreck, S. 1983. "A Partnership Farmland Ethic." *Environmental Ethics* 5 (1): 33-45.

Edwards, C., and H. Regier. 1988. *An Ecosystem Approach to the Integrity of the Great Lakes in Turbulent Times*. Proceedings of a 1988 workshop supported by the Great Lakes Fishery Commission and the Science Advisory Board of the International Joint Commission, Toronto, Great Lakes Fishery Commission.

Edwards, S. 1981. "Environmental Policy: Bounded Rationality Applied to Unbounded Ecological Problems." In *Environmental Policy Formation*, ed. D. Mann. Lexington, MA: Lexington Books.

Ehrenfeld, D. 1978. *The Arrogance of Humanism*. Oxford: Oxford University Press.

Ehrlich, P.R. 1982. "Human Carrying Capacity, Extinctions and Nature Reserves." *BioScience* 32 (5): 331.

–. 1988. "Why Put a Value on Biodiversity?" In *Biodiversity*, ed. E.O. Wilson. Washington, DC: National Academy Press.

Ehrlich, P.R., and A.H. Ehrlich. 1991. *Healing the Planet*. Reading, MA: Addison-Westley.

–. 1997. "Ehrlich's Fables." *Technology Review* 100 (1): 39-47.

Ehrlich, P.R., J.P. Holdren, and A.H. Ehrlich. 1977. *Ecoscience: Population, Resources, Environment*. San Francisco: W.H. Freeman.

Ehrlich, P.R., and P.H. Raven. 1965. "Butterflies and Plants: A Study of Coevolution." *Evolution* 18: 586-608.

Elden, M., and M. Levin. 1991. "Cogenerative Learning: Bringing Participation in Action Research." In *Participatory Action Research*, ed. W.F. Whyte, 127-142. Newbury Park: Sage Publications.

Elden, M., and R.F. Chisholm. 1993. "Emerging Varieties of Action Research." Introduction to the special issue. *Human Relations* 46 (2): 1-23.

Emery, F.E., and E.L. Trist. 1965. "The Causal Texture of Organizational Environments." *Human Relations* 18: 21-31.

–. 1972. *Towards a Social Ecology: Contextual Appreciation of the Future in the Present*. London: Plenum Press.

Emmett, B. 1998. *Report of the Commissioner of the Environment and Sustainable Development to the House of Commons*. Ottawa: Minister of Public Works and Government Services.

–. 1999. *Report of the Commissioner of the Environment and Sustainable Development to the House of Commons*. Ottawa: Minister of Public Works and Government Services.

Environics Research Organization. 1995. *Focus Canada: 4*. Toronto: Environics.

Environment Canada. 1992. *State of the Environment Report 1991*. Ottawa: Supply and Services Canada.

Erikson, K. 1994. *A New Species of Trouble: The Human Experience of Modern Disasters*. New York: W.W. Norton and Company.

Estes, R.J. 1993. "Toward Sustainable Development: From Theory to Praxis." *Social Development Issues* 15 (3): 1-29.

Everden, N. 1985. *The Natural Alien*. Toronto: University of Toronto Press.

Ewald, P.W. 1994. *Evolution of Infectious Disease*. Oxford: Oxford University Press.

FAO and Government of Netherlands. 1991. Main documents presented at FAO/Netherlands Conference on Agriculture and the Environment, Nertogenbosch, Netherlands, 14-19 April.

FAOSTAT. 1997. FAOSTAT Statistics Database. Rome: FAO. www.fao.org.

Farnsworth, N.R. 1988. "Screening Plants for New Medicines." In *Biodiversity*, ed. E.O. Wilson, 83-97. Washington, DC: National Academy.

Faucheux, S., D. Pierce, and J. Proops. 1996. *Models of Sustainable Development*. Cheltenham, UK: Edward Elgar.

Findlayson, A.C. 1994. *Fishing for Truth: A Sociological Analysis of Northern Cod Stock Assessments from 1977 to 1990*. Institute for Social Economic Research, Social and Economic Study No. 52, Memorial University, Newfoundland.

Finkle, P., K. Webb, T. Stanbury, and A. Pross. 1994. *Federal Government Relations with Interest Groups: A Reconsideration*. Ottawa: Supply and Services.

Fish, H. 1988. "What Goes Up: Science, Politics, Dead Lakes and Dying Trees. Will the Adirondacks Survive the Fallout?" *Adirondack Life* 19 (1): 34-41.

Fiske, J. 1994. "Audiencing: Cultural Practice and Cultural Studies." In *Handbook of Qualitative Research*, ed. N.K. Denzin and Y.S. Lincoln. London: Sage Publications.

Folke, C. 1991. "Socioeconomic Dependence on the Life-Supporting Environment." In *Linking the Natural Environment and the Economy: Essays from the Eco-Eco Group*, ed. C. Folke and T. Kaberger. Dordrecht, The Netherlands: Kluwer Academic Publishers.

Folke, C., C.S. Holling, and C. Perrings. 1996. "Biological Diversity, Ecosystems, and the Human Scale." *Ecological Applications* 6 (4): 1018-1024.

Folke, C., and F. Berkes. 1992. *Cultural Capital and Natural Capital Interrelations*. International Institute of Ecological Economics, the Royal Swedish Academy of Sciences, Beijer Discussion Paper Series No. 8.

Foucault, M. 1980. *Power/Knowledge: Selected Interviews and Other Writings, 1972-1977*. New York: Pantheon.

–. 1986. *The Core of the Self*. Trans. Robert Henley. New York: Pantheon.

Fox, M. 1980. *Returning to Eden*. New York: Viking Press.

Francis, G. 1994. "Ecosystems." Paper presented to the Social Science Federation of Canada, Ottawa, 17-19 February.

Francis, G., and S. Lerner. 1995. "Making Sustainable Development Happen: Institutional Transformation." In *Achieving Sustainable Development*, ed. A. Dale and J. Robinson. Vancouver: UBC Press.

Freire, P. 1970. *Pedagogy of the Oppressed*. New York: Seabury Press.

Fritz, R. 1996. *Corporate Tides: The Inescapable Laws of Organizational Structure*. San Francisco: Barrett-Koehler.

Funtowicz, S.O., and J. Ravetz. 1991. "A New Scientific Methodology for Global Environmental Issues." In *Ecological Economics: The Science and Management of Sustainability*, ed. R. Costanza, 137-152. New York: Columbia University Press.

–. 1993. "Science for a Post-normal Age." *Futures* 25 (7): 735-755.

Furkiss, V. 1974. *The Future of Technological Civilization*. New York: Brazillier.

Gardner, G., and B. Halweil. 2000. *Underfed and Overfed: The Global Epidemic of Malnutrition*. Worldwatch Paper 150. Washington, DC: Worldwatch Institute.

Gare, A.E. 1995. *Postmodernism and the Environmental Crisis*. London: Routledge Press.

Geuer, C. 1998. In *Sustainable Development: A Framework for Governance*, ed. A. Dale. http://www.sdri.ubc.ca/addialogue.

Gibson, R.B., and R. Tomalty. 1995. "An Ecosystem Approach to Planning for Urban-Centered Regions." *Cornell Journal of Planning and Urban Issues* 10: 1-10.

Gleick, P.H., ed. 1993. *Water in Crisis: A Guide to the World's Fresh Water Resources*. New York: Oxford University Press.

Gordon, A., and D. Suzuki. 1990. *It's a Matter of Survival*. Toronto: Stoddart Press.

Gowdy, J.M. 1994. *Coevolutionary Economics: The Economy, Society and the Environment*. Boston: Kluwer Academic Publishers.

Gramsci, A. 1971. *Selections from the Prison Notebooks of Antonio Gramsci*. New York: International Publishers.

Gray, B. 1989. *Collaborating: Finding Common Ground for Multiparty Problems*. San Franciso: Jossey-Bass Publishers.

Gregory, R., and R.L. Keenery. 1994. "Creating Policy Alternatives Using Stakeholder Values." *Management Science* 40 (8): 1035-1048.

Gruen, A. 1986. *The Betrayal of the Self: The Fear of Autonomy in Men and Women*. New York: Grove Press.

Guba, E.G. 1990. "The Alternative Paradigm Dialog." In *The Paradigm Dialog*, ed. E.G. Guba, 17-30. Newbury Park, CA: Sage Publications.

Guba, E.G., and Y.S. Lincoln. 1994. "Competing Paradigms in Qualitative Research." In *Handbook of Qualitative Research*, ed. N.K. Denzin and Y.S. Lincoln, 105-117. London: Sage Publishers.

Gunderson, L.C., C.S. Holling, and S. Light. 1995a. "Lessons from the Everglades: Learning in a Turbulent System." *BioScience Supplement* 45 (16): 66-73.

Gunderson, L.C., C.S. Holling, and S. Light, eds. 1995b. *Barriers and Bridges to the Renewal of Ecosystems and Institutions*. New York: Columbia University Press.

Habermas, J. 1972. *Knowledge and Human Interests*. Boston: Beacon Press.

–. 1990. *Moral Consciousness and Communicative Action*. Cambridge: MIT Press.

Hanna, S., and S. Jentoft. 1996. "Human Use of the Natural Environment: An Overview of Social and Economic Dimensions." In *Rights to Nature: Ecological, Economic, Cultural, and Political Principles of Institutions for the Environment*, ed. S. Hanna, C. Folke, and K.-G. Maler. Washington, DC: Island Press.

Haraway, D.J. 1991. *Simians, Cyborgs and Women: The Reinvention of Nature*. New York: Routledge Press.

Hardin, G. 1969. "Not Peace, But Ecology." In *Diversity and Stability in Ecological Systems*, U.S. Brookhaven National Laboratory, Report of the Symposium, 26-28 May, Upton, New York.

–. 1986. *Cultural Carrying Capacity: A Biological Approach to Human Problems*. Acceptance speech, 10 August, AIBS Annual Meeting at the University of Massachusetts, Amherst.

–. 1993. *Living within Our Means: Ecology, Economics and Population Taboos*. New York: Oxford University Press.

Harding, S. 1987. *Feminism and Methodology*. Bloomington: Indiana University Press.

Hardy, P., and T. Zdan. 1997. *Assessing Sustainable Development Principles in Practice*. Winnipeg: International Institute for Sustainable Development.

Harmon, D. 1995. "Losing Species, Losing Languages: Connections between Biological and Linguistic Diversity." Paper presented at the Symposium on Language Loss and Public Policy, Albuquerque, New Mexico, 30 June-2 July.

Hawken, P. 1993. *The Ecology of Commerce: A Declaration of Sustainability*. New York: HarperCollins Publishers.

–. 1997. "Natural Capitalism." *Mother Jones* March/April, 40-62.

Hawken, P., A. Lovins, and H. Lovins. 1999. *Natural Capitalism: Creating the Next Industrial Revolution*. Boston: Little, Brown and Company.

Hayward, T. 1995. *Ecological Thought: An Introduction*. Cambridge: Blackwell Publishers.

Head, I. 1992. *On a Hinge of History. The Mutual Vulnerability of South and North*. Toronto: University of Toronto Press.

Hefner, J.M., B.O. Wilson, T.E. Dahl, and W.E. Frayer. 1994. *Southeast Wetlands: Status and Trends, mid-1970s to mid-1980s*. Atlanta, GA: U.S. Dept. of the Interior, Fish and Wildlife Service.

Henderson, H. 1991. *Paradigms in Progress: Life Beyond Economics*. Indianapolis: Knowledge Systems, Inc.

Hengeveld, H. 2000. "The Science: Global Temperature Is on the Rise and the Dangers Are Real and Significant." *Alternatives* 26, 2 (Spring): 15-16.

Hern, W.M. 1990. "Why Are There So Many of Us? Description and Diagnosis of a Planetary Ecopathological Process." *Population and Environment: A Journal of Interdisciplinary Studies* 12 (1): 9-39.

Heron, J. 1981a. "Experiential Research Methodology." In *Human Inquiry. A Sourcebook of New Paradigm Research*, ed. P. Reason and J. Rowan, 153-166. New York: John Wiley and Sons.

–. 1981b. "Philosophical Basis for a New Paradigm." In *Human Inquiry: A Sourcebook of New Paradigm Research*, ed. P. Reason and J. Rowan, 19-36. New York: John Wiley and Sons.

–. 1989. *The Facilitator's Handbook*. London: Kogan Page.

–. 1996. *Co-operative Inquiry: Research into the Human Condition*. London: Sage Publications.

Hill, S.B. 1973. "Ecology, Ethics and Feelings." In *The Re-evaluation of Exisiting Values and the Search for Absolute Values*. Boston, MA: ICUS.

–. 1975. "Ecosystem Stability in Relation to Stresses Caused by Human Activities." *Canadian Geographer* 19: 206-220.

–. 1979. "Interdisciplinary Approaches to Synthesis." In *Symposium on Foundations Research and New World Models*. The Society for Common Insights and the Bionic Studies Group of Sweden.

–. 1980. "Observing Stressed and Unstressed Ecosystems and Human Systems: Means for Recovery and Value Identification." In *Absolute Values and the Search for the Peace of Mankind*. Vol. 2. Proceedings of the Ninth International Conference on the Unity of the Sciences, Miami Beach, Florida, 22-30 November.

–. 1985. "Redesigning the Food System for Sustainability." *Alternatives* 12 (3/4): 32-35.

–. 1991. "Ecovalues-Ecovision-Ecoaction: The Healing and Evolution of Person and Planet." In *Absolute Values and the Reassessment of the Contemporary World*. New York: ICUS.

–. 1993. "Science, Scientists and the Evolution of Responsible Systems of Personal and Planetary Management." In *Ethical Management of Science as a System*, ed. R. Packham. Proceedings of the Thirty-seventh Annual Meeting of International Social Systems Scientists, University of Western Sydney at Hawkesbury, Australia.

–. 1996. *What I Don't Know About Social Ecology: Unknowing as a Process of Social Change*. Sydney: University of Western Sydney at Hawkesbury.

–. 1998. "Redesigning Agroecosystems for Environmental Sustainability: A Deep Systems Approach." *Systems Research and Behavioral Science* 15: 391-402.

Hill, S.B., and J.C. Henning. 1992. "Competing Green." *CGA Magazine* (October): 391-402.

Hill, S.B., R.J. MacRae, and J. Pinn. 1994. "The Key to Sustainability and Health of Agroecosystems." Presentation to the First International Symposium on Ecosystem Health and Medicine, 19-23 June, Ottawa, Canada.

Hilborn, R., C.J. Walters, and D. Ludwig. 1995. "Sustainable Exploitation of Renewable Resources." *Annual Review of Ecology and Systematics* 26: 45-67.

Hilborn, R., and D. Ludwig. 1993. "The Limits of Applied Ecological Research." *Ecological Applications* 3: 550-552.

Hirst, P. 1994. *Associative Democracy: New Forms of Economic and Social Governance*. Cambridge: Polity.

Holdgate, M. 1996. *From Care to Action. Making a Sustainable World*. London: Earthscan Publications Limited.

Holdren, J., G. Daily, and R. Ehrlich. 1995. "The Meaning of Sustainability: Biogeophysical Aspects." In *Defining and Measuring Sustainability: The Biogeophysical Foundations*, ed. M. Munasinghe and W. Shearer, 3-17. Washington, DC: The United Nations University.

Holdren, J., and P. Ehrlich. 1974. "Human Population and the Global Environment." *American Scientist* 62: 282-292.

Holling, C.S. 1973. "Resilience and Stability of Ecological Systems." *Annual Review of Ecology and Systematics* 4: 1-23.

–. 1978. *Adaptive Environmental Assessment and Management*. New York: John Wiley and Sons.

–. 1986. "Resilience of Ecosystems: Local Surprise and Global Change." In *Sustainable Development of the Biosphere*, ed. W.C. Clark and R.E. Munn. Cambridge, UK: Cambridge University Press.

–. 1989/90. "Integrating Science for Sustainable Development." *Journal of Business Administration* 19 (1-2): 73-83.

–. 1993a. "An Ecologist's View of the Malthusian Conflict." Presented to the Population-Environment-Development Lecture Series, the Royal Swedish Academy of Sciences, Stockholm.

–. 1993b. "Investing in Research for Sustainability." *Ecological Applications* 3: 552-555.

–. 1994. "Simplifying the Complex: The New Paradigms of Ecological Function and Structures." *Futures* 26 (6): 598-609.

–. 1996. "Surprise for Science, Resilience for Ecosystems, and Incentives for People." *Ecosystem Applications* 6 (3): 733-735.

Holling, C.S., and G.K. Meefe. 1996. "Command and Control and the Pathology of Natural Resource Management." *Conservation Biology* 10 (2): 328-337.

Holling, C.S., and S. Sanderson. 1996. "Dynamics of (Dis)harmony in Ecological and Social Systems." In *Rights to Nature: Ecological, Economic, Cultural, and Political Principles of Institutions for the Environment*, ed. S. Hanna, C. Folke, and K.-G. Maler. Washington, DC: Island Press.

Homer-Dixon, T., J.H. Boutwell, and G.W. Rathjens. 1993. "Environmental Change and Violent Conflicts." *Scientific American* 268 (2): 38-45.

Hooks, B. 1984. *Feminist Theory: From Margin to Center.* Boston: South End Press.

Houghton, R.A. 1990. "Global Effects of Tropical Deforestation." *Environmental Science Technology* 24 (414): 414-420.

Hutchings, J.A., C. Walters, and R.L. Haedrich. 1997. "Is Scientific Inquiry Incompatible with Government Information Control?" *Canadian Journal of Fisheries Aquatic Science* 54: 1198-1210.

Hutchings, J.A., and R.A. Myers. 1994. "What Can Be Learned from the Collapse of a Renewable Resource? Atlantic Cod, Gadus Morhua, of Newfoundland and Labrador." *Canadian Journal of Fisheries Aquatic Science* 51: 2126-2146.

Independent Commission on Future Population and Quality of Life (ICFPQL). 1996. *Caring for the Future.* Oxford: Oxford University Press.

International Development Research and Policy Task Force. 1996. *Connecting with the World: Priorities for Canadian Internationalism in the 21st Century.* Ottawa: International Development Research Centre.

Issacs, S. 1946. *Social Development in Young Children: A Study of Beginnings.* London: George Routledge and Sons.

IUCN (International Union for the Conservation of Nature and Natural Resources). 1980. *World Conservation Strategy: Living Resource Conservation.* With the United Nations Environment Programme and the World Wildlife Fund. Gland, Switzerland: IUCN.

IUCN (International Union for the Conservation of Nature and Natural Resources), World Wildlife Fund, and United Nations Environment Programme. 1991. *Caring for the Earth.* Gland, Switzerland: IUCN.

Jacobs, M. 1994. "Toward a Methodological Critique of Sustainable Development." *Journal of Developing Areas* 28: 237-252.

Jagtenberg, T., and D. McKie. 1997. *Eco-Impacts and the Greening of Postmodernity: New Maps for Communication Studies, Cultural Studies, and Sociology.* London: Sage Publications.

Jansson, A.M., M. Hammer, C. Folke, and R. Costanza, eds. 1994. *Investing in Natural Capital: The Ecological Economics Approach to Sustainability.* Washington, DC: Island Press.

Jantsch, E. 1980. *The Self-Organizing Universe. Scientific and Human Implications of the Emerging Paradigm of Evolution.* Oxford: Pergamon Press.

Jantsch, E., and C. Waddington, eds. 1976. *Evolution and Consciousness: Human Systems in Transition.* Reading, MA: Addison-Wesley Publishing Company.

Jickling, R. 1994. "Why I Don't Want My Children to Be Educated for Sustainable Development." *Journal of Environmental Education* 23 (4): 5-8.

Jiggins, J. 1994. *Changing the Boundaries: Women-Centered Perspectives on Population and the Environment.* Washington, DC: Island Press.

Jordan, W.R., M.E. Gilpin, and J.D. Aber. 1987. *Restoration Ecology: A Synthetic Approach to Ecological Research.* Washington, DC: Island Press.

Josselson, R. 1996. *The Space between Us: Exploring the Dimensions of Human Relationships.* Thousand Oaks, CA: Sage Publications.

Kagan, J. 1958. "Socialization of Aggression and the Perception of Parents in Fantasy." *Child Development* 29 (2): 311-318.

Kanter, R. 1983. *The Change Makers: Innovation and Entrepreneurship in the American Corporation.* New York: Simon and Schuster.

Karlberg, M. 1997. "How Adversarial News Frames Limit Public Understanding of Environmental Issues." *Alternatives* 23 (Winter): 1.

Kasperson, R.E., O. Renn, P. Slovic, H. Brown, J. Emel, R. Goble, J. Kasperson, and S. Ratick. 1988. "The Social Amplification of Risk: A Conceptual Framework." *Risk Analysis* 8: 177-187.

Kaufman Hall, V. 1995. Women Transforming the Workplace: Collaborative Inquiry into Integrity in Action. PhD diss., University of Western Sydney, Hawkesbury.

Kay, J.J. 1994. Some Notes on the Ecosystem Approach: Ecosystems as Complex Systems. Unpublished report. Dept. of Environment and Resource Studies, University of Waterloo.

Kay, J.J., and E. Schneider. 1994. "The Challenge of the Ecosystem Approach." *Alternatives* 20 (3): 32-39.

Kay, J.J., and G. Francis. 1995. Applying Complex Systems Theory as an Ecosystem Approach. Unpublished discussion draft. University of Waterloo.

Keeley, M. 1992. "Values in Organizational Theory and Management Education." In *Classics of Organization Theory,* ed. J. Shafritz and J. Ott. Pacific Grove, CA: Brooks/Cole Publishing Company.

Keeney, R.L. 1996. *Value-Focused Thinking: A Path to Creative Decisionmaking.* Cambridge: Harvard University Press.

Kellert, S., and E. Wilson, eds. 1993. *The Biophilia Hypothesis.* Washington, DC: Island Press.

Kendall, H.W., and D. Pimentel. 1994. "Constraints on the Expansion of the Global Good Supply." *Ambio* 23 (3): 198-205.

Kerr, S.R., and R.A. Ryder. 1997. "The Laurentian Great Lakes Experience: A Prognosis for the Fisheries of Atlantic Canada." *Canadian Journal of Fisheries Aquatic Science* 54: 1190-1197.

Kiel, D.L. 1991. "Lessons from the Nonlinear Paradigm: Applications of the Theory of Dissipative Structures in the Social Sciences." *Social Science Quarterly* 72 (3): 431-443.

Koestler, A. 1978. *Janus: A Summing Up.* London: Hutchinson.

Korten, D. 1995. *When Corporations Rule the World.* West Hartford, CT: Berrett-Koehler Publishers.

Kuhn, T. 1962. *The Structure of Scientific Revolutions.* Chicago: Chicago University Press.

Kuznik, F. 1997. "How to Be an Orangutan." *International Wildlife* (January/February) 27 (1).

Lahaye, N., and D. Llerena. 1996. "Technology and Sustainability: An Organizational and Institutional Change." In *Models of Sustainable Development,* ed. S. Faucheux, D. Pierce, and J. Proops, 205-227. Cheltenham, UK: Edward Elgar.

Lakoff, G. 1987. *Women, Fire, and Dangerous Things: What Categories Reveal about the Mind.* Chicago: University of Chicago Press.

Lal, R. 1990. "Soil Erosion and Land Degradation: The Global Risks." In *Advances in Soil Science.* Vol. 2: *Soil Degradation,* ed. R. Lal and B.A. Stewart. New York: Springer-Verlag.

La Porte, T.R., ed. 1975. *Organized Social Complexity: Challenge to Politics and Policy.* Princeton, NJ: Princeton University Press.

Lardner, J. 1999. "World Class Workaholics." *U.S. News & World Report,* 13 December.

Lather, P. 1986. "Issues of Validity in Openly Ideological Research: Between a Rock and a Hard Place." *Interchange* 17 (4): 63-84.

–. 1991. *Getting Smart: Feminist Research and Pedagogy with/in the Postmodern.* New York: Routledge.

Lauder, H., and G.I. Kahn. 1988. "Democracy and the Effective Schools Movement in New Zealand." *International Journal of Qualitative Studies in Education* 1 (1): 51-68.

Lear, W.H., J.W. Baird, J.C. Rice, J.E. Carscadden, G.R. Lilly, and S.A. Akenhead. 1986. *An Examination of Factors Affecting Catch in the Inshore Cod Fishery of Labrador and Eastern Newfoundland.* Canadian Technical Report of Fisheries and Aquatic Sciences. Ottawa: Fisheries and Oceans Canada, Fisheries Research Branch.

Lee, K.N. 1993. *Compass and Gyroscope: Integrating Science and Politics for the Environment.* Covelo, CA: Island Press.

Lele, S. 1991. "Sustainable Development: A Critical Review." *World Development* 19 (6): 607-621.

Leopold, A. 1949. *A Sand County Almanac and Sketches Here and There.* New York: Oxford University Press.

Levin, S.A. 1997. "Management and the Problem of Scale." *Conservation Ecology.* http://www.consecol.org/Journal/vol1/iss1/art13/.

Lewin, K. 1946. "Action Research and Minority Problems." *Journal of Social Issues* 2: 34-46.

–. 1951. *Field Theory in Social Sciences.* New York: Harper and Row.

Lewin, R. 1991. *Life at the Edge of Chaos.* New York: Macmillan Publishing Company.

Lincoln, Y.S., and E.G. Guba. 1985. *Naturalistic Inquiry.* Newbury Park, CA: Sage Publications.

Lindblom, C. 1959. "The Science of 'Muddling Through.'" *Public Administration Review* 19: 81-86.

Lipsey, R. 1995. In *Reconciling Human Welfare and Ecological Carrying Capacity,* ed. A. Dale, J. Robinson, and C. Massey. Vancouver: Sustainable Development Research Institute.

Lister, N.-M. 1997. Workshop at Lac Maskinonge, Quebec.

–. 1998. In *Sustainable Development: A Framework for Governance,* ed. A. Dale. http://www.sdri.ubc.ca/addialogue.

Livingston, J. 1994. *Rogue Primate: An Exploration of Human Domestication.* Toronto, ON: Key Porter Books.

Lovejoy, T.E. 1980. "A Projection of Species Extinctions." In *The Global 2000 Report to the President: Entering the Twenty-First Century.* Washington, DC: Council on Environmental Quality, U.S. Government Printing Office.

Lowry, K., and R.A. Carpenter. 1984. *Holistic Nature and Fragmented Bureaucracies: A Study of Government Organization for Natural Systems Management.* Based on discussions and conclusions of a seminar entitled Alternative Organizations for Managing Natural Systems, held in June-August 1983 at the East-West Environment and Policy Institute of the East-West Center, Honolulu, Hawaii.

Ludwig, D. 1996. "The End of the Beginning." *Ecological Applications* 6 (1): 16-17.

Ludwig, D., R. Hilborn, and C. Walters. 1993. "Uncertainty, Resource Exploitation, and Conservation: Lessons from History." *Science* 260: 35-36.

Lyotard, J.F. 1984. *The Postmodern Condition.* Trans. Geoff Bennington and Brian Massumi. Minneapolis: University of Minnesota Press.

MacDonald, M. 1995. "Promises, Promises: Canadian Campaign Rhetoric, Agenda 21, and the Status of Women." In *Achieving Sustainable Development,* ed. A. Dale and J. Robinson, 182-203. Vancouver: UBC Press.

MacDonald Commission. 1985. *Royal Commission on the Economic Union and Development Prospects for Canada.* Report, 3 volumes. Ottawa: Minister of Supply and Services Canada.

McElroy, S.C. 1997. *Animals as Teachers and Healers.* New York: Ballantine Books.

McLaren, D.J. 1991. "Humankind: The Agent and Victim of Global Change in the Geosphere-Biosphere System." Paper delivered at Planet Earth: Problems and Prospectus, Queen's University symposium, Kingston, ON, 7-8 June.

McMichael, A.J. 1995. *Planetary Overload: Global Environmental Change and the Health of the Human Species.* Cambridge: Cambridge University Press.

McNeely, J.A., K.A. Miller, W.V. Reid, R.A. Mittermeir, and T.B. Werner. 1990. *Conserving the World's Biodiversity.* International Union for the Conservation of Nature and Natural Resources, World Resources Institute, Conservation International, US World Wildlife Fund, and the World Bank.

MacNeill, J. 1989. *Sustainable Development, Economics and the Growth Imperative.* Report to the World Resources Institute and the United Nations Economic Commission for Europe.

–. N.d. "Reforming Government Distortions of the Market: Eco-efficiency – An Aim for OECD Governments." Speech delivered in Paris, France.

MacNeill, J., P. Winsemius, and T. Yakushiji. 1991. *Beyond Interdependence: The Meshing of the World's Economy and the Earth's Ecology.* New York: Oxford University Press.

McNeill, W.H. 1992. *The Global Condition: Conquerors, Catastrophes, and Community.* Princeton, NJ: Princeton University Press.

MacRae, J., S.B. Hill, J. Manning, and A. Bentley. 1990. "Policies, Programs and Regulations to Support the Transition to Sustainable Agriculture in Canada." *American Journal of Alternative Agriculture* 5 (2): 76-92.

Maguire, P. 1987. *Doing Participatory Research: A Feminist Approach*. Amherst, MA: Center for International Education.

Mallet, D. 1991. *The Green Grassroots: Small Business and the Environment*. Toronto: Canadian Federation of Independent Business.

Malley, D.F. 1993. "Raising Consciousness in Ecosystem Health." *Journal of Aquatic Ecosystem Health* 2: 317-327.

Malley, D.F., and S.C. Lawrence. 1994. "A Quantum Leap to Sustainable Development: Assimilating the Knowledge of 20th Century Physics." Paper prepared for the Women and Science Panel at the Women and Sustainable Development (Canadian Perspectives) Conference, University of British Columbia, Vancouver, 27-31 May.

Mangel, M., L.M. Talbot, G.K. Meffe, M.T. Agardy, D.L. Alverson, J. Barlow, D.B. Botkin, G. Budowski, T. Clark, J. Cooke, R.H. Crozier, P.K. Dayton, D.L. Elder, C.W. Fowler, S. Funtowicz, J. Giske, R.J. Hofman, S.J. Holt, S.R. Kellert, L.A. Kimball, D. Ludwig, K. Magnusson, B.S. Malayang III, C. Mann, E.A. Norse, S.P. Northridge, W. F. Perring, C. Perrings, R.M. Peterman, G.B. Rabb, H.A. Regier, J.E. Reynolds III, K. Sherman, M.P. Sissenwine, T.D. Smith, A. Starfield, R.J. Taylor, M.F. Tillman, C. Toft, J.R. Twiss, J. Wilen, and T.R. Young. 1996. "Principles for the Conservation of Wild Living Resources." *Ecological Applications* 6 (2): 338-362.

Maruyama, M. 1981. "Endogenous Research: Rationale." In *Human Inquiry: A Sourcebook of New Paradigm Research*, ed. P. Reason and J. Rowan, 227-238. New York: John Wiley and Sons.

Maser, C. 1992. *Global Imperative: Harmonizing Culture and Nature*. Walpole, NH: Stillpoint Publishing.

Massey, C. 1997. In *Sustainable Development A Framework for Governance*, ed. A. Dale. http://www.sdri.ubc.ca/addialogue.

Master, L.L., S.R. Flack, and B.A. Stein, eds. 1998. *Rivers of Life: Critical Watersheds for Protecting Freshwater Biodiversity*. Arlington, VA: The Nature Conservancy.

Maturana, H.R., and F. Varela. 1987. *The Tree of Knowledge: The Biological Roots of Human Understanding*. Boston: New Science Library.

May, P.J., R.J. Burby, N.J. Ericksen, J.W. Handmer, J.E. Dixon, S. Michaels, and D.I. Smith. 1996. *Environmental Management and Governance: Intergovernmental Approaches to Hazards and Sustainability*. London: Routledge.

May, R.M. 1974. "Biological Populations with Nonoverlapping Generations: Stable Points, Stable Cycles, and Chaos." *Science* 186 (4164): 645-647.

May, R.M., and G.F. Oster. 1976. "Bifurcations and Dynamic Complexity in Simple Ecological Models." *American Naturalist* 110: 573-599.

Mayntz, R. 1978. "Intergovernmental Implementation of Environmental Policy." In *Interorganizational Policy Making*, ed. K. Hanf and F.W. Scharpf. Beverly Hills, CA: Sage Publications.

Meadows, D.H., D.L. Meadows, and J. Randers. 1992. *Beyond the Limits: Confronting Global Collapse, Envisioning a Sustainable Future*. Toronto: McClelland and Stewart.

Meadows, D.H., D.L. Meadows, J. Randers, and W.W. Behrens III. 1972. *Limits to Growth*. New York: Universe Books.

Meadows, D.L., ed. 1977. *Alternatives to Growth-l: A Search for Sustainable Futures*. Cambridge: Ballinger.

Merchant, C. 1980. *The Death of Nature: Women, Ecology and the Scientific Revolution*. New York: Harper and Row.

–. 1992. *Radical Ecology: The Search for a Livable World*. New York: Routledge.

–. 1996. *Earthcare: Women and the Environment*. New York: Routledge.

Meredith, T. 1999. "Concepts, Cosmologies and Commitments: Using Biodiversity Indicators in Critical Zones, Models." In *Communities, Development, and Sustainability across Canada*, ed. J. Pierce and A. Dale, 243-274. Vancouver: UBC Press.

Merton, R.K. 1936. "The Unanticipated Consequences of Purposive Social Action." *American Sociology Review* 1: 894-904.

Michael, D.N. 1993. "Governing by Learning: Boundaries, Myths and Metaphors." *Futures* 25 (1): 81-89.

–. 1995. "Barriers and Bridges to Learning in a Turbulent Human Ecology." In *Barriers and Bridges to the Renewal of Ecosystems and Institutions,* ed. L.H. Gunderson, C.S. Holling, and S.S. Light. New York: Columbia University Press.

Middleton, J. 1998. In *Sustainable Development: A Framework for Governance,* ed. A. Dale. http://www.sdri.ubc.ca/addialogue.

Miles, M.B., and A.M. Huberman. 1993. *Qualitative Data Analysis: A Sourcebook of New Methods.* Newbury Park, CA: Sage Publications.

Miller, D.J. 1989. "Introductions and Extinction of Fish in the African Great Lakes." *Trends in Ecology and Evolution* 4 (2): 56-59.

Miller, J.G. 1965. "Living Systems: Basic Concepts." *Behavioral Science* 10 (3): 193-237.

Mintzberg, H. 1983. *Power in and around Organizations.* Englewood Cliffs, NJ: Prentice-Hall.

Mintzberg, H., D. Dougherty, J. Jorgensen, and F. Westley. 1996. "Some Surprising Things about Collaboration: Knowing How People Connect Makes It Work Better." *Organizational Dynamics* 25 (1): 60-71.

Mishan, E.J. 1969. *The Costs of Economic Growth.* New York: Pelican.

–. 1977. *The Economic Growth Debate: An Assessment.* London: George Allen and Unwin.

Mitroff, I., and R. Kilmann. 1975. On Organizational Stories: An Approach to the Design and Analysis of Organizations through Myths and Stories. Unpublished manuscript, University of Pittsburgh.

Mitsch, W.J., and S.E. Jorgensen, eds. 1989. *Ecological Engineering: An Introduction to Ecotechnology.* New York: John Wiley and Sons.

Mooney, M.A., and P.R. Ehrlich. 1997. "Ecosystem Services: A Fragmentary History." In *Nature's Services: Societal Dependence on Natural Ecosystems,* ed. G.C. Daily. Washington, DC: Island Press.

Morgan, G. 1986. *Images of Organization.* Newbury Park, CA: Sage Publications.

Morrissey, J.B. 1993. "Biological Reference Points: Some Opening Comments." In "Risk Evaluation and Reference Points for Fisheries Management," ed. S.J. Smith, J.J. Hunt and D. Bivard. *Canadian Journal of Fisheries and Aquatic Sciences* 120: 1-4.

Myers, N. 1979. *The Shrinking Ark.* Oxford: Pergamon Press.

–. 1990. "Mass Extinctions: What Can the Past Tell Us About the Present and the Future?" *Global Planet Change* 82: 175-185.

Natural Resources Defense Council (NRDC). 1996. *Green Auto Racing: National Efforts and International Cooperation to Promote Advanced Cars and Fuels.* Washington, DC: NRDC.

Norgaard, R. 1988. "Sustainable Development: A Co-Evolutionary View." *Futures* 20 (16) (December): 606-620.

–. 1994. *Development Betrayed: The End of Progress and a Co-Evolutionary Revisioning of the Future.* New York: Routledge.

–. 1989. "The Case for Methodological Pluralism." *Ecological Economics* 1: 37-57.

North, D.C. 1990. *Institutions, Institutional Change and Economic Performance.* Cambridge: Cambridge University Press.

Norton, B.C. 1987. *Why Preserve Natural Variety?* Princeton, NJ: Princeton University Press.

Odum, E.P. 1969. "The Strategy of Ecosystem Development." *Science* 164: 262-270.

–. 1970. "Optimum Population and Environment: A Georgian Microcosm." *Current History* 58 (June): 355-366.

–. 1972. "Ecosystem Theory in Relation to Man." In *Ecosystem Structure and Function,* ed. J.A. Wiens. Oregon: Oregon State University Press.

–. 1975. *Ecology: The Link between the Natural and the Social Sciences.* New York: Holt, Rinehart and Winston.

–. 1985. "Trends to Be Expected in Stressed Ecosystems." *BioScience* 35 (7): 419-422.

–. 1989. *Ecology and Our Endangered Life-Support Systems.* Sunderland, MA: Sinquer Associates.

Odum, E.P., and H.T. Odum. 1972. "Natural Areas as Necessary Components of Man's Total Environment." In *Transactions of the 37th North-American Wildlands and Natural Resources Conference,* 178-179. Washington, DC: Wildlife Management Institute.

Odum, H.T. 1971. *Environment, Power and Society*. New York: John Wiley and Sons.
–. 1973. "Energy, Ecology and Economics." *Ambio* 2 (6): 220-227.
–. 1983. *Systems Ecology: An Introduction*. New York: John Wiley and Sons.
Odum, H.T., and E.P. Odum. 1981. *Energy Basis for Man and Nature*. New York: McGraw-Hill.
O'Hara, S.U. 1995. "Sustainability: Social and Ecological Dimensions." *Review of Social Economy* 52 (4): 529-551.
Ophuls, W. 1977. *Ecology and the Politics of Scarcity: Prologue to a Political Theory of the Steady State*. San Francisco, CA: W.H. Freeman.
O'Riordan, T. 1988. "The Politics of Sustainability." In *Sustainable Environmental Management: Principles and Practice*, ed. R.K. Turner. Boulder, CO: Westview Press.
Ornstein, R., and P. Ehrlich. 1989. *New World, New Mind: Moving Toward Conscious Evolution*. New York: Doubleday.
Orr, D. 1994. *Earth in Mind: On Education, Environment and the Human Prospect*. Washington, DC: Island Press.
Pal, L. 1990. "Official Language Minorities and the State: Dual Dynamics in a Single Policy Network." *Policy Communities and Public Policy in Canada*, ed. A. Coleman and G. Skogstad, 170-190. Toronto: Copp Clark Pitman.
Paquet, G. 1997. "Straws in the Wind: Slouching toward a New Governance." *Optimum: The Journal of Public Sector Management* 27 (3): 44-50.
Park, P., M. Brydon-Miller, B. Hall, and T. Jackson. 1993. *Voices of Change: Participatory Research in the United States and Canada*. Toronto: Ontario Institute for Studies in Education.
Parsons, T. 1947. "Introduction." In *Max Weber: Theory of Social and Economic Organization*, ed. A.M. Henderson and T. Parsons, 1-5. New York: Oxford University Press.
Pauly, D., and V. Christensen. 1995. "Primary Production Required to Sustain Global Fisheries." *Nature* 374: 255-257.
Pearce, D.W. 1993. *Economic Values and the Natural World*. Cambridge, MA: MIT Press.
Pearce, D.W., and R.K. Turner. 1990. *Economics of Natural Resources and the Environment*. Baltimore, MD: Johns Hopkins University Press.
Peavey, F. 1986. *Heart Politics*. Montreal, QC: Black Rose Books.
–. 1994. *By Life's Grace: Musings on the Essence of Social Change*. Gabriola Island, BC: New Society Press.
Peccei, A. 1978. *World Futures – Which Way is Forward?* The Seventh International Conference on the Unity of the Sciences, Boston, MA, 24-26 November.
Pepper, D. 1996. *Modern Environmentalism: An Introduction*. London: Routledge.
Perlmutter, H., and E. Trist. 1986. "Paradigms for Societal Transition." *Human Relations* 39 (1): 1-27.
Perrings, C.A., C. Folke, and K.-G. Maler. 1992. "The Ecology and Economics of Biodiversity Loss: The Research Agenda." *Ambio* 21: 201-211.
Perrings, C.A., K.-G. Maler, C. Folke, C.S. Holling, and B.-O. Jansson, eds. 1995. *Biodiversity Conservation: Problems and Policies*. Dordecht, The Netherlands: Kluwer Academic Publishers.
Pestel, E. 1989. *Beyond the Limits to Growth: A Report to the Club of Rome*. New York: Universe Books.
Peterson, D., and J. Goodall. 1993. *Visions of Caliban: On Chimpanzees and People*. Boston: Houghton Mifflin Company.
Piaget, J. 1953. *The Origin of Intelligence in the Child*. London: Routledge.
Pierce, J.T. 1999. "Making Communities the Strong Link in Sustainable Development." In *Communities, Development and Sustainability across Canada*, ed. J.T. Pierce and A. Dale, 277-290. Vancouver: UBC Press.
Pimentel, D. 1968. "Population Regulation and Genetic Feedback." *Science* 159 (3822): 1432-1438.
Pimentel, D., C. Wilso, C. McCullum, R. Huang, P. Owen, J. Flack, Q. Tran, T. Saltman, and B. Cliff. 1996. Environmental and Economic Effects of Biodiversity. Unpublished manuscript.

Pinter, L. 1998. In *Sustainable Development: A Framework for Governance*, ed. A. Dale. 2 April. http://www.sdri.ubc.ca/addialogue.

Plant, C., and J. Plant, eds. 1990. *Turtle Talk: Voices for a Sustainable Future.* Lillooet, BC: New Society Publishers.

Plant, J., and C. Plant. 1992. *Putting Power in Its Place: Create Community Control.* Lillooet, BC: New Society Publishers.

Platt McGinn, A. 1999. "Safeguarding the Health of Oceans." Worldwatch Paper 145, March. Washington, DC: Worldwatch Institute.

Plumwood, V. 1983. *Feminism and the Mastery of Nature.* London: Routledge.

Pope, S. 1998. In *Sustainable Development: A Framework for Governance*, ed. A. Dale. 15 April. http://www.sdri.ubc.ca/addialogue.

Popper, K.R. 1974. *Open Society and Its Enemies.* London: Routledge and Kegan.

Postel, S. 1987. *Defusing the Toxics Threat: Controlling Pesticides and Industrial Waste.* Washington, DC: Worldwatch Institute.

–. 1992. *Last Oasis: Facing Water Scarcity.* New York: W.W. Norton and Company.

Prigogine, I., and I. Stengers. 1984. *Order out of Chaos.* New York: Bantam.

Pronk, J., and M. Haq. 1992. *Sustainable Development: From Concept to Action.* The Hague Report. New York: United Nations Development Programme.

Pross, P. 1992. *Group Politics and Public Policy.* Toronto: Oxford University Press.

Putnam, R. 1993a. *Making Democracy Work: Civic Traditions in Modern Italy.* Princeton, NJ: Princeton University Press.

–. 1993b. "The Prosperous Community: Social Capital and Public Life." *American Prospect* 13: 1-8.

–. 1996. "The Decline of Civil Society: How Come? So What." The 1996 John L. Manion Lecture. *Optimum* 27 (2): 27-42.

Quinn, D. 1992. *Ishmael.* New York: Bantam/Turner Press.

Reason, P. 1993. "Reflections on Sacred Experience and Sacred Science." *Journal of Management Inquiry* 2 (3): 273-283.

–, ed. 1994. *Participation in Human Inquiry.* London: Sage Publications.

Reason, P., and J. Rowan. 1981a. "Issues of Validity in New Paradigm Research." In *Human Inquiry. A Sourcebook of New Paradigm Research*, ed. P. Reason and J. Rowan, 239-250. New York: John Wiley and Sons.

–, eds. 1981b. *Human Inquiry: A Sourcebook of New Paradigm Research.* New York: John Wiley and Sons.

Redclift, M. 1988. "Sustainable Development and the Market: A Framework for Analysis." *Futures* 20 (6) (December): 635-650.

Rees, W.E. 1989. "Defining 'Sustainable Development.'" CHS Research Bulletin. Vancouver: UBC Centre for Human Settlements.

–. 1991. "Economics, Ecology and the Limits of Conventional Analysis." *Journal of the Air and Waste Management Association* 41: 1323-1327.

–. 1992. "Ecological Footprints and Appropriated Carrying Capacity: What Urban Economics Leaves Out." *Environment and Urbanization* 4 (2).

–. 1996. "Revisiting Carrying Capacity: Area-Based Indicators of Sustainability." *Population and Environment: A Journal of Interdisciplinary Studies* 17 (3): 195-201.

Rees, W.E., and M. Wackernagel. 1994. "Ecological Footprints and Appropriated Carrying Capacity: Measuring the Natural Capital Requirements of the Human Economy." In *Investing in Human Capital*, ed. A.M. Janson, M. Hammer, C. Folke, and R. Costanza. Washington, DC: Island Press.

Regan, T., and P. Singer, eds. 1976. *Animal Rights and Human Obligations.* Englewood Cliffs, NJ: Prentice-Hall, Inc.

Regier, H.A. 1995a. "Ecosystem Integrity in a Context of Ecostudies as Related to the Great Lakes System." In *Perspectives on Ecological Integrity*, ed. L. Westra and J. Lemmons. Dordrecht, The Netherlands: Kluwer Academic Publishers.

–. 1995b. In *Reconciling Human Welfare and Ecological Carrying Capacity*, ed. A. Dale, J. Robinson, and C. Massey. Vancouver, BC: Sustainable Development Institute.

Regier, H.A., and G. Baskerville. 1986. "Sustainable Redevelopment of Regional Ecosystems

Degraded by Exploitative Development." In *Sustainable Development of the Biosphere*, ed. W.C. Clark and R.E. Munn. London: Cambridge University Press.

Reid, W., and K. Miller. 1989. *Keeping Options Alive: The Scientific Basis for Conserving Biodiversity*. Washington, DC: World Resources Institute.

Repetto, R. 1986. *Economic Values and the Natural World*. London: Earthscan.

Rifkin, J. 1995. *The End of Work: The Decline of the Global Labor Force and the Dawn of the Post-Market Era*. New York: G.P. Putnam's Sons.

Robinson, J.B. 1992a. "Of Maps and Territories: The Use and Abuse of Socioeconomic Modelling in Support of Decision Making." *Technological Forecasting and Social Change* 42: 147-164.

–. 1992b. "Risks, Predictions and Other Optical Illusions: Rethinking the Use of Science in Social Decision Making." *Policy Sciences* 25: 237-254.

–. 1988. "Unlearning and Backcasting: Rethinking Some of the Questions We Ask about the Future." *Technological Forecasting and Social Change* 33: 325-338.

–. 1996. "In Defence of Sustainable Development." Paper delivered at University of British Columbia, Vancouver, BC.

Robinson, J.B., G. Francis, R. Legge, and S. Lerner. 1991. "Defining a Sustainable Society: Values, Principles, and Definitions." *Alternatives* 17: 36-46.

Roe, D., W. Pierce, K. Florian, and E. Sibbergeld. 1997. *Toxic Survey*. Washington, DC: Environmental Defense Fund.

Roe, E. 1998. *Taking Complexity Seriously: Policy Analysis, Triangulation and Sustainable Development*. Dordrecht, Netherlands: Kluwer Academic Publishers.

Rogers, R.A. 1994. *Nature and the Crisis of Modernity: A Critique of Contemporary Discourse on Managing the Earth*. Montreal: Black Rose Books.

Rollin, B. 1981. *Animal Rights and Human Morality*. Buffalo, NY: Prometheus Books.

Rolston, H. 1980. *Environmental Ethics: Duties to and Values in the Natural World*. Philadelphia: Temple University Press.

Rorty, R. 1979. *Philosophy and the Mirror of Nature*. Princeton: Princeton University Press.

Rosaldo, R. 1989. *Culture and Truth: The Remaking of Social Analysis*. Boston: Beacon.

Roseland, M. 1999. "Natural Capital and Social Capital: Implications for Sustainable Community Development." In *Communities, Development, and Sustainability across Canada*, ed. J.T. Pierce and A. Dale, 190-207. Vancouver: UBC Press.

Roszak, T., M. Gomes, and A. Kanner. 1995. *Ecopsychology: Restoring the Earth, Healing the Mind*. San Francisco: Sierra Club Books.

Rothman, D. 1998. In *Sustainable Development: A Framework for Governance*, ed. A. Dale. http://www.sdri.ubc.ca/addialogue.

Rowan, J. 1981. "A Dialectical Paradigm for Research." In *Human Inquiry: A Sourcebook of New Paradigm Research*, ed. P. Reason and J. Rowan, 19-36. New York: John Wiley and Sons.

Ruddick, S. 1989. *Maternal Tinkering: Towards a Politics of Peace*. Boston, MA: Beacon.

Rueggeberg, H., and J. Griggs. 1993. "Institutional Characteristics which Support Sustainability." In *1995 Environmental Scan for the Canadian Council of Ministers of the Environment*. Toronto: Thompson, Gow and Associates.

Ruether, R. 1979. "Mother Earth and the Megamachine." In *Womanspirit Rising: A Feminist Reader in Religion*, ed. C. Christ and J. Plaskow. San Franciso: Harper and Row.

Sahl, J.D., and B.B. Bernstein. 1995. "Developing Policy in an Uncertain World." *International Journal of Sustainable Development* 2: 124-135.

Sale, K. 1991. *Dwellers in the Land: The Bioregional Vision*. Philadelphia, PA: New Society Publishers.

Salwasser, H. 1993. "Sustainability Needs More than Better Science." *Ecological Applications* 3: 5875-5887.

Sanders, C. 1992. *Surviving Grief and Learning to Live Again*. New York: John Wiley and Sons.

Sapa, A. 1999. *A Penny Better Spent May Save the World*. IOL News Article, 22 September.

Schaffer, W.M., and M. Kot. 1985. "Do Strange Attractors Govern Ecological Systems?" *BioScience* 35 (6): 342-350.

Schmidheiny, S., with the Business Council for Sustainable Development. 1992. *Changing Course: A Global Business Perspective on Development and the Environment.* Cambridge, MA: MIT Press.

Schneider, E.D., and J.J. Kay. 1994. "Complexity and Thermodynamics: Towards a New Ecology." *Futures* 24 (6): 626-647.

Schön, D. 1971. *Beyond the Stable State.* New York: W.W. Norton and Company.

–. 1983. *The Reflective Practitioner.* New York: Basic Books.

Schulz, A. 1964. *Studies in Social Theory.* Collected Papers 2. The Hague, the Netherlands: Martinus Nijhoff.

Schumacher, E.F. 1973. *Small is Beautiful. Economics as if People Mattered.* New York: Harper & Row.

Schutz, A., and M. Weber. 1967. *The Phenomenology of the Social World.* Evanston, IL: Northwestern University Press.

Schweder, R.A., and R.A. LeVine. 1984. *Culture Theory: Essays on Mind, Self and Emotion.* Cambridge, MA: Cambridge University Press.

Science Council of Canada. 1977. *Canada as a Conserver Society: Resource Uncertainties and the Need for New Technologies.* Ottawa: Minister of Supply and Services.

Scoones, I., and J. Thompson. 1994. *Beyond Farmer First: Rural People's Knowledge, Agricultural Research and Extensions Practice.* London: Intermediate Technology Publications.

Sears, R., E. Maccoby, and H. Levin. 1957. *Patterns of Child Rearing.* New York: Harper.

Shairo, S. 1989. "Towards a Language of Educational Politics: The Struggles for a Critical Public Discourse of Education." *Educational Foundations* 3 (3): 79-100.

Shiva, V. 1989. *Staying Alive: Women, Ecology and Development.* London: Zed Books.

Siegel, B. 1990. *Peace, Love and Healing: Bodymind Communication and the Path to Self-Healing – An Exploration.* New York: Harper and Row.

Sims, D. 1998. In *Sustainable Development: A Framework for Governance,* ed. A. Dale. 10 August. http://www.sdri.ubc.ca/addialogue.

Skogstad, G., and P. Kopas. 1992. "Environmental Policy in a Federal System." In *Canadian Environmental Policy: Ecosystems, Politics and Process,* ed. R. Boardman. Toronto: Oxford University Press.

Smuts, J.C. 1926. *Holism and Evolution.* New York: Macmillan Company.

Soule, J.D., and J.K. Pipper. 1992. *Farming in Nature's Image: An Ecological Approach to Ecotechnology.* New York: John Wiley and Sons.

Soule, M.E. 1991. "Conservation: Tactics for a Constant Crisis." *Science* 253: 709-824.

Spangler, D. 1996. *Everyday Miracles: The Inner Art of Manifestation.* New York: Bantam Books.

Study of Critical Problems (SCEP). 1970. *Man's Impact on the Global Environment.* Cambridge, MA: MIT Press.

Sutherland, S., and B. Doern. 1985. *Bureaucracy in Canada: Control and Reform.* Toronto: University of Toronto Press.

Suzuki, D. 1995. "Disconnected Economics?" *Ecodecision* 16 (Spring): 19-21.

Tandon, R. 1981. "Dialogue as Inquiry and Intervention." In *Human Inquiry: A Sourcebook of New Paradigm Research,* ed. P. Reason and J. Rowan, 293-301. New York: John Wiley and Sons.

Taylor, F.W. 1911. *Principles of Scientific Management.* New York: Harper and Row.

Thompson, M. 1993. The Meaning of Sustainable Development. Paper presented at the Conference on Global Governability, London, England, 20 April.

Thompson, P., and W.T. Stanbury. 1984. "Looking Out for No. 1: Incumbency and Interest Group Politics." *Canadian Public Policy* 27 (1): 37-51.

Tietenberg, T. 1992. *Environmental and Natural Resource Economics.* New York: HarperCollins.

Toffler, A. 1970. *Future Shock.* New York: Bantam Books.

Tomkins, S. 1962. *Imagery, Affect, Consciousness.* New York: Springer.

Torbert, W.R. 1987. *Managing the Corporate Dream: Restructuring for Long-term Success.* Holmwood, IL: Dow Jones-Irwin.

–. 1991. *The Power of Balance: Transforming Self, Society, and Scientific Inquiry.* Newbury Park, CA: Sage Publications.

Torrie, R. 1996. *Business Strategies for Sustainable Development in the Canadian Energy Sector.* Ottawa: National Round Table on the Environment and the Economy.

Trainer, F.E. 1996. *Towards a Sustainable Economy.* Oxford: Jon Carpenter.

Trist, E. 1976. "Action Research and Adaptive Planning." In *Experimenting with Organizational Life: The Action Research Approach,* ed. A.W. Clark. New York: Plenum Press.

–. 1983. "Referent Organizations and the Development of Interorganizational Domains." *Human Relations* 36: 269-284.

Trist, E., and H. Murray. 1990. "Historical Overview: The Foundation and Development of the Tavistock Institute." In *The Social Engagement of Social Science: A Tavistock Anthology.* Volume 1: *The Socio-Psychological Perspective,* ed. E. Trist and H. Murray. Philadelphia: University of Pennsylvania Press.

Turner, R.K. 1988. "Sustainability, Resource Conservation and Pollution Control: An Overview." In *Sustainable Environmental Management: Principles and Practice,* ed. R.K. Turner. London: Bellhaven Press.

–. 1992. "Speculations on Weak and Strong Sustainability." CSERGE GEC Working Paper 92-96. London: CSERGE and UCL.

Tyrchniewicz, A., and A. Wilson. 1994. *Sustainable Development for the Great Plains: Policy Analysis.* Winnipeg: International Institute for Sustainable Development.

Umpleby, S.A. 1990. "The Science of Cybernetics and the Cybernetics of Science." *Cybernetics and Systems* 21 (1): 109-121.

UNEP (United Nations Environment Programme). 1995. *Global Biodiversity Assessment.* New York: Cambridge University Press.

–. 2000. *Global Environmental Outlook 2000.* London: Earthscan Publications.

Union of Concerned Scientists. 1993. *World Scientists' Warning to Humanity.* Cambridge, MA.

United Nations Development Programme. 1995. *Human Development Report.* Oxford: Oxford University Press.

–. 1997. *Human Development Report.* New York: Oxford University Press.

United Nations Population Division. 1995. *World Urbanization Prospects: The 1994 Revision.* New York: United Nations.

Vainio-Matilla, A. 1998. In *Sustainable Development: A Framework for Governance,* ed. A. Dale. 8 March. http://www.sdri.ubc.ca/addialogue.

Van Gelder, S. 1995. "The Next Reformation: An Interview with Paul Hawken." *Context* 41: 17-24.

–. ed. 2000. "The Page that Counts." *Yes! A Journal of Positive Futures* 14 (Summer): 11 (for child poverty stats, Casa Alianza, www.casa-alianza.org; and for worker stats, Smith, S. *Undernews,* February 2000: James Lardner, "Worldclass Workaholics," *U.S. News and World Report,* 13 December 1999).

Van Manen, M. 1990. *Researching Lived Experience: Human Science for an Action Sensitive Pedagogy.* New York: State University of New York Press.

Vickers, G. 1972. *Freedom in a Rocking Boat: Changing Values in an Unstable Society.* London: Penguin Books.

Vig, N.J., and M.E. Kraft, eds. 1990. *Environmental Policy in the 1990s: Toward a New Agenda.* Washington, DC: Congressional Quarterly.

Vitousek, P., H.A. Mooney, J. Lubchenco, and J.M. Melillo. 1997. "Human Domination of Earth's Ecosystems." *Science* 277: 494-499.

Vitousek, P., P. Ehrlich, A. Ehrlich, and P. Matson. 1986. "Human Appropriation of the Products of Photosynthesis." *BioScience* 36: 368-373.

von Bertalanffy, L. 1968. *General Systems Theory.* New York: Brazillier.

Wackernagel, M., and W. Rees. 1996. "Ecological Footprints and Appropriated Carrying Capacity: Measuring the Natural Capital Requirements of the Human Economy." In *Investing in Natural Capital: The Ecological Economics Approach to Sustainability,* ed. A.M. Jansson, M. Hammer, C. Folke, and R. Costanza. Washington, DC: Island Press.

Walters, C.J. 1986. *Adaptive Management of Renewable Resources.* New York: McGraw Hill.

Walters, C.J., and C.S. Holling. 1990. "Large-Scale Management Experiments and Learning by Doing." *Ecology* 71 (6): 2060-2068.

Walters, C.J., and J.-J. Maguire. 1996. "Lessons from Stock Assessment from the Northern Cod Collapse." *Reviews in Fish Biology and Fisheries* 6: 125-137.

Waring, M. 1995. *Sex, Lies and Globalization*. Ottawa: National Film Board.

Weick, K.E. 1976. "Educational Organizations as Loosely Coupled Systems." *Administrative Science Quarterly* 21: 1-19.

–. 1985. "Sources of Order in Underorganized Systems: Themes in Recent Organizational Theory." In *Organizational Theory and Inquiry*, ed. Y.S. Lincoln, 106-136. Newbury Park, CA: Sage Publications.

Westley, F. 1995. "Governing Design: The Management of Social Systems and Ecosystem Management." In *Barriers and Bridges to the Renewal of Ecosystems and Institutions*, ed. L.H. Gunderson, C.S. Holling, and S.S. Light. New York: Columbia University Press.

Westley, F., and H. Vredenburg. 1996a. "Strategic Bridging: The Collaboration Between Environmentalists and Business in the Marketing of Green Products." *Journal of Applied Behavioral Science* 27 (1): 65-90.

–. 1996b. "Sustainability and the Corporation: Criteria for Aligning Economic Practice with Environmental Protection." *Journal of Management Inquiry* 5 (2): 104-119.

Wexler, P., R. Martusewics, and J. Kern. 1987. "Popular Educational Politics." In *Critical Pedagogy and Cultural Power*, ed. D. Livingston. South Hadley, MA: Bergin and Garvey.

White, L. 1967. "The Historical Roots of Our Ecologic Crisis." *Science* 155 (3767): 1203-1207.

Whitehead, A.N. 1925. *Science and the Modern World*. Middlesex: Penguin Books.

–. 1929. *Process and Reality: An Essay in Cosmology*. Cambridge: Cambridge University Press.

Wiens, J.A. 1997. "Scientific Responsibility and Responsible Ecology." *Conservation Ecology*. http://www.consecol.org/Journal/vol1/is1/art16/.

Williamson, G.S., and I.H. Pearse. 1980. *Science, Synthesis and Sanity: An Inquiry into the Nature of Living*. Edinburgh: Scottish Academic Press.

Wilson, A.T.M., E.L. Trist, and A. Curl. 1952. "Transitional Communities and Social Reconnections: A Study of Civil Resettlement of British Prisoners of War." In *Readings in Social Psychology*, ed. N.E.G. Swanson, T.M. Newcombe, and E.L. Hartley. Second ed. New York: Holt.

Wilson, E. 1992. *Diversity of Life*. Cambridge, MA: Kelknap Press.

–, ed. 1988. *Biodiversity*. Washington, DC: National Academy Press.

Winters, G.H. 1986. *Aide-memoire on 2J3KL Assessment: No Gratum Anus Rodentum?* CAF-SAC Research Document, Department of Fisheries and Oceans, St. John's, Newfoundland.

Wolzar, M. 1983. *Spheres of Justice: A Defense of Pluralism and Equality*. New York: Basic Books.

Wood, D., and B. Gray. 1991. "Toward a Comprehensive Theory of Collaboration." *Journal of Applied Behavioral Science* 27 (2): 139-162.

Woodley, S., J. Kay, and G. Francis. 1993. *Ecological Integrity and the Management of Ecosystems*. Delray Beach, FL: St. Lucie Press.

Woollard, R., and W. Rees. 1999. "Social Evolution and Urban Systems: Directions for Sustainability." In *Communities, Development and Sustainability across Canada*, ed. J.T. Pierce and A. Dale, 27-45. Vancouver: UBC Press.

World Bank. 1997. *The State in a Changing World: The World Development Report*. Washington, DC: The World Bank.

World Resources Institute. 1992-93. *A Report by the World Resources Institute*. New York: Oxford University Press.

World Resources Institute, International Union for the Conservation of Nature and Natural Resources, and United Nations Environment Programme. 1992. *Global Biodiversity Strategy: Guidelines for Action to Save, Study, and Use the Earth's Biotic Wealth Sustainably and Equitably*.

World Resources Institute, United Nations Environment Programme, United Nations Development Programme, and the World Bank. 1996. *World Resources: A Guide to the Global Environment, 1996-97*. New York: Oxford University Press.

Worster, D. 1993. *The Wealth of Nature: Environmental History and the Ecological Imagination*. New York: Oxford University Press.

Wright, S., T. Dietz, R. Borden, G. Young, and G. Guagnano. 1993. *Human Ecology: Crossing Boundaries.* Fort Collins, CO: The Society for Human Ecology.

Young, O., and K. von Moltke. 1993. "To Avoid Gridlock: Governance without Government." *Working Progress* 14 (2): 4.

Zussman, D., and J. Jabes. 1989. *The Vertical Solitude: Managing in the Public Sector.* Ottawa: Institute for Research on Public Policy.

Index

Set in Stone by Brenda and Neil West, BN Typographics West
Printed and bound in Canada by Friesens
Copy editor: Joanne Richardson
Proofreader: Deborah Kerr
Indexer: Patricia Buchanan